EVE WAS FRAMED

Baroness Helena Kennedy QC is Chair of the British
Council, Chair of the Human Genetics Commission and
a member of the Bar Association's International Task
Force on Terrorism. Her most recent book is *Just Law:
The Changing Face of Justice – and Why it Matters to
Us All*.

'When an operatic diva holds her audience spell-
bound, she is greeted with cries of *bravissima*. Similarly, when a well-known barrister and broadcaster,
Helena Kennedy, writes a book as compelling as this,
bravissima is her due. This is a cogently argued
examination of how the British legal system ignores,
downgrades, underrates and discriminates against
women . . . Kennedy has properly argued that a
profession that practices law and pursues justice must
be seen to be just, reasonable, unprejudiced, and open
to public scrutiny. *Bravissima!*'

Julia Neuberger,
Sunday Times

'Do women get a fair deal at the hands of the criminal
justice system in Britain? That is Helena Kennedy's
central question. Her answer is an unequivocal 'no'.
Her book is a sober and sobering explanation of why
this is so. She puts her case, and suggests remedies,
with compelling clarity. This is an important book; if
it gets the wide readership it deserves it will make a
substantial difference to public debate about Britain's
legal system'

A C Grayling,
Financial Times

'This powerful and authoritative polemic, cannot be
dismissed (though some men will admittedly try) as a
hysterical tirade by a paranoid feminist. Kennedy cites
precedents and incontrovertible evidence to show how
a "web of prejudice, privilege and misinformation
affects women" in all their dealings with the law . . .
brave, forceful and eloquent. It may even change
things'

Jessica Mann,
Sunday Telegraph

'*Eve Was Framed* is timely, persuasive and highly readable. If it occasionally induces a sense of despair, that is not Helena Kennedy's fault but a reflection of the antiquated nature of the system she is assessing. The law, on the evidence presented here, is not so much an ass as an Oxbridge-educated ex-public school boy with a sentimental attachment to Victorian values'

Joan Smith,
Independent on Sunday

'Kennedy's stimulating and constantly informative book covers all aspects of women in the justice system. That they are unfairly treated, at every level, is beyond any real debate. How to reverse the habits and attitudes of centuries is a more difficult question. Kennedy has no quick and easy answer; nor is there one. There are, though, a number of smaller reforms, the accumulation of which would make a real difference to women. Kennedy lists them all, from the trivial – the abolition of the very male-culture dinners which all aspiring barristers have to attend – to the way judges are chosen, so as to remove it from the all-male decision-making process that governs appointments today. To be fair, the legal system has, in recent years, reacted perceptibly to the pressures for change ... It is all too slow for Kennedy. The practical effect of all these good intentions will be too long in coming; but her book deserves to hasten the process of change. She may not have proved that Eve was framed, but a miscarriage of justice there certainly has been'

Marcel Berlins,
Literary Review

Helena Kennedy

EVE WAS FRAMED

WOMEN AND BRITISH JUSTICE

VINTAGE BOOKS
London

Published by Vintage 2005

32

First published in Great Britain in 1992 by
Chatto & Windus

Vintage
Random House, 20 Vauxhall Bridge Road, London SW1V 2SA

www.vintage-books.co.uk

Addresses for companies within The Random House Group Limited
can be found at: www.randomhouse.co.uk/offices.htm

The Random House Group Limited Reg. No. 954009

A CIP catalogue record for this book
is available from the British Library

ISBN 9780099224419

The Random House Group Limited supports The Forest Stewardship
Council (FSC), the leading international forest certification organisation.
All our titles that are printed on Greenpeace approved FSC certified paper
carry the FSC logo. Our paper procurement policy can be found at:
www.rbooks.co.uk/environment

Typeset by SX Composing DTP, Rayleigh, Essex
Printed and bound in Great Britain by
Clays Ltd, Elcograf S.p.A.

CONTENTS

To women in prison

Acknowledgements

A formidable body of learned work does exist to support the view that women are still disadvantaged in the law and in the courts. I am very conscious of my indebtedness to the many wonderful women and men who have given me insights into the workings of the criminal justice system over the years. I cannot possibly name them all, but I would first like to mention some of the criminologists and academic lawyers in the field because their books, which are still available to inspire others, lent me reassurance that all was not in the mind and provided me with a sound theoretical base for my professional life: Pat Carlen, Rebecca and Russell Dobash, Frances Heidensohn, Susan Edwards, Carol Smart, Jennifer Temkin, Susan Atkin, Brenda Hale, Lorna Smith, Kathleen Donovan, Catherine MacKinnon, Jocelynne Scutt, Betsy Stanko, Kate Mallinson and Nicola Lacey. In preparing this new volume I want also to thank Baroness Vivien Stern, Sue Stapely, Joanna Phoenix, the psychologist Anna Motz and a director at the CPS, Seamus Taylor, who provided many new insights. A special mention must go to my great friend Albie Sachs, who is renowned as a judge on the South African Constitutional Court. He was imprisoned and almost killed in an explosion because of his political commitment to a new South Africa. He also deserves acknowledgement as a leading contributor to feminist jurisprudence.

I also want to remember with gratitude the late Chris Tchaikovsky of Women in Prison, and to thank Southall

Black Sisters for continued inspiration. They are a spectacular group of women from whom I have learned so much. And I am grateful to many practitioners and friends, especially Geoffrey Bindman, Jane Hoyal, Quincy Whittaker and Dr Gillian Mezey. Over the years I have been given particular help by one of our finest forensic psychiatrists, Dr Nigel Eastman, who has worked with me on many cases. He has a profound understanding of the interface between law and psychiatry and knows how to make that relationship work in the courtroom. I have learned greatly from our collaboration. Three of the new crop of formidable women at the Bar have been a great support in pulling together the changes which have taken place since *Eve* was first published. They are Rebecca Lee, Allison Bailey and Katherine Rainwood. I thank them all.

Faith Evans, my literary agent, was the prime mover behind the original creation of this book. She sat on a jury in one of my cases and later wrote urging me to put pen to paper. It took many years before I took the plunge but this book would not have been possible without her generous support, friendship and belief that it was possible. Jenny Uglow, my editor, was the midwife to this endeavour: her insight, intelligence, skill and support were crucial. Also, a tribute to the now retired publisher Carmen Callil, who helped me so much first time round and is still a source of great encouragement. For this second edition I am greatly indebted to Rachel Cugnoni, Ali Reynolds, Liz Foley, Beth Humphries and Patrick Hargadon of Random House for making it happen. Thank you all. And finally, my eternal gratitude goes to Iain Hutchison whose tolerance, encouragement and love sustain me.

Introduction: The Illusion of Inclusion

After the publication of the first edition of *Eve Was Framed* in 1992 I took part in many debates about women and the criminal justice system. Elderly judges were paraded through television studios to take issue with my claim that the system failed women. They would all insist that justice was blind; the gender of an accused was of no consequence and, if anything, being female worked in her favour. To reassure me that he was not a misogynist one told me that he had voted for women to be allowed to join the Kennel Club!

In the years that have followed a lot has happened. There is now greater awareness of the ways in which discrimination works. The institutions have been forced into reforms. Women are more visible in the courts and the legal establishment talks a good talk on domestic violence. It is tempting to swallow the claim that we have moved into a post-feminist era; the battles having been won, the picture is completely changed, and women have the world at their feet. Any attempts to document the continuing problems facing women, or the entrenched attitudes which persist, evoke a dismissive insistence that gender bias has been addressed and remaining pockets of resistance are few.

However, re-reading *Eve Was Framed* I realised that while a lot has happened not enough has changed. With the increased numbers of young women in the law schools and the legal profession, with a growing number of women receiving appointments to the Bench, we can be seduced into the premature conclusion that the systemic problems have been solved and it is now just a question of more women working their way through the profession. The illusion of inclusion can deny the reality that professional structures still do not adequately accommodate the reality of women's lives; the conjuring trick done with numbers can disguise the fact that certain attitudes to women remain unchanged and that women coming before the courts still encounter myths and stereotypes which disfigure the legal process. Yes, as the seventies Virginia Slims cigarette advert used to say, 'We've come a long way, baby' but the journey is as yet unfinished.

Over 50% of students in law schools are female. They come out with great degrees and are fabulous women. The competition for places in professional practice is now so fierce that many use their degrees to go into other activities, but, for those determined to enter legal practice, the majority are steered towards public service law, by which I mean fields largely funded out of legal aid. Two women for every one man now apply for a place in sets of chambers doing publicly funded work. The same is happening with traineeships in legal aid solicitors' practices. The men make career choices much more related to money and prestige and head for the high-rewarding areas of practice, but women find their place doing poor folks' law. Women invariably do the ill-rewarded work in all walks of life and what follows is a lowering of the esteem of that professional activity. I have always worked as a legal aid lawyer myself and without regret but I mind that women are denied the choices that are open to so many of their male colleagues because doors are not oiled for them.

The reward gradient between the litigant who is legally aided and the one who is privately funded is huge. This is particularly noticeable when legally aided wives are up against privately funded husbands trying to hide away their wealth and assets, and it is invariably the privately funded male barrister doing battle with the publicly funded female barrister. However, when governments justify taking the scythe to legal aid they summon up for the public the notion of the fat cat lawyer, bloated male barristers dining out on public funds, when in fact those who will suffer will largely be committed young women who work tirelessly for little reward, and their clients.

There is public trumpeting every time a woman is made a senior judge and private harrumphing that she is probably not up to it.

The pace is slow and explained by the insistence that only the best will do, as though mediocre men have never adjudicated and that women still do not have what it takes. It is as though evolution might sort out our deficiencies, like fish growing feet. There is still insufficient recognition that the merit principle has to be examined to ensure that it is underpinned by criteria which also value the particular skills and experience women could bring to the role. As Dame Brenda Hale, our only woman judge in the House of Lords, has said, 'we need to forge a new picture of a judge who does not fit the traditional model but is still recognisably a judge'.

The failure is that we still do not take sufficient account of the ways that women's experience is different from that of men whether as practitioners or as people forced to use the law, as victims of crime or as defendants. Women of my generation have to take some of the blame because in all our talk of equality we crowded out some important arguments about difference. The reason was our own sensitivity to difference; it had been used so successfully to exclude women from public life – our psychological wiring was considered inappropriate for the logical requirements of legal decision-making or medicine or governing and our feminine vulnerability was used to explain why we should be kept in the domestic arena. We were so cagey about special pleading that we started out by arguing simply for fair treatment. We argued for equality as 'equal treatment' not realising the cul-de-sac this would create. Equalisation has almost invariably been towards a male norm. The public standards already in place were assumed to be valid so, instead of our attempting to order the world differently, women have been expected to shape up, whether as lawyers or as people before the courts.

There are still too many in the law who believe that the law is an objective set of rules, that law is neutral. The point of *Eve Was Framed* was to show that this claim of neutrality was bogus. Law was male because it was made by men and only when lawmaking was reconsidered could law become just. But reforming the law with some legislative changes and the appointment of a few women will not resolve the deeply embedded problems of the law. There has to be a serious acknowledgement that legal cultures are premised on notions which are themselves excluding rather than including.

When women of my generation began to turn the spotlight on the treatment of women by law and in the law, we argued for law reform but what has become increasingly clear is that law reform of itself is not the answer. Law is often part of the problem. We argued for equality but of course treating as equal those who are unequal does not produce equality. We have to start talking about substantive equality which acknowledges the historic imbalances between men and women in our society rather than formal equality. Real equality means treating 'as equals' while taking account of the context of our lives.

I had a perfect example recently when, in the spirit of equality, some very decent liberal peers supported a reactionary call to provide men in rape cases with the cover of anonymity. The call came in response to a small number of high-profile cases where celebrities had to undergo tabloid hysteria and public humiliation only to have cases of a sexual nature dropped before charging. The police should never have released the names of the men to the press in the first place but leaks of this sort can create a nice little earner for errant police officers. Instead of insisting that names should not be published until after charging, 'good for the goose, good for the gander' arguments were made. The undertow of the arguments questioned the rationale for protecting the identity of women complainants who could be malicious liars. In fact, the provision of anonymity was introduced to help women to come forward after rape because it was recognised that the shame of the experience had such serious implications for women. The slow lifting of the taboo around rape has meant that some women waive the protection and speak publicly about their horrifying experience, but for many women it is still such a source of humiliation and degradation that public attention would be the final straw. In some communities exposure will affect the safety of women and their prospects as wives and mothers; rape is still such a source of dishonour it may even lead to family rejection.

There is no doubt that men wrongly accused suffer too, but openness as a principle is in the public interest. Crime is not a private matter. The rape of women concerns us all and should not be swept under the carpet any more than any other crime. An accusation of murder if unsubstantiated also has terrible consequences for the accused but public hearing of alleged wrongdoing is a crucial element of a democracy, where openness of the process prevents abuse by the authorities. The police have also been able to clear up serial rapes because the publication of a man's name can encourage other women to come forward. A time may come when women who seek justice after being raped will not feel they are the ones on trial and our cultures may evolve so that women who are violated are not themselves blamed, but until those anomalies are resolved a differential in treatment is justified. It is worth noting that the very same people who argued 'difference' to keep women in their box, hate its invocation when it is a remedy for disadvantage. Suddenly equality is the byword.

Rape is the perfect example of the inadequacy of legal reform to challenge the more immutable forces operating in the law: all the changes designed to secure justice for women who have been raped – from removal of the corroboration requirement to restrictions on the right to cross-examine – have amounted to little. The conviction rate for rape in Britain is still the lowest for all serious crime, and despite increased reporting the convictions are falling. Over the past decade the number of reported rapes has doubled but only 7% of complaints ever lead to conviction. Sometimes it is as low as 5.8% (Home Office, *Safety and Justice: The Government's Proposals on Domestic Violence, 2003*). Very few rape cases proceed to court, for a huge number are withdrawn. This is often because women cannot face the legal process. Despite all the efforts to improve the system, the stumbling block is that the woman knows that cross-examination will expose her to all the double standards that confront women and it will be her word against his. Women know that it is difficult to secure a conviction; they make their own calculations as to whether they are prepared to go through with it. Of the cases which do proceed to trial the conviction rate in rape is 41% when the general conviction rate for crime across the board is 73%. The reason for law reform's failure is because rape is the ultimate buffer; it is where the law crashes up against the rawest display of the continuing power imbalance between men and women.

The mythologies around rape are still present although the judiciary is much more circumspect about making the kinds of public utterances which they did with frequency right up to the mid-1990s. The cases which used to hit the news are legendary: the guardsman who walked free after his conviction because of his fine service record, although his victim's vagina was torn by the rings on his hand; the woman who was judged 'contributory negligent' because she was walking alone at night; and so on. It was often in their unguarded moments when passing sentence that judges disclosed their prejudices. I remember blanching early on in my practice when I heard Sir Melford Stevenson, a judge who was extravagant in doling out long sentences, being generous to a rape defendant because, he said, the girl was 'asking for it'. She had been hitch-hiking, a far more serious offence in His Lordship's view. The rape was described as 'an anaemic affair as rapes go', as though something a bit more colourful might be expected from a red-blooded rapist. The sentence was suspended. Some of the most notorious cases gave rise to extensive criticism of the particular judges involved. In 1990, Mr Justice Jupp passed a suspended sentence on a man who twice raped his ex-wife, explaining that this was 'a rare sort of rape. It is not like someone being jumped in the street. This is within the family and does not impinge on the public.' Mr Justice Leonard, in the Vicarage rape case, passed sentences of five years and three years on the defendants because the victim had apparently made a 'remarkable recovery'. Lucky defendants! They had repeatedly raped the victim at knifepoint, forced her to have oral sex, and penetrated her anally with the handle of a knife. Any recovery was no thanks to them. Since the trial the young woman has courageously written and spoken publicly about her experience, and has been deeply critical of the judge.

In 1986 two paratroopers had their sentences of 18 months reduced because their victim was 'dissolute and sexually depraved'. In July 1991 Mr Justice Alliot gave a rapist a three-year jail sentence, although the recommended minimum for someone found guilty of the offence is five years, because his victim was a 'common prostitute' and a 'whore'. In passing sentence he explained, 'While every woman is entitled to complain about being violated, someone who for years has flaunted their body and sold it cannot complain as loudly as someone who has not . . . '

As late as 1990 in his *Textbook of Criminal Law*, Professor Glanville Williams asserted the relevance of the fact that women frequently enjoy fantasies of rape. He cited as his authority Helene Deutsch's *The Psychology of Women* (published forty-five years before) and Paul H. Gebhard's *Sex Offenders: an Analysis of Types* (published twenty-five years before). He included no contemporary references and seemed to take no account of the possibility that a woman might enjoy a private fantasy where she is in control, whilst not welcoming the reality.

Women's organisations from townswomen's guilds to church groups, from the Women's Institute to student unions, increased the volume of their discontent with the law. The arrival of over 100 women on the Labour benches after the 1997 election undoubtedly shifted the debate. These MPs, in coalition with women in other parties, have fought hard to place women's issues on the agenda and, despite attack and accusations of political correctness, they have instigated legal reform. Women like Vera Baird QC, Fiona Mactaggart, Margaret Hodge and many others. As Solicitor-General, Harriet Harman has heroically pushed for better systems to deal with domestic violence and Patricia Hewitt has championed the case for a change in parent leave and the work/life balance. Unfortunately two successive Home Secretaries recognised the value to be drawn from women's support and harnessed women's issues to their own regressive programmes on law and order. We should have realised the downside when legislation introduced to deal with stalking was used to curb picketing. Women's requests that magistrates should be able to exclude men who batter their partners from the family home and imprison them for breach of the order has given birth to the Anti-Social Behaviour Order, which is now used extensively in alarming ways by the police. There are concerns that young people who could have been diverted from crime are acquiring criminal records and experience of prison too readily because of ASBOs. Women's plea that men whose lawyers insidiously cross-examine rape complainants about their sexual history should have their own previous convictions or history placed before the courts has now led to a generalised legal change to disclose the convictions of an accused in theft cases. Women's campaigns for a power of arrest to be attached to common assault was designed to deal with domestic violence – to give women in the absence of their partner the opportunity to seek help and advice before violence escalated and to stop the police dismissing a 'domestic' unless there was blood on the walls. Instead of confining it to domestic violence, all common assault now carries a power of arrest for the first time ever and we can be sure it will be used most actively against boys on street corners.

The hijacking of women's movement campaigns for attacks on civil liberties is now commonplace. After he was appointed to a Home Office Advisory Panel on Law and Order by the Labour Minister Paul Boateng, the right-wing columnist, Simon Heffer, took great joy in describing how he was making common cause with hairy feminists to put iron in the Home Office soul.

It is always worth noting who your bedfellows are when embarking on campaigns for change. More justice for women cannot be bought at the price of less justice for men. The lowering of standards to improve conviction rates and introduction of increased police powers always end up affecting women too because their use becomes generalised. With the best of intentions Harriet Harman, in her role as a law officer of the Crown, began appealing the sentences passed on men convicted of manslaughter of their wives because she thought they were too lenient. Her argument was that infidelity by a wife or an announcement that she is leaving the home should not be a justification or mitigation in the contemporary world for outbursts of rage. She is right, but arguing for increased sentences at that time simply fed into the current clamour for increased punishment generally. The outcome has been the ratcheting up of sentences across the board for domestic killing so that women who were receiving appropriate, compassionate sentences are now less likely to walk free from the court, even when they have killed after being battered for years. The law of unintended consequences is not one that is on the statute books.

The lesson for all of us is that improving justice requires careful strategies. The law is undoubtedly an instrument of change but it can be a blunt instrument when the context in which it operates is not fully understood. Understanding and acknowledging the cultural, physical and societal disadvantages women experience are crucial to doing justice but sometimes even women are oblivious to those effects. Women who have never themselves experienced such obstacles are just as immune as any man to their meaning. I have a successful woman colleague at the Bar, whom I like enormously, who is very dismissive of arguments about 'a woman's perspective'. She has little truck with women's complaints of sexual harassment because she thinks young professional women are not tough enough to be in the law if they cannot deal with unwelcome overtures. Her education and upbringing have inducted her into seeing the world from the perspective of men and no experience to date has provided the awakening electric shock. Paradoxically, some men instinctively recognise gender and race disparities although they are far outside their personal experience and are the most effective advocates of dynamic shifts in legal custom and practice.

Domestic violence is an area where the law is still being dragged into the real world. The argument that violence against women is an abuse of their human rights is now being understood but there is an increasingly vocal claim of equivalency – that women also hit men, that men are abused by women but tell no one out of shame. We are being led to believe that battered men are suffering in silence just as women once did. While there are no doubt such cases they are not the norm and they distract us from the really serious problems which blight women's lives and make equality impossible. At public meetings, the police and officials often talk about 'people' who experience domestic violence, using language which disguises the reality that in our society it is women who are most often battered, women who are killed by their partners at a rate of two a week, women and their children who are all slain by a vengeful partner who then turns the gun on himself, girl children who are disproportionately the victims when we read of cruelty and neglect leading to death. According to the Home Office statistics at least a quarter of all violent crime is domestic violence and it is perpetrated against women. The refusal to acknowledge the gendered nature of violence is a continuing problem.

In the last decade a number of high-profile miscarriages of justice have reminded us that women still face special kinds of risk within the system. In 2003, three criminal cases involving the prosecution of mothers for causing the deaths of their babies created public consternation. Sally Clark and Angela Cannings were both convicted of murder and sentenced to life imprisonment before being finally released by the Court of Appeal. Trupti Patel's case was a miscarriage of justice waiting to happen had the courts not become alert to the potential problem of expert testimony in cases involving the deaths of babies. The common feature in these trials was that each concerned a mother who had suffered the loss of more than one infant. The repetition of sudden deaths without explanation raised suspicion amongst professionals and, in the absence of eyewitness evidence of harmful conduct, the police investigations relied upon medical expertise, particularly that of paediatricians and pathologists. The courts were provided with the spectacle of professional men of high status condemning mothers who had suffered the terrible trauma of losing their children on evidence of a highly questionable kind, often buttressed by spurious judgements about the appropriateness of the woman's response to her loss. The assumption was that the babies had been suffocated when in fact pointers in other directions were over-looked. Ninety per cent of babies who die unexpectedly do so from natural causes and in some families genetic factors may explain more than one infant death. However, the presumption of innocence was ignored and hawkish beliefs about the propensity of certain mothers to kill their babies took hold. All the old stereo-types about appropriate behaviour for women and traditional mothering permeated the courts, and it was as though we had learned nothing in the last decade. Travesty was added to tragedy for these women and they will never recover.

In 2004, after the conviction of Ian Huntley for the Soham murders, an inquiry was launched into the police failure to keep records of numerous previous complaints against him of rape and sex with underage girls, all of which had been dropped by police. Huntley had applied for a job as a caretaker at a school close to the homes of the two young girls he subsequently murdered: a security check revealed no past history because the police in Humberside had destroyed the records. They claimed unconvincingly that this had been done to comply with the Data Protection Act. On that basis no police intelligence on suspects would ever be kept. The reality was that police took the sexual complaints with a pinch of salt. They claimed the underage sex was not prosecuted because the girls consented, which is not actually a defence to underage sex. One of the alleged rapes had not been pursued because the police were able to show from CCTV footage that the alleged victim had danced closely with Huntley before the sexual encounter in an alley. Consent to any intimacy is still consent to all, in the minds of some police officers.

In characterising the law's shortcomings I am aware that powerful cultural forces are at work. It is claimed that the law only reflects public attitudes which are prejudicial to women. However, we are entitled to expect more. The law transmits powerful messages, which construct and underpin our social relations. It is important that those messages do not reinforce stereotypical images of womanhood and femininity or endorse notions of masculinity which are detrimental to women and indeed negative for men. Judges say to me that one minute I want equality for women, yet the next minute I want the law to treat them differently. All I am really asking is that the law should be capable of transcending difference by first acknowledging it. The Supreme Courts in Canada, Australia and South Africa all now accept that formal equality is not good enough. Ameliorative or substantive equality requires courts in those jurisdictions to take account of the ways that women or other groups in society have endured discrimination.

The law regulates our social relations. In doing so it issues messages which resonate throughout society. Those messages are internalised, which is why the law is so important. The law can never be completely out of step with public feeling or it will be held in contempt but it should be capable of taking a lead in reshaping attitudes to violence, in challenging double sexual standards and in addressing gender disparities. This two-step which the law has to conduct, of leading public opinion yet also reflecting it, is a difficult manoeuvre. What does *not* work is for the law to lag behind public concerns or to dismiss their value.

Women up and down the country still feel that the law does not address their concerns. The perception that the courts are simply out of touch with the reality of people's lives poses a serious threat to justice. When the legal system fails, or is seen to fail, in the fulfilment of its practical function, society reaps the consequences. 'But the law cannot be subject to fashion' is the judicial refrain. No one would dispute this, but it can become an excuse for atrophy and blinkered vision. Real and generous shifts in attitudes are required to maintain confidence in the law.

The ritual and mystique of court procedure is itself out of date. A recurrent theme, heard from prisoners and witnesses alike when talking about their courtroom experiences, is the terror of the witness box, the intimidation of the procedure, made worse by the paraphernalia of wigs and gowns and a language which obfuscates rather than illuminates. Some people feel they are unable to give a good account of themselves because of disadvantage in the face of articulate middle-class lawyers. Self-consciousness then interferes with their ability to recollect events accurately. They are often unsure of the questions asked, but answer them as best they can because they do not want to be told off. That makes many defendants and victims, particularly women, feel like children again, undoubtedly because they often are treated as children.

The criminal trial is a terrifying process. Those who are most affected by it, the victims and defendants, are those who are most alienated by the ambience and the procedures.

The courtroom mystique is not unintentional: the participants are supposed to feel in awe of the process for its magic to work. But for many it brings back some of the nightmares of childhood. For the witness or defendant it means having the focus of attention turning on them in an environment which is comfortable only to a small class of people. It means speaking aloud in front of everyone. It means being scrutinised and perhaps being found wanting.

The number of jurors who cannot read the oath is often cited as a sign of our illiterate times; in fact the problem is more likely to be the difficulty of enunciating the words in public. The performance is the inhibitor. In an important trial with racial overtones the Crown asked for one of the few black jurors to be 'stood by' (released from service) because of his difficulty with reading; it was later discovered that he had no problem at all but was terrorised by the process. The *faux pas* had in the meantime wiped out confidence in the prosecution team, whose insensitivity was seen as an example of biased white justice.

Many people have misapprehensions about how the courts work. Schooled on American films, they do not realise that our system is different. They also fail to appreciate the degree of dramatic licence which operates. To the victim of a crime, for example, it comes as a shock that the person they see as conducting 'their' case almost never sits down and has a chat with them. Because the victim in a case is a witness the code of professional conduct in relation to witnesses comes into force, which means the prosecuting lawyer cannot speak to them about their evidence. Prosecuting counsel is counsel for the state. Defence barristers are also prohibited from talking directly to witnesses other than experts. Indeed, defence counsel should only really talk to his or her client in the presence of a solicitor. There is some flexibility about the rules in lower courts.

Obviously prosecutors could introduce themselves to witnesses, and many counsel for the Crown are now doing this, but there is still a large number of practitioners who feel that their impartiality should not be impugned. They do not want to run the risk of allegations that they said something inappropriate or tried to coach a witness, so the violated woman or child is left bewildered as to who is who amongst the bigwigs.

Even expert witnesses at times complain of their treatment as either patronising or dismissive. Psychiatrists, psychologists and sociologists have a particularly rough ride. They come like lambs to the slaughter if their reports are full of references to 'cycles of deprivation' or 'cognitive dissonance'. We have our own arcane language in the courtroom and we do not want anyone else's creeping in.

Justice can be compromised because people who are caught up in an already flawed legal process are often judged on grounds which have nothing whatsoever to do with the facts of the case. Those who are most susceptible are the young and the working-class, the immigrant, Muslim, Irish, black, homosexual or female: when we look at the problems facing women, we should always keep these other groups in mind.

In reviewing cases within these chapters, I have concentrated on women and crime because this is the field in which I practise, but the same fundamental problems operate in the other areas of the law in varying degrees. I am especially aware of the ways that immigration and asylum laws can discriminate against women because their lives are so poorly understood. I have also restricted my ambit to the courtroom and reflected on my own branch of the profession, which until recently had a monopoly of the right to conduct trials.

It is often the way with discriminatory practice that its victims know full well what is happening whilst those who perpetrate it are oblivious. Denying women their experience is one of the ways in which male power is maintained – which brings us back to the central issues addressed in this book. Is the criminal justice system sensitive to the reality of women's lives? If women as victims have cause for complaint what about women in the dock? And if this happens to women, are other citizens similarly disadvantaged?

Blame for the lack of confidence in the law cannot be placed at the door of judges or any one group of people. Nor is there any conspiracy afoot. It is the nature of the beast that needs reassessment, and the attitudes which support the survival of the status quo. Creating a legal framework which is truly equitable means a real overhaul of our legal thinking. The institution itself has to change. Only then will the law be just.

I

Eve was Framed

Law does not spring out of a social vacuum. My maternal grandmother had her own line in moralising, and one of the old wives' maxims that fell from her lips was that there would be no bad men if there were no bad women. This world view, which would usually be expounded as she swept vigorously around me while I attempted homework on the kitchen table, filtered through our days and was certainly absorbed by my mother. As we struggled through Glasgow Central Station past a group of well-soused merrymakers on our way home from paying the rent, she would tighten her grip on my hand and mutter that there was only one thing worse than a drunk man, and that was a drunk woman.

Even as a child it seemed to me that if there was one body of people who were tougher on women than on men it was other women, a puzzling contradiction given the strength of the female bonds in my community. However, for the most part I just accepted that there were higher expectations of women. At every point in my Catholic girlhood the Virgin Mary was presented to us as our role model. Men were simply victims of their own appetites, hardly capable of free will when it came to sex or violence, and it was up to us to act as the restraining influence. After all, woman was responsible for the original sin. It was only later that I came to the conclusion that Eve had been framed.

I swallowed the idea that women should generally be expected to behave better than men, since there seemed ample evidence that they did so anyway, and I could see no harm in keeping up the standard. However, my sense of natural justice balked at the idea of holding women responsible for male transgressions. Why should women be considered the moral cornerstones of society? Does motherhood really carry with it such an overwhelming obligation? Transportation from Paradise is one thing, but a sentence of eternal damnation when the conviction had to be based on the uncorroborated testimony of a co-accused must surely constitute a breach of international standards on human rights. Poor old Eve. I wonder if she would have done *any* better with a good defence lawyer. Here is the speech for the prosecution:

> To me a thoroughly criminal woman is a most repugnant crea-ture. Although male criminals largely outnumber females, there exist many more of the latter than appear in published statistics. That is to say, women are the cause of, directly or indirectly, a large amount of crime in men for which they receive no statisti-cal credit. Personally I feel quite convinced that some women wield a hypnotic influence over men, and it is invariably a malign influence . . . obeying that instinct for working mischief to the opposite sex which women would seem to have inherited from Mother Eve . . . Speaking generally, women have less willpower than men and therefore less self-control upon emergency. One of the most staggering and repugnant attributes of man exhibited by bad women is their perfectly fiendish cruelty. It is all the more startling by being displayed by one who is supposed to be gentle by nature. It is certainly a matter for meditation that the cruellest forms of crime are invariably committed by women. The only consolation is that they are not women in the ordinary acceptation of the word and something malign happened at their begetting which sets them apart from ordinary human beings.

Who could resist Hargrave L. Adams? I fell upon his *Woman and Crime* in a bookshop just off Chancery Lane, and read it aloud for the entertainment of friends in my early years of practice at the Bar. His Gothic descriptions of the devilish power of women and their abject wickedness were supplemented by photographs of women looking for all the world like pantomime dames. Traces of moustache visible around some of their mouths supported his hinted contention that an excess of male hormone must account for their behaviour. Others were flagrant in their seductiveness, heavy-lidded temptresses who lured good men to their doom.

Adams wrote his book around 1910, and his parade of poisoners, baby-farmers and vitriol throwers seemed a long way from the female offenders who crossed my path in my first years of practice. By and large, these women had come before the court because they lacked money and the opportunity to live a decent life. In the cells cigarettes were exchanged like salt in the desert, and we would talk the hours away in the long wait for cases to be called on.

A probation officer at Holloway Prison told me she thought that most women were in jail either because of a man or because of not having a man. This sounded like the flip-side of holding women responsible for male misdeeds, with men this time carrying the can. However, she was highlighting the reality of many women's lives, where involvement in crime arises out of doing something at the behest of a man, or as a result of the hardship of dealing with children alone when their man has left, or of the mess created by sexual abuse suffered when they were children or their experience of violence at the hands of husbands. The descent into alcohol and drug abuse or prostitution is almost invariably linked to those common threads. Women's pathways into crime are usually quite distinct from men's. According to commissioned research for the Fawcett Society by J. Rumgay *When Victims Become Offenders* (2004) 'coercion by others, particularly males, upon whom women may become economically dependent, often introduces them to lifestyles in which criminal activity plays a strong part'. A survey conducted by the criminologist, Pat Carlen, in the same year showed that six out of ten women coming out of prison had been inside for offences committed at the behest of men.

One of the main reasons why men commit crime is because it enhances their sense of masculinity, but the reverse is not true; far from it. Femininity is diminished by crime, and women who commit crime are reduced as women by the process of criminalisation because they know that they are perceived differently from their male counterparts.

Why is it that we feel differently about women committing crime? It always seems to me that crime is seen as an inevitable extension of normal male behaviour, whereas women offenders are thought to have breached sacred notions of what is deemed to be truly female. There is also a sense that criminal women poison the fount of youth. Rather like the old aphorism that educating a man means just that, whilst educating a woman means educating a whole family, the phrase 'criminal woman' induces fears of little potential criminals cowering behind her skirts.

All this was new to me. I did not come to the Bar in the early seventies as a feminist looking for slights against women. Indeed, I was not particularly conscious of women's issues at all, except inasmuch as they were part of my general concern about what happened to working-class people when they sought justice. I felt extreme irritation at the lengthy discussions about chairpersons when I wanted to get on with whatever was the business in hand. I did not know then about the power of language and the subtle means used to maintain control. I knew about the power that came with hiring and firing, owning and letting, having an education and being unschooled. I also knew about powerlessness in the face of that.

Powerlessness has inevitably meant that women have had to secure advantage by less crude methods than men, and – not just in the area of crime – have as a result often been labelled devious and Machiavellian, as though such traits are never present in the chaps. Female criminals are also portrayed as a rare species, and rarity quickly becomes translated into abnormality.

One of the major criminology studies conducted in the nineteenth century, by Lombroso and Ferrero, described women as congenitally less inclined to crime than men. However, it seems that they make up for this by the excessive vileness of the crimes they do commit. 'Rarely is a woman wicked,' wrote Cesare Lombroso, 'but when she is she surpasses the male.' Believing that the female criminal could be identified by certain physiological features, the two men examined the skull of Charlotte Corday, murderer of Marat, and pronounced it a truly criminal type. They did not seem to apply rigorous scientific standards to these tests and would most likely have said the same about the skull of a canonised nun if fed suggestive information. The fantasy of cross-examining them with a trunkful of skeletons at the ready brightens the odd moment.

A more recent student of female crime, the American Otto Pollak, contended in his study *The Criminality of Women* (1950) that women manipulate men into committing offences while remaining immune from prosecution themselves. He claimed that women are intrinsically cunning, as exemplified by the passive role they assume during intercourse, a passivity which allows them to fake orgasms in a way that men cannot. This ability, it seems, endows women with the master status of liars and deceivers. To those contemporary women who are confident and comfortable with their sexuality it all seems risible but remnants of such thinking remain. The fear of the manipulative, dissembling female lives on.

When it comes to 'economy with the truth' my own experience is that men are quite as good at dishing out the phoney baloney or sexing up the dossier as women. Women are rare amongst the ranks of confidence tricksters. Yet if you listen to many a judge directing the jury in a rape case, you would think most women suffered from an inherent defect which he feels he must reluctantly spell out. We are not always trustworthy, is the insidious message.

As I continued to practise, it became increasingly clear to me that women in court still had less credibility than men. As soon as it was announced that the alibi witness was a wife, girlfriend or female family member, eyes would often roll to the heavens in tacit agreement that her testimony would be worthless.

I used to think that women police officers would be seen as especially worthy of trust, given that they have not been tainted by police corruption scandals and are portrayed in television dramas like *Prime Suspect* as tough but tender and ethically unimpeachable. Yet, women in the police force tell me this is not true. It is assumed that, like women in the family, they will lie to save the skin of male colleagues, or be even more ruthless when on a crusade to convict an accused.

Wherever they stand in the courtroom, women have to fight harder to gain the same authority or credibility as their male counterparts. Female lawyers often describe being patronised and marginalised, their legal arguments given greater weight when repeated in the mouths of male colleagues. We see this same phenomenon in relation to women in politics. In September 2004

Patricia Hewitt mentioned the demographic problem facing Britain with so few babies being born, suggesting that a better work–life balance and improved childcare might affect the choices women make; she was attacked as a totalitarian nanny, advocating enforced breeding. The same insight from David Willetts, another politician, was greeted with acclaim.

Because we feel differently about women committing crime, we have gone to some lengths to avoid defining them as criminal, preferring the idea that they have emotional problems; they are mad rather than bad. The truth is that our desire to seek psychiatric explanations for women's crime is a way of trying to make it invisible, a profound expression of our worst fears about the social fabric falling apart. Women are still the glue that cements the family unit, providing cohesion and continuity, and we do not like to admit to the possibility that there is a potential for crime in us all. There is much less willingness to invoke the workings of the psyche to explain male wrongdoing. Even today scepticism about the role of the psychiatrist creeps into courtroom discussions, and judges adopt the tone of Lady Bracknell as soon as you dare to mention the unhappy childhood of the brute in the dock. With women the attitude is noticeably different.

The mystery of women's birth-giving properties obviously plays a part in sustaining judicial attitudes, and any disorder or disability linked to childbearing or the menstrual cycle has traditionally been treated sympathetically: postnatal depression or menopausal blues, post-abortion *tristesse* or premenstrual tension. However, medicalising and pathologising women is a way of perpetuating the myth that they are victims of their own physiology and that the function of all women might be intrinsically impaired. In 1991 a planning appeal was mounted in Australia on the grounds that the presiding member of the Appeals Tribunal was pregnant and, according to the appellant's affidavit, 'suffering from the well-known medical condition (placidity) which detracts significantly from the intellectual competence of all mothers-to-be'.

In the nineteenth century menstruation was a prominent explanation in cataloguing women's crime, especially if the offences were atypical or if the woman was not lower-class. Most women who stole could not afford a lawyer who would have them diagnosed as kleptomaniac, but for any woman with enough funds for a doctor as well as a lawyer, nymphomania, pyromania and all manner of manias were invented to explain their aberrant behaviour. Hysteria was the Latin word for the womb.

The suffragettes met with the same insistence that their behaviour was due to menstrual dysfunction, problems with their ovaries or chronic spinsterhood. In recent times the exaggerated attention given to premenstrual tension has fed into the theory that women's biology may be to blame for their behaviour; most defence advocates will be happy to exploit PMT, leaving aside the impact of this for women generally: it is the lawyer's imperative to prevent people going to jail.

In circumstances which defy this simple psychiatric labelling and where the offence is heinous, there is a very different response. Women not only become 'unsexed' in the way that Lady Macbeth felt was necessary to steel herself for crime, but take on monstrous proportions in the collective mind.

Myra Hindley's name is still one that springs to everyone's lips as soon as criminals come into the conversation, regardless of sex. Crimes involving children always engage our deepest emotions and we all feel a particular empathy with the families of the victims. But although the Moors Murders must come near the top of any catalogue of atrocities, public horror concentrated more and more on the female of the two offenders, and I think that, while this is partly because Hindley did not avoid visibility, it is largely because of her gender. The same was true in relation to Rose West who with her husband Fred West was involved in a catalogue of terrible sexual crimes including rape, torture and murder, culminating in her receiving multiple life sentences in 1995. We still find it mystifying that women should engage in such depravity.

After the Soham murder case in 2003, where two young girls were cruelly murdered by a school caretaker, Ian Huntley, public hostility remained disproportionately high towards his girlfriend Maxine Carr, who was in no way involved in the killings but who provided him for a period with an alibi, out of ignorant loyalty. On release from prison she had to be given a fresh identity and a rare court injunction was invoked to secure her protection from reprisals. Since then she has had to move house several times because she was recognised and at risk of attack. Even if women do not themselves have children, society expects them to embody the nurturance and protectiveness associated with mothering, and there is a heightened outrage when they seem to run in the face of those ideas.

Society still has higher expectations of women and it is one of the reasons why women have such a hard time securing justice in rape cases: they end up being judged by unspoken social laws about what is deemed acceptable behaviour for women.

The debate about rape which has now raged for over 30 years has opened many people's eyes to the workings of the legal system. If such incredible stereotyping of women works against them when they are victims of crime, what happens to women who appear in the dock charged with offences? The answer is not simple, and it is not heartening either. Some would have you believe that judges fall prey to the charms of women and are soft on them out of misguided chivalry, that women get away with murder and that a snub nose, high cheekbones and a shapely pair of legs would probably be of more benefit to the accused than an able defence lawyer.

The attitude of the court to a female accused still depends on the kind of woman she is perceived to be. In itself this is no different from the conscious and unconscious approach to any defendant, who is judged according to all sorts of hidden criteria, such as whether they are employable or whether they show enough respect to the court. But for a woman, the assessment of her worth is enmeshed in very limiting ideas. If she challenges conventions in any significant way, she is seen as threatening or, at the least, disappointing. A mere hint in court that a woman might be a bad mother, a bit of a whore or emotionally unstable, and she is lost. And whether she is victim or offender it is very hard to withstand the attack of an inventive cross-examiner. There is, for instance, a double edge to the seemingly uncontroversial question about how long before the alleged rape a woman had sexual intercourse. A long time before implies sexual loneliness, a reason for seeking out intercourse with almost anyone, whereas an active sexual life implies a voracious, indiscriminate, appetite. There is no winning.

The chivalry hypothesis has little substance. Indeed, the view of many judges today is 'you want equality? well, you'll get equality'. Taking insufficient account of the fact that women are still the primary carers of children and other family members, they ignore the way women are still discriminated against in the job market and fail to see that the sentencing system is formulated with men in mind. The organisation Women in Prison reports that women, ironically, sometimes receive harsher sentences than men because they are mothers. They may be deemed unsuitable for community service because they have young children, but then the courts, unable or unwilling to come up with an alternative punishment, send them to jail.

In the gamut of crime women usually commit less serious offences. They also tend to play supportive roles: harbouring and handling stolen goods, carrying drugs, providing safe houses, cashing stolen cheques. As in the world of legitimate enterprises, they are still on the payroll but are rarely the paymaster, a syndrome that is usually reflected in shorter sentences but has nothing to do with the kindness of judges. While Joyti De-Laurey, the personal assistant to a director of Goldman Sachs the bankers, may have spirited away over £4 million without her boss noticing, few women embark on such bold embezzlement. White collar criminals usually have a wife at home laundering their shirts. Women are a minority of those suspected or convicted of crime, representing just one in five of known offenders. However, the escalation of the numbers of women being sent to prison is shocking – in the last decade the female prison population has trebled. According to Home Office statistics on 2 July 2004 there were 4,475 women in prison. Ten years ago in 1994 the average female population was 1,811. Five years ago in 1999 it stood at 3,247. During the course of 2002, 12,650 women were received into prison. Yet there has been no equivalent rise in the number of women committing offences or women committing more serious offences. Two-thirds of of the women who enter custody in a year are on remand; that means they are as yet unconvicted. Of these, 58% do not receive a custodial sentence and one in five is acquitted altogether. It is obvious that they should not have been in custody in the first place but the question as to why this is happening is rarely asked. Fifteen per cent of suicides in prison in 2003 (14 out of 94) were committed by women, according to the Prison Service Safer Custody group yet they account for only 6% of the average daily population. In 1993 there was only one female suicide in custody.

What is bizarre is that of sentenced female prisoners, the majority are held for non-violent offences despite the constant refrain that prison should really only be used for violent offenders or those committing serious crime. Over 70% of women in prison are on short sentences of less than 12 months, sentences which serve no earthly purpose other than retributive punishment. Half of all imprisoned women have dependent children. More women were sent to prison in 2002 for shoplifting than any other crime. Shoplifters accounted for nearly a third of all women sentenced to immediate custody in that year. A woman convicted of theft or handling at the Crown Court is now twice as likely to go to prison as in 1991. At the Magistrates' Courts the chance of a woman receiving a custodial sentence has risen sevenfold.

Why are we seeing this disproportionate punishment of women? While some of it can be explained by an increase in the severity of sentences generally, this cannot adequately account for such a meteoric rise. I have no doubt that in part it is the result of the crude equation that equality means no soft-soaping of women, even if they have babies and young children or a history of being abused. Our call for gender equality has led to a hamfisted, literal interpretation of equality with no consideration of the context of the women's lives.

I happen to be of the unfashionable school that thinks that crime for the most part has its roots in social or emotional deprivation, whether you are male or female. I also see little value in imprisoning those whose offending is rooted in social problems, when support and treatment in the community is going to wreak far less damage on everyone concerned. I certainly think that imprisoning for low-level crime is ludicrous as well as cruel. But increasingly prisons are being used as the dumping ground for those whose needs are not being met by underfunded public services. As Singleton et al reported in 1998, two-thirds of women in prison suffer from mental health problems; over half have suffered domestic violence and one in three has experienced sexual abuse. Around 40% of women in prison are dependent users of drugs.

Given the nature of our legal system and the history of its development, it is hardly surprising that women have special problems in our courtrooms.

The common law upon which our legal system is based developed in the Middle Ages when, drawing on the Roman law tradition, women and children were placed under the jurisdiction of the paternal power, the head of the household, and were deemed to be his property.

As communities grew in size and as the nature of the state changed, legal proceedings became formalised. The records of the previous decisions of the courts were called upon to declare the state of the law, and it was this body of cases and the principles inferred from them which became known as the common law.

The main tribunal in which women initially figured was the ecclesiastical court, where allegations of witchcraft were tried. All sorts of behaviour thought to be aberrant for a woman were defined as sorcery and contrary to canon law. The Church had a low opinion of women at the best of times, and those who seemed to have abandoned the control of men or who were licentious or of independent mind rarely survived to sell their story to the local minstrel. In time the jurisdiction over witchcraft transferred to the Assizes, the ordinary criminal courts, and like other serious felonies was met with execution.

As the law developed it began to flow from other sources: the writings and opinions of legal commentators and statutes passed by parliament. Until comparatively recently women played no part at all in the construction and content of the law, and even now their role in lawmaking is barely significant. Until 2003 there was no woman at all in the House of Lords – the British supreme court – and the appointment of the brilliant Brenda Hale to their lordships' ranks was long overdue. This has inevitably meant that law has been made from a male perspective with little female input. Fortunately, the parliamentary role in lawmaking has been improved by the increasing presence of women in the legislature as MPs and peers. However, there are still few women in positions of power and influence, despite women being 52% of the population.

Until the late nineteenth century, under the common law a husband and wife were treated as one person and marriage meant the surrender of separate legal rights for a woman. From this unity of husband and wife sprang all the disabilities of the married woman. She could own no property in her own right and commence no legal action because either would imply she had a separate legal existence. Wives then and until very recently could not be raped by their husbands, because they were supposed to have contracted to provide sex whenever their husbands wished it. Women had no custodial rights of the children they bore in wedlock; rights of custody belonged to fathers alone. They were long excluded from being witnesses, save in exceptional cases, and even after it became acceptable for women to testify they could not give evidence against their husbands. They were generally deemed to be under the control of their spouse. In the words of one legal commentator quoted in Radcliffe & Cross's *The English Legal System* (1964):

> It was a doctrine of elegant simplicity and one capable of remarkable results. It was a doctrine that removed, in theory, the burdens of responsibility and the sanctions of morality from any woman who entered the holy state of matrimony. Logically considered, all her crimes and all her sins emanated from the duplicated brain of her husband and her lord. Not only did she convey to him her person and her worldly goods, but she added the entire responsibility of her personality to the weight of his own. The Creator took from Adam a rib and made it Eve; the common law of England endeavoured to reverse the process, to replace the rib and to remerge the personalities.

The nineteenth century saw a revolutionary change in women's status, brought about (as is always the case), not by the generous bequest of the powerful, but by the pressure of women's demands. The Married Women's Property Acts of 1870 and 1882 were historic victories, allowing married women a legal identity and removing in part their invisibility. But the task of pulling the weight of this legal monolith into the twenty-first century, when people

have very different roles and expectations, seems H\
especially when well nigh all of the powerful positions wi\
law are held by the kind of men who roll their eyes at tl ↙ery
mention of gender bias. In the old days they laughed and scoffed at
the very word 'sexism' but a new culture prevents such open
dismissal. Most legislation and case law nowadays has the
semblance of neutrality, and some legislative changes are designed
to improve the position of women, but the letter of the law can too
easily become a cloak for the reality.

Discriminatory practices still surface in many areas of the law. In
the Family Courts, there have been enormous improvements,
culminating in recent judgments recognising the value of a
woman's contribution to her husband's financial success by caring
for the family over the years. Settlements may now take account of
a spouse's future earnings in reaching a fair disposition of assets.
But still the courts are often ignorant of the kinds of jobs and
salaries available to women, the costs of childcare and the particular
employment problems of the displaced homemaker. In judicial
training sessions in the USA groups of judges are asked to put the
value on a bag of groceries. Few are able to do so and I am sure our
own judges would not fare any better.

The claim is currently made by the lobbying group Fathers 4
Justice that the Family Courts now discriminate against men in
child custody disputes; they maintain that feminists have a
stranglehold on family law and the pendulum has swung so far that
men are now an oppressed minority. While it is true that there are
injustices around access, with some embittered, vengeful wives
blocking visiting rights to children, the picture is often more
complex. If there has been a history of domestic violence towards a
partner, the court has to perform a hard balancing act, recognising
that the abuse of a mother is almost invariably abusive of the
children who witness it, especially if she insists that she faces
continuing harassment. Judges are also faced with a serious
problem about how they enforce orders against women. Sending a
woman to jail when she is the mainstay in the lives of her children
is a choice Family Court judges resist, while their brothers in the
Criminal Court seem to have less inhibitions. The courts are

expected to place the well-being and interests of children at the centre of their deliberations. However, rather than a display of feminism, leaving children with a mother can often be the result of deeply entrenched ideas amongst judges about appropriate roles for men and women. When I did my stint of family work I saw decisions being made about custody in which women were penalised if they were the ones who had walked out of the matrimonial home, leaving children behind, even when they did so to escape abuse. This was particularly true if a woman had found a boyfriend. It was the same test which had been applied over a century before to Annie Besant, the pioneer of contraception, who was prosecuted in 1871 for publishing pamphlets on family planning. Her sexual politics was seen as a sign of her unsuitability as a mother, and she too suffered the slings of courtroom bias, by being denied custody of her daughter. Colleagues practising in the family courts say there are still residues of those attitudes around, which are based on stereotypes of gender roles and double sexual standards.

Sometimes the victories which are achieved for women have bizarre consequences because the wrongs they are seeking to redress are not fully understood by those who are asked to put the changes into practice. The Parlour decision in 2004 was greeted by women as a significant breakthrough for wives and partners who stay at home to care for children, making significant personal sacrifices in their own careers and contributing to their man's success. Ray Parlour is a celebrity footballer playing in the Premier League who commands a huge salary which is likely to increase; he also receives very high increments for promotions and advertising. The court in the Parlour settlement decided that Mrs Parlour should receive not only a division of current assets but also a portion of Ray Parlour's future earnings. The same principle should apply where a male partner assumes the domestic role. However, in the spirit of gender equality the courts now interpret this to mean that when a couple divorces after their children are grown and both have had careers, if the woman earns more and has better prospects for the future she has to fork out to her husband even if he never took a greater role in childcare than she did. There is also a failure to acknowledge that even where both partners work, mothers usually bear the responsibility of organising childcare and most of the domestic scene.

Translating these principles into the reality of people's lives seems to defy judges for whom, like the past, gender inequality is a foreign country. For the same reasons, women also have problems in obtaining realistic damages for personal injuries, because awards are so closely tied to wage-earning and those who work in the home often receive ridiculously low sums: the real economic value of housework is never explored.

In many areas of the law women still suffer from antiquated views. Most of the time these are quite unconscious and unspoken, and therefore hard to challenge. In this book I have concentrated on the criminal justice system, partly because it is the area in which I have now practised, woman and girl, for thirty years, but also because, affecting as it does the liberty of the subject, it is an area of the law which needs to be addressed with the greatest urgency.

The web of prejudice, privilege and misinformation that affects women is, of course, compounded for the poor. The experience of women is a paradigm of that which faces any person, male or female, who is not part of the dominant culture. There is no conspiracy. Often the assumptions arise simply from a lack of insight into the lives lived by people of a different class. A woman who practises in the field of childcare says that over the years, whenever judges have expressed concern about working mothers not spending enough time with their children, she has always made the simple comparison with children who are sent to boarding-school. She says that the discomfort can be tangible.

Judging is not an easy task, and in the face of criticism some judges wonder whether it is worth the candle. In press reports that cause uproar after a trial, complex details are often overlooked. But because it is considered undignified and unproductive, judges are encouraged to say nothing in the face of public criticism, even when there may well be good reasons for some of their remarks. That is why open explanations for decisions should, in my view, almost always be given in court. Judges also suffer from being misreported and having their words taken out of context.

If any single category of human being is unaccustomed to being treated as inferior or subordinate, it is a white, male, British judge. It has rarely been part of his life's experience. In broad terms, even today four out of five full-time professional judges in the higher courts are the product of public schools and of Oxford and Cambridge. Very occasionally the less privileged have joined the ranks, and that number is slowly growing. It is barely possible to mention the narrow background of the judiciary now without some fellow jumping up and informing you that his father was a coalman or a garage owner. Products of the grammar schools are becoming thicker on the ground as the beneficiaries of expanded university education in the 1960s and '70s progress through the Bar. However, the men on the Bench often find it hard even to imagine the lives of the really disadvantaged or the young. The retirement age for judges has only just been reduced to 70. The average age of judges in this country is between 60 and 65, which coincides with the time when most other people are retiring. And according to statistics presented by the Department for Constitutional Affairs in autumn 2004, only nine High Court judges out of 108 are women. Of these, one is black. She is the only black judge in the High Court.

Being told that you may be unfair, even unconsciously, is not something any of us welcome. Many judges find it hard to accept that they are ever affected by extraneous considerations. The former Lord Chancellor, Lord Mackay, who is sensitive to these issues, tells a story about his days as a lecturer at Edinburgh University when he was required to mark a register of student attendance. For the most part he would call out the names of students, but on a number of occasions he marked off the name of the one black student without calling it out, partly because he was well aware of the student's presence but also because he was hesitant about the pronunciation. The student challenged him about it and Lord Mackay was wretched to think he had been hurtful to a student whom he liked and regarded well. It must be emphasised that there are many decent judges who are keen to take on board new learning and who think deeply about the power and authority they wield.

The law mirrors society with all its imperfections and it therefore reflects the subordination of women, even today. But holding up a mirror can never be its sole function. The law affects as well as reflects, and all of those involved in the administration of justice have a special obligation to reject society's irrational prejudices.

The law is symbolic, playing an important role in the internalising of ideas about what is right and natural. If the men of law say sexily dressed women have it coming to them, they reinforce that view in the man on the street. The law constructs beliefs about roles of men and women in the home and at work which feed back into generally held attitudes about women.

True justice is about more than refereeing between two sides. It is about breathing life into the rules so that no side is at a disadvantage because of sex or race or any of the other impediments which deny justice.

It is no answer to make a simple call for equal treatment. Dealing equally with those who are unequal creates more inequality. Justice is obtained by giving a fair and unbiased appraisal of each person and situation, without relying on preconceived notions, whether the defendant is black or white, male or female, straight or gay. Justice recognises the tension between the ideal of equality and the reality of people's lives. There are those who claim that the true classical symbol of Justice has her wearing a blindfold of impartiality, but I prefer the image of an all-seeing goddess, as she appears above the Central Criminal Court at the Old Bailey.

2

Playing Portia

Myths are tent pegs which secure the status quo. In the law, mythology operates almost as powerfully as legal precedent in inhibiting change. Women are particularly at its mercy, although men do not escape its force, especially when issues of class and race emerge.

Sometimes the myths conflict. The myth that women are arch-deceivers, prone to making false allegations, blights many rape trials – unless the defendant is black, when the myth of his rampant sexuality emerges in competition. The old belief that it is only working-class men who abuse their wives sits comfortably with the belief that women are masochists anyway. The assumption that men do women's thinking for them, prevailing on them to provide false alibis and bail, does battle with the myth that it is women who incite criminal enterprise.

Mythology is a triumph of belief over reality, depending for its survival not on evidence but on constant reiteration. Myths are not the same as lies, in that they do not involve deliberate falsification. They endure because they serve social needs. The notion that judges are invariably impartial is also pervasive and unreal, but it is supposed to sustain our faith in the legal system.

Mythologies do change. They also vary between different groupings, but what matter are the dominant myths which receive institutional reinforcement daily in the administration of justice.

I had not been in criminal practice for long before I realised that special rules apply in, for example, rape cases. I saw some male jurors winking their support for my male client before the alleged victim had even finished her evidence, and I learned very quickly, like every other lawyer worth her salt and a brief fee, that the nearer I could get to painting my female client as a paragon of traditional womanhood, the more likely she was to experience the quality of mercy. If a woman with a weakness for bovver boots could be persuaded into wearing pearls and a *broderie anglaise* blouse she might just tip the judicial scales in her favour. Of course, male clients are also encouraged to present themselves smartly, but for women the purpose is much more complex.

The first case I ever did was for a woman who was pleading guilty in the Magistrates' Court to shoplifting. The items were children's clothes, and I was reassured by all the old hands in chambers that nothing much would happen to her: women always got off lightly and she would probably be fined, even if she did have a couple of previous convictions. I arrived at court and found my client in a state of great anxiety because she had not been able to make any arrangements for her children. It turned out that she had a suspended sentence of imprisonment outstanding which, in some bid to deny the inevitability of going to prison, she had failed to mention to my instructing solicitor. Like so many poor women, she had no resources to pay a fine and the courts had on previous occasions run through what they saw as the alternatives: a conditional discharge, then a probation order, then a suspended sentence and now the full McCoy. In this miserable first experience, as I watched my despairing client being taken off to Holloway, weeping for her children, I saw what we all now know from the research. Because their lack of resources makes financial penalties unsuitable, and because there are so few community programmes suited to women, female offenders end up in prison, despite the often trivial nature of their offending. Three times as many women as men go to prison for a first offence (*Guardian*, 21 November 1991).

It does not do wonders for your confidence when your first client is packed off to jail, however hopeless the case, but I hung on in there, doing a particularly active trade (which I thoroughly enjoyed) in my early years representing fellow Scots, marauding tartan-clad supporters who had been involved in displays of male camaraderie after Cup Finals. I suppose I was instructed on the assumption that I would be able to translate. While every other woman in the law tells stories of being taken for the solicitor's secretary, I was generally taken for the defendant's sister. Young black women in the law tell me the same assumption is made about them. I also had a significant clientele of Glaswegian prostitutes, whose families all thought they were down south working with the Civil Service. Some of them sent home money for babies their mothers were rearing for them; others had children living with them whom they looked after perfectly well, despite all belief to the contrary.

The early years of every barrister's practice are spent gaining experience in the lower courts. As a woman intent on criminal work I often found myself in the Juvenile and Magistrates' Courts representing women and children, because in the dispersal of legal crumbs by solicitors or more especially chambers' clerks the soft end of offending went to the girls. Even as I have progressed up the ladder into serious crime I have always represented a proportionately higher number of women and young people, because in the expectations of the courtroom it is an appropriate role to play.

Women are also often sought to act for men in rape and other sexual assaults, because of the involuntary endorsement they give to the male defendant. A recurring moan of pain is uttered in the women's robing room at the Old Bailey by female barristers who are force-fed a diet of sexual offence cases to the exclusion of all else. The men either make themselves scarce or say they can't hack it if children are involved. In a skewed effort to flaunt their professionalism women not only find themselves conducting these cases but sometimes do them with as much machismo as any man.

I too have done my share of sexual cases. Inevitably I have been able to watch the dynamics of the court as well as participate in them, and I have no doubt that sexuality and reproduction play a role in the judging of women which is not only irrelevant but unequalled by anything that happens to men.

For me, coming to the Bar was almost an accident. It was an escape route from the original plan to study in Glasgow, and was devised after weeks of panic in London. I was doing a summer job and had breathed the air of other possibilities, a world beyond. But the pleasure my family had taken in the first of us going to university meant that any proposed alternative had to satisfy their anxieties about the unknown, and fulfil their hopes that I might end up with a good job.

The only professional women they or I had ever known were schoolteachers, who in those days seemed to have a better material life than any other women we knew. For my own part, doing an English degree seemed like the most wonderful chance to read as much as you wanted without anyone accusing you of shirking. I had spent my childhood hearing aunts rebuke my mother for failing to take my nose out of a book and insisting that too much reading made you ill. Yet there was a certain predictability in heading towards teaching which made me want to resist it. I wanted to do what was not expected of me. The only other person I knew with a degree had read law, and its mysteries had caught my imagination.

In the United Kingdom and in Ireland, unlike in the United States and other jurisdictions, the legal profession is divided into two distinct parts. Barristers, of whom there are now 11,000, provide specialist advice and courtroom advocacy, and solicitors, of whom there are around 90,000, provide a range of services from drawing up contracts, doing the conveyance on a property, writing a will, and representing suspects in the police station to preparing cases and representing defendants in mainly lower courts. I was seduced by the heightened drama of the Bar.

My father, a soft-hearted, intelligent man, had left school, like my mother, at 14. He worked as a dispatch hand in the print industry and was active in his union. I remember his passionate belief in the Labour movement and his pride in the changes which had been won in his lifetime. He thrilled to the idea of my doing law, especially when I said I wanted to be a trade union lawyer. I'm not sure where I picked up that idea from, but it seemed like a way of being professional without sounding too high-falutin'.

When some of my relatives were told I had joined 'Gray's Inn' and was studying for the 'Bar' they imagined I had gone in for hotel management or catering and could not understand why anyone would pass up Glasgow University to do such a thing.

The Inns of Court – Lincoln's Inn, Gray's Inn, Middle Temple and Inner Temple – are the four old-established centres for barristers which act both as colleges which you have to join and workplaces where groups of barristers have chambers (offices). The Inns of Court have since the beginning of their existence in the fourteenth century enjoyed the sole right to admit, train and, in general, control the professional life of the barristers. The constitution of the Inns has been described by Sir Frederick Pollock in his *Essays in the Law* as 'a survival of medieval republican oligarchy, the purest to be found in Europe'.

The Inns are governed by the Benchers, who are not elected but who themselves choose their fellows and successors. They act as landlords of the Inns' properties. The Inns are also responsible for the education and training of barristers.

The requirements for qualification as a barrister have changed since I did my training. Today, once the aspiring barrister has done a law degree or the post-graduate diploma in law, he or she must complete a period of vocational training at one of a handful of institutions around England and Wales. The hopeful barrister must also be admitted to one of the four Inns of Court. As a requisite for being called to the Bar, the professional body of practitioners, the student must eat 12 dinners in the Inn's Hall. In my day it was 24 dinners.

If a barrister practises in London, he or she will usually do so from chambers which are located in one of the four Inns. When not doing a case out of London, many barristers continue to eat regularly in the Inn, which runs on the lines of the best London clubs.

The arrangements and language would bemuse any bystander, and when you add to that the whole complicated system of courts, with its different divisions ranging from the local magistrates' court to the Court of Appeal, it was no wonder my relatives were bewildered. Their confusion was not helped by my father trying to explain to them that for some reason I had to eat all these dinners in order to qualify. It sounded like a queer way to learn a profession, something only the English could have thought up.

The mysteries of the legal system in Scotland, let alone England, had rarely impinged on our lives, save for shamed references to cousin Bertie, who had ingeniously wired up his electricity to the street-lighting and seen the inside of Barlinnie.

My mother was surprisingly quiet at my decision. To her, London was purgatory, if not hell, and she muttered about things coming to a sorry pass. She had had her own run-in with lawyers when she tried to get compensation for a head injury after a falling slate had nearly blinded her. She had gone to a solicitor only after much cajoling, sure that just asking questions would cost her money and that lawyers were not for the likes of her. She had much more faith in holy water than the legal system, and merely getting involved in that world frightened her. Her line was that any normal person would be thrilled at the chance of being a lady teacher, and she ignored my refrain about not knowing any boys who had that ambition.

Against this well-meaning resistance I just had to succeed; however miserable I was, there could be no complaining. And was I miserable! Like childbirth, nothing had really prepared me for it.

I stepped from the equivalent of a comprehensive school in no mean city into the pages of an Evelyn Waugh novel. Like a foreigner abroad, I smiled a lot to cover my bewilderment, and my benevolence was totally misread by hordes of public-school boys who did not know what it meant to have a girl as a friend.

Lectures were the least of my problems, providing a happy respite from social contact. The Inn robing room, where we put on a legal gown for dining, was the real class divider. Here, like the Queen, women carefully knotted silk headscarves in front of their chins rather than under them, and talked about weekend house parties and 'cockers-pees', which after enough eavesdropping I realised were nothing more vulgar than cocktail parties.

Sixties radicalism had certainly not had its way in the Inns of Court. Down the road at the London School of Economics, students were in revolt about the way the school was governed; everywhere young people were demonstrating – against the war in Vietnam, then at its height, and against apartheid, demanding disinvestment in South Africa. Meanwhile at Gray's Inn, except amongst a very few, the main topics of conversation were the Field Club Ball and the Fencing Club. There was even a Smoking Concert after dinner during each Trinity Term, from which women were excluded because of the ribald nature of the proceedings. I remember a great uproar when Clarissa Dickson Wright, disguised in a bear outfit, gatecrashed the event. The wrath of one Judge Thesiger was wrought upon her and she was expelled from the Hall.

Hall was supposed to represent the heart of life as a Bar student. Here, in the rarefied atmosphere of the beautiful wood-panelled hall, dining was to present the opportunity for exchanging learned legal footnotes and scholarly opinions on case law. It was all supposed to be made real by our sitting alongside fellows who were actually doing the business of practising in court, though in reality anyone who had a halfway decent practice and a reasonable family life was not whiling away his nights eating Gray's Inn dinners.

The idea behind the anachronistic process of dining is that it creates a camaraderie amongst the profession in which familiarity will help in the maintenance of high ethical standards, somewhat in the nature of the college spirit at Oxford or Cambridge. It is also expected that these events will provide the opportunity for new entrants to a profession to make contacts which will serve them well throughout practice, and may help them find out about the different chambers to which they might apply as a pupil or as a tenant. Patronage was an insidious feature of life at the Bar.

Across the refectory tables trainee lawyers are meant to imbibe the barristerial ethos along with their port, hearing courtroom anecdotes, Inns of Court gossip and, if they are very lucky, learned legal exchanges. For most students, 'dining in hall' or 'keeping term' is an inconvenience, to be endured rather than enjoyed. For me Gray's Inn was another planet. I remember taking my place tentatively in Hall as one of the relatively few women studying for the Bar at that time. I had been forewarned to avoid the seat at the farmost corner, as a special rite fell upon the person placed there. As soon as the plates were cleared a clamour went up, remnants of bread roll were jettisoned towards the corner, spoons were rung against the glasses and the call of 'Up, junior!' resounded through the Hall. The unfortunate student seated at the end of the last row was expected to request permission to smoke from the 'Senior in Hall'. Projecting the voice above such a din was all part of the oratorical practice for some future advocate as great as Edward

Marshall Hall, the Victorian supremo. But woe to the woman who unsuspectingly arrived last and was required to sit in this hellish place. The noise levels were then insurmountable. The demand was that she stand on the table to be heard above the ribaldry and catcalls. I remember expressing my horror to a more worldly table-mate, asking him what was wrong with these people. He laughingly warned me if I started calling such ancient tradition into question I would be accused of having a chip on my shoulder.

My avoidance of this seat did not save me from humiliation. Gray's Inn maintained another strange formula for giving students the opportunity of practising their skill as advocates. Prissy rules of etiquette obliged diners to square themselves off into sets of four along the lengthy trestles. Within your 'mess' of four you had to toast each other in a special order and pass the port according to ship's rules. Breach of this etiquette entitled a diner to act as plaintiff and bring a charge against his colleague, who was then required to defend himself. The Senior in Hall sat in judgment.

I unwittingly became the recipient of such a charge, made by a blustering public-school boy. Fingers in his lapels, he denounced me for entering the hallowed halls inappropriately dressed; what was more, he confided conspiratorially, he could 'see through' my 'little scheme'. This attempt at wit was directed at the black crocheted dress I was wearing under my student gown. It was the one black garment I possessed and fulfilled the colour requirement for dining. Appropriate to the fashion of the time, it was about six inches above my knees, but it was worn over a black petticoat. I still remember my puzzlement and then mortification as the thundering cacophony built up in the Hall. Spoons hit the table and feet stamped the floor for what seemed like an eternity as they demanded a display of my clothing. Finally, quiet was called for by our 'judge', who asked if I wished to defend myself.

I sat motionless, not recognising the court, and maintaining my right to silence. Calls of 'bad sport' went up, and then the Senior suggested that this was a case where the judge should have a view of the *locus in quo*. He requested that I come up to the front and, after hesitating, I obligingly mustered as much dignity as I could and complied. I was made to parade in front of him with neither of us exchanging a word. On my returning to my place he chivalrously found for me and awarded me a decanter of port. At what a price. For months I tossed in my bed re-creating those events, and in my dreams I did not play the game but made the perfect crushing statement and resisted the pressure that is always applied to women to 'see the fun'.

Like everyone else I completed my dinners. I became engulfed in practice at the Bar and, apart from the occasional lunch in Hall, returned to dine only ten years later. The occasion was a debate, and I was responding to a request from some young women students who felt a motion put before the House was offensive. I can no longer remember the exact wording – something like 'A woman's place is on her back' or 'Woman is her own worst enemy'. In solidarity, I turned up to oppose the motion, optimistic that the majority of male law students would have changed. As the evening wore on, my heart sank. All the same old ritual persisted. The buffoon who proposed the motion had a huge claque of puerile supporters in the audience who thought it enormously funny to say rude words usually found in relation to women's secondary sexual characteristics. When one woman student in the Hall expressed indignation, Mr Proposer's response was, 'What's the matter with you, Stephanie, are you having your period?' Visions of him and his cronies got up in full-bottomed wigs and judicial robes flooded my brain. If this was the flower of tomorrow's legal profession, the problem required more than hope and a prayer.

Before long I began gravitating towards other outsiders, many of whom were carefully referred to as 'Commonwealth students', and found a happy home in their midst. Some had interesting political backgrounds and were studying law during periods of enforced exile. Whenever there was a coup in some African state my father would expect the ousted leader to end up at the Inns of Court, and he was often right. Amongst these men and women there were white and black South Africans, people from the Caribbean, Malaysia, India and Pakistan, who opened my eyes to the world and its wider politics. The only time there was ever any real political action amongst the students was when there was an organised student sit-in in resistance to a ploy by the Inns of Court which would have prevented overseas law students staying on after they qualified to get experience in pupillage; they were being asked to undertake to leave as soon as they passed their exams. The campaign was successful, and I have a lasting sense of the solidarity which developed. I became actively involved in the Debating Society, which in Gray's Inn substituted for the student politics you find in other academic institutions. The ticket we ran on for election as office-holders of the society was mildly progressive, and succeeded only because of the general lack of interest of most of the students. I was eventually elected vice-president of the society and found a niche in this 'foreign country' that was the forcing house for tomorrow's legal establishment, but I had to fight damned hard for my foothold. Pity any child of the lower orders who does not have a mother sitting in Glasgow waiting to remind them that they had been warned about taking up with Sassenachs and fancy things like law.

In this world of insiders and outsiders I was often content to be a watcher, a student of social mores, which may explain why I see so much of what goes on in the law through the eyes of the consumer. When people criticise the law or lawyers I rarely feel defensive, because I do not feel they are talking about me. Yet for many within the profession it is an unforgivable betrayal to criticise one's brothers in law. You may be allowed to do it with restraint within the profession, but woe betide the fool who breaks rank. I suppose it is one of the lessons that lives on long after public school, that whatever happens you owe it to your House to defend its good name, even if there is the odd bully or pederast in it generally making life hell.

In the insider/outsider scenario there is often no one more desperately protective of the legal environment than the outsider who now belongs, just as there is no one who loves the Garrick more than the tabloid editor, or the House of Lords more than a New Labour peer. You should always worry about the barrister who wears the black jacket and pinstriped trousers or who carries one of those cloth bags with their kit in it. It is a sure sign he has only just qualified or that he rarely gets a brief but desperately wants the world to know he is a barrister. Those who need the comfort of a *Brüderbond* insist on the little rituals which set the barrister apart: the silly refusal to shake hands on introduction because we barristers are part of a fraternity where such a formality is not required.

The Bar can be a very seductive place. Once you have got over the hurdles and have established yourself in practice, and once your colleagues know that, despite your politics, you are not really that bad after all, it can be wonderful. There is a general tolerance of the other view, and certainly at the Criminal Bar the camaraderie is one of the most pleasurable parts of the job. The fight in court can be tough and the locking of horns can be serious stuff, but only rarely does the wrangle live on beyond the case.

However, there are hurdles, and these should not be forgotten.

Sadly, too many people do forget, or did not encounter them because of the oil of privilege, which works a treat in most institutions and to which the law is particularly susceptible. I did not know anyone in practice at the English Bar when I started, which is the experience of most ordinary folk, and I did not know where to begin when it came to finding pupillage. Fortunately, the system is now much more transparent and open. Applications to chambers can rarely now be done through the old boy network. Chambers are now required by Bar rules to invite competitive application and they have interviewing panels which are given clear guidance on proper interviewing practice. Back then, anyone whose family had no professional connections was at a serious disadvantage.

Once called to the Bar, the new barrister is still not fully qualified but must embark on a 12-month period of pupillage, during which they are attached as an apprentice to a practising barrister. The pupil will go to court with their pupil-master to learn how to conduct a case, and will read all his or her briefs and have a try at writing opinions or drafting pleadings; the pupil will also look up points of law for the master and prepare notes for him (or her, though there were very few women around at the time when I was a pupil) to use in court.

I persuaded a friend who qualified the year before to introduce me to his pupil-master, whom I then bludgeoned into taking me on, despite his warning that I would hate it in his chambers. He was absolutely right.

Chambers are the rooms in which barristers work, traditionally cloistered within the Inns. There is an architectural coherence about these male institutions: public schools, Oxbridge colleges, Inns of Court, Houses of Parliament. They combine opulence with austerity. The entrances to many sets of chambers resemble the closes of Scottish tenements, stark and bare-boarded. The conditions within are usually cramped like a book- and leather-bound womb. The lavatories might interest the public health inspectorate.

Within sets of chambers, as the rooms are called, each barrister is self-employed, but there is a unity and interdependence particularly in the early stages of practice, with work switching between barristers. Chambers, therefore, means more than shared offices and involves embracing the corporate identity of your brethren.

The clerks in my pupillage chambers did not like women and acted as though I were a piece of flotsam that had drifted in by mistake. Standing in the clerk's room trying to secure their attention was like trying to get served in the Harrods perfume department when you are wearing your old anorak. There were no other women, and the male barristers minded the invasion of their all-male sanctum. The discrimination was blatant, and sets of chambers openly declared a no-women policy.

The story for black barristers was even worse. In 1979 there were only 200 ethnic minority barristers in independent practice. Most of those practised from chambers entirely comprised of those from ethnic minorities, and their work came largely from the minority communities. A committee was set up at the Bar to look at racial discrimination. In 1989 the Bar Council commissioned a survey which showed that in multi-racial Britain more than half of the total of all chambers did not have a single black or Asian tenant and that 53% of non-white barristers were ghettoised in a small number of chambers. This empirical research led to the fiercely debated Bar policy of setting a target of at least 5% ethnic minority lawyers in all chambers. This positive action has made a huge change, although racial discrimination still operates in dark crevices. It also galvanised women in the profession to do something about the discrimination they experienced.

No research has ever been undertaken into the class background of barristers, but it goes without saying that still too few working-class men and women find their way into practice; although a reasonable proportion of Bar students are now coming from the new universities, that is not a clear indicator of social background. While there has been an increase in the numbers of people entering higher education, particularly of women, the numbers of students from lower socio-economic groups has been slower to increase. Indeed, after years of campaigning by some of us for pupils to receive grants or payment so that those without private incomes could survive, we are now finding that the scheme which was introduced has its downside. While chambers are now obliged to provide financing for a number of pupils, the effect of this has been to reduce the numbers of pupillages because of the cost to chambers, and since conventional criteria are used in assessing ability the few places that exist are going to conventional candidates. In the highly competitive market for pupillages and tenancies in chambers, the Oxbridge graduate is still too often preferred. Students coming from the new universities have a harder time getting a place.

I survived pupillage by doing odd jobs and running up a frightening overdraft but it is much worse for students today who come out of university with huge debt before they ever embark on pupillage. My fear is that the combined deterrents of financial burden and scarcity of places will turn the Bar back into a preserve of the well-to-do. To their shame, it was rich commercial barristers who vetoed a proposal to create a levy at the Bar to help fund the entry of people from disadvantaged backgrounds into the profession.

When I ran into financial problems in 1972 I wrote to my MP, Dr Jack Cunningham, to complain about the unavailability of grants or other support, and he in turn raised the matter with the then Minister of Education. Having herself qualified at the Bar, she suggested I might turn my hand to a bit of freelance journalism to see me through the lean times. She herself had apparently had a column in the *Daily Express.* She failed to mention her millionaire husband, whose name was Denis.

It was clear to me that I was not likely to be taken on as a tenant, a fully paid up member who has his name on the door and thus officially becomes one of the barristers practising from those chambers. Obtaining a tenancy is extremely difficult, because the number of those emerging from pupillage and looking for tenancies considerably outstrips that of available spaces.

I had moved chambers for my second six months and my pupil-master was about to leave the Bar to become an MP. Rather than begin the miserable process which faces young barristers of applying endlessly to different chambers with constant rejection, I joined forces with five other novice practitioners and decided to establish a new set of chambers. A notice appeared on the information board in Middle Temple Lane advertising three tiny rooms in Lincoln's Inn as available for a large set of chambers to use as an annexe. We purloined the notice and became the only candidates for the tenancy, found a very junior clerk to manage our work, and innocently launched into practice, servicing by and large the newly emergent law centres, to which we were very committed.

Many of the problems women and others have faced in the legal profession are similar to those encountered in any occupation. The law was not the only profession in which people got jobs through having the right social connections, or knowing the right people or having gone to Oxbridge. Nor is it the only activity in which style, appearance, demeanour and self-confidence play a large part in success. However, as well as the traditional legal and cultural handicaps, there are also structural problems within the profession itself. Women have to overcome the handicaps created by the already established tracks which divide the profession into élite and non-élite areas, and find themselves, as I did, more readily functioning in areas that are undeservedly less prestigious, such as family law, child protection and low-level crime.

But change has taken place. It became too silly and unfashionable to keep certain chambers as bastions of chauvinism, and there are now none which bar women barristers. The days are gone when the majority feared that the male sanctum would be destroyed by high-pitched voices and repositories for sanitary towels. I laughed out loud in the early 1990s when I found a letter from Inner Temple in my pigeonhole telling me that women's personal hygiene was causing a problem for the ancient sewage system of the Inn, which had never been designed to deal with women. Could we legal women desist, or insist on suitable bins being introduced into the lavatories? I saw it as a victory for women that we were here in sufficient numbers now to block the drains, but pitied the isolated female souls who would have to be very brave indeed to raise the issue at a chambers meeting.

However, despite protestations that discrimination is a thing of the past, change has not gone to the core. Today women represent 40% of solicitors and 30% of barristers. The Law Society has found that women starting a training contract to become a solicitor in a law firm are paid on average 7% less than men, and the gap is widening. Throughout their careers women in the law earn on average less than men. This is partly explained by the areas of law in which they function and the fact that they are less well represented in the big City firms. Of solicitors with 10–19 years' experience in law firms over 80% of men are senior partners or run their own business as a sole practitioner compared with only 55% of women. At the Bar too, women are clustered in the areas of law which are less well paid and the numbers of women in commercial law and other highly remunerated specialisms are still small. As I explained in the Introduction, this is mainly because women are steered away from such practice or find it uninviting.

Research conducted and published in 1998 showed that between the ages of 29 and 36 a disproportionate number of women leave the Bar. The ratio is two women for every man. We can all guess that the differential wastage relates to the difficulties for women of combining practice with having children. A survey is now being conducted into why people leave and I will lay a pound to a penny that the research will confirm that women still face problems around maternity leave and the long hours culture of the Bar. As self-employed professionals, barristers do not receive maternity rights or benefits, so time out greatly reduces income. In addition many chambers still require a woman on maternity leave to pay rent to chambers even though she has no income. Chambers like my own provide rent-free periods for maternity and paternity leave and this should be the course adopted by all chambers. With the advent of new technology it is increasingly possible to prepare cases at home. Once a trial is under way the court days are clearly not negotiable. No one can job-share a murder trial or ask for a three-day week if they are a trial lawyer but if chambers were amenable it should be possible for women and men to adjust or reduce their caseload to allow space between cases for a well-adjusted family life. The problem remains that chambers often maintain a culture in which saying no to a case is sacrilege. There is a particular machismo at the Criminal Bar which means success is measured by being constantly in court without a day to catch breath. Losing women in significant numbers at this stage also dilutes the pool from which judges will be drawn five or ten years down the road.

The accounting of progress, under the tutelage of the public relations experts, is done through a number count rather than through any profound shift in established thinking or significant change in the legal culture. The heads of chambers know that it is important to claim that their chambers have an equal opportunities policy, but further questioning shows that there are often inadequate structures to make that a reality. In the Law Schools there have been more female law students than men for a number of years now, and they are coming through with excellent qualifications, often far better than the men. Some of those now coming to the Bar are mature women making a courageous career change. They deserve to be in a profession which is flexible enough to embrace their domestic responsibilities as well as their talent. A new generation of men at the Bar also think differently about fatherhood. They too want to spend time with their children and many are living with women who expect them to take their share of the domestic load.

The days of jokes in Latin had largely passed by the time I was called to the Bar. It is during the early days of pupillage that the mysteries of legal practice are fathomed and the strange language of the courtroom is learned. Out of the mouths of the babes who are new barristers came learned incantations – 'May it please, My Lord' and the like – taken from some bygone era and fed into the mouths of old Etonians. They seemed a wholly inappropriate means of communication for me, a Glaswegian who spoke with the voice of the people. I decided that I could live without some of the verbal ritual and perhaps still achieve a measure of *gravitas*.

The whole business of deciding who is any good as an advocate is fraught with value judgements. As in the theatre, styles change, and nowadays Marshall Hall, the great Edwardian advocate, would be considered a terrible old ham. Advocacy is about communicating and persuading, something women are not only as good at as men, but often in fact better – more down to earth and less pompous. It requires the marshalling of material, research, the ability to charge your argument with imagery. It involves an interplay of the cerebral and the emotional, with a shifting of emphasis between the two, depending on your recipients. You have to be quick on your feet and have a good memory.

The extraordinary thing about the Bar is that large numbers of practitioners rarely do the thing which most members of the public imagine must be their daily bread and butter – i.e. persuade a jury that someone is innocent or guilty. Many are civil practitioners, whose days are largely spent behind a desk working on a brief, advising in the capacity of consultant and only occasionally making a foray into court. Criminal advocacy is to my mind crucial work in the courts because the liberty of the subject is at stake, but there are parts of the Bar which are quite sniffy about crime, as though there is something unpleasantly contagious about the clientele.

Every barrister is asked regularly by perplexed lay people how they feel about representing someone they know to be guilty. I am told that each profession elicits a parallel classic enquiry: doctors are asked if they ever feel squeamish about blood; actors are quizzed about being able to learn their lines; dentists about being sadists. For my own part, representing clients who are probably guilty is rarely a problem; it is representing those you think are innocent which induces sleepless nights. However, the polite answer we all give is that it is not our role to judge guilt or innocence; we concentrate instead on evaluating and testing the evidence and putting our clients' cases as they would themselves if they were acting in person.

The reason, of course, for the question is the public feeling of distaste for the 'hired gun', the courtroom mercenary who will defend the indefensible – the challenge is invariably about representing terrorists, child abusers and rapists. What is misunderstood is the moral basis for advocacy; it is somehow assumed that representing those who are charged with terrible crimes is a mark of amorality. If every lawyer refused to act for those whose conduct is reprehensible, many unpopular people might go unrepresented or be represented by a limited section of the profession. But there is another important consideration. If a barrister was able to pick and choose his or her clients, endorsement would follow from having a certain counsel and, conversely, failing to secure eminent counsel would emit a damning message. The principle was expounded by Erskine when he represented Tom Paine on a charge of sedition in 1792:

> If the advocate refuses to defend from what he may think of the charge or of the defence, he assumes the character of the judge; nay, he assumes it before the hour of judgement; and in proportion to his rank and reputation puts the heavy influence of perhaps a mistaken opinion into the scale against the accused.

Alternatively, if the 'cab rank' principle of taking all-comers did not exist, advocates might avoid a case for fear that acting for particular clients might identify them with the allegations. Even so, when Lord Hooson defended in the Moors Murders case, some of his political opponents (not the candidates, he hastened to add) tried to use it against him in an election campaign. Those of us who have acted in the Irish cases have always been subjected to allegations of being terrorist sympathisers.

The longer I practise the more wholeheartedly committed I become to the cab-rank principle, not only because of its constitutional significance in protecting civil liberties, but because of the incoherence of any other course for criminal practitioners. Picking over the horrors of crime to settle for those which are least offensive is hardly a worthwhile pursuit. In any event it is by no means always possible to tell whether your client is indeed guilty. Often I read the papers in a case and think it sounds ridiculous until I meet the client, whose personal account is so compelling that my original view changes. And there are also occasions when I think a case is terrific – until ten minutes into the consultation.

The Bar is not an easy choice for women, for reasons other than the old prejudices. It can be very hard to compete publicly and enter into open debate with men. We are still not educated adequately for it. We are still training women not to offend.

Women on public platforms or around board tables are still not heard because they rarely make full use of their authority and too often use language which men do not hear. A woman can start a sentence with 'I feel that . . .' and be ignored, only to hear her opinion reiterated by a male colleague who says 'From my wide experience' and receives applause. There is no reason why men should fully understand that ambivalence about the public forum because, although most advocates, regardless of gender, have occasional anxiety attacks, that is very different from standing up in a predominantly male environment and finding your voice.

Confidence and skill in advocacy come from doing it repeatedly, but irascible old men don't make the going easy. I am no oratorical genius, but I try to encourage female pupils to watch other women in court, just to reassure them that they do not have to behave like men or function in any way that feels unnatural. I have always believed that modern advocacy should be about clear, unpatronising communication. And it has to be attractive.

The criminal courts also demand a rather different style, because here barristers are trying to persuade a jury rather than a judge. The pleasure of working with a jury is hard to describe, and for those who are addicted there is nothing like it. It is one of the reasons why good advocates often make lousy judges. As I have already indicated, they continually want to step down into the ring and spar with one side or the other (usually the other), and they grieve for the old days when the adrenaline surged. From time to time the Court of Appeal is compelled to quash a conviction because a trial judge takes over the role of prosecutor.

But criminal advocacy can raise a particular problem for women precisely because it is the most adversarial arena in the court system. You have to enjoy the taste of blood and some men on the Bench feel uncomfortable with assertive women, an ambivalence that becomes very clear when arguments are heated. If there is a woman on both sides, interventions of the 'Come now, ladies' variety are common, said in a tone which suggests that some kind of catfight is breaking out. Genteel charm is still the expected role; aggression is considered phallic, certainly unattractive in a woman. Those messages are in the air and can be very undermining for young women struggling to feel comfortable as professionals. It is especially hard on those whose femininity is still dependent on approval from male authority figures. The way we continue to socialise girls means they are taught to avoid confrontation and encouraged to please. Both can be useful skills in advocacy, but in courtroom battles you also have to be bold, and having a cross Daddy figure up there on the Bench can create a real identity problem.

The speech to the jury is the criminal barrister's opportunity to persuade and captivate. It should ebb and flow, full of story and rhythm. The jury should never be bored and throughout the trial the advocate should be building the blocks for that speech. It is important for women to show juries that they too are textured, real human beings. There is a stereotype of the woman barrister which must also be unpicked. If you have to spend most of a trial giving witnesses a tough grilling, I always advise women to find a witness to whom they can be charming so that they can confront the negative caricature that might be in the ether.

Quite unjustly, women are still not rated highly as advocates. Samuel Johnson's old adage still holds: like performing dogs, the surprise is not that they might do it well but that they do it at all. In my student days Glanville Williams, *Learning the Law*, was set reading and in it he unabashedly asserted that women were not usually suited to the Bar because their voices did not have the right timbre and were hard on the ear. Subsequent versions were trimmed of the offending remarks but not before their poison had been swallowed by generations of women. Yet, as recently as 2001, a civil judge in the Royal Courts of Justice, Master Robert Turner, wrote a guide to advocacy which criticised women lawyers for being too quietly spoken. The possibility that he might be a touch deaf had not occurred to him.

'Show me the woman barrister who can laugh a case out of court,' was the challenge made to me by one of the men at the Bar. I was pushed to think of one – but nor could I think of many men with the power and control to mock a whole state prosecution. That particular abandoned style is not available to most advocates, least of all to women.

Fortunately, women are becoming much less vulnerable to the criticism that only tough old boots survive in the criminal courts or that female criminal lawyers have to be as hard as nails. I was constantly told by colleagues that the word amongst certain judges was that I was a terrible harridan who ate small boys for breakfast. Whoever this woman was that filled them with terror, she became particularly confusing when she became pregnant. The contradictory myths about women are profoundly in conflict when a woman advocate fighting her corner is also a symbol of fecundity. There is a tangible difference in atmosphere. Juries are bemused and interested; judges are benign, and worry about being seen to argue with you. I was tempted to make it a permanent state in the interests of my clients.

Stereotypes are more likely to emerge when women are scarce than when they are common. For women lawyers they tend to eclipse demonstrations of competence and make it harder for them to show professional strength. To some extent the examples of stereotyping are trivial and have little to do with one's performance as a lawyer. But to the extent that women have to learn to ignore the comments they elicit, or to respond to them, or are made to feel trapped in uncomfortable roles, the prevailing images are handicaps which men do not share – unless they are black.

The casting of a woman as the protagonist lawyer in films of courtroom dramas has established a fashionable new persona: the message is that we can be tough, assertive and all-woman as well. A lawyer's womanliness is shown by giving her a sex life, children and snazzy little suits nipped in at the waist, and she shows signs of being compassionate about her clients as well as passionate about winning. But never far behind is that terrible female give-away: overidentification with her clients. Women face this accusation much more frequently than men because explanations have to be found for why they fight so hard to win. Men performing with the same vigour are merely described as passionate advocates.

Overidentification is a charge rarely made of corporate lawyers: after all, it's hard to overidentify with a trust fund or the Credit Union. And while committed and zealous prosecutors do exist, I do not imagine that there are many who would be described as identifying too closely with the Queen. It is only ever said of defence lawyers who fight hard for their clients; and it is never a complaint from the customer. In my experience, professional distance is often used as an excuse for having no bedside manner. It is also a way of excluding women's values from notions of professionalism: caring is interpreted as partial; it is impartiality that is the male, legal, ideal.

It is however perfectly possible to feel for a client's anguish without losing the ability to judge the appropriate tactic. In fact the opposite – denial of the ways in which their cases affect them emotionally – is the problem with most male barristers and judges. You cannot remain unaffected in a criminal case involving child sexual abuse which goes on for several months, with detailed and repeated evidence from damaged children, in a courtroom awash with pornographic evidence. It may be that learning to acknowledge ways in which they are touched by different kinds of cases would enable lawyers to function more effectively as professionals.

Many barristers love the wig and gown. They are part of the élitism of the profession. Although the Commercial Bar are keen to abandon the wig, and recent Lord Chancellors would have been happy to see it go, the suggestion has created an uproar amongst many criminal barristers, who came to the Bar for the outfit. I would certainly be thrilled to see an end to the wig, which is ridiculous and uncomfortable but especially liked by men who are going bald. It is maintained that the wig provides a degree of welcome anonymity, apparently not needed by our friends in the Chancery division, who have a better class of clientele, unlikely to seek them out if they lose the case.

One of the real reasons the wig is being clung to the more earnestly now is to distinguish the barrister from that mere mortal the solicitor advocate, who as a result of a challenge to the Bar's monopoly rights of audience is able to conduct cases in most courts. Protectionism comes instinctively to the professions.

Although I think the wig should be relegated to ceremonial occasions, some sort of robe which covers clothes is probably very useful for women, and I would favour a closed gown like that worn by French advocates. This provides protection against the con-clusions drawn from women's dress or the constant commenting on appearance which can blight the lives of American women lawyers. When I was a novice at the Bar, I had a judge ask me to put my hair up in a chignon because he thought I was flicking my ponytail at the jury and gaining advantage. Even after I became a Queen's Counsel, a judge wrote to my head of chambers to complain about my bracelets, which he considered inappropriate for court. He said not a word to me, but using the insidious mechanisms which operate at the Bar, was making an attempt to bring me into line. (Male barristers festooned with gold watch-chains would never raise an eyebrow.) I can well imagine the problems there would be for women more fully exposed to view.

There is far too much pomp and circumstance in British courts, but after discussing courtroom experience with female attorneys in the USA I can appreciate that there are benefits to be gained from some degree of formality. It is a question of getting the balance right. One of the major complaints by American women lawyers is that they are often undermined in court by being referred to as 'honey' by their male colleagues, and even by judges – not a problem I have ever encountered in the Old Bailey, where the hardship is much more likely to be about being acknowledged at all, lawyers too often being collectively referred to as 'gentlemen'.

Language generally is a problem. Perhaps with too much accommodation, I learned to live with the assertion that the male pronoun includes the female before realising that, if the law and courtroom analogies are always couched in male pronouns, it is more difficult for juries to see women embraced by their application. Even the new Sexual Offences Act 2004 uses the pronoun 'he' throughout when referring to the complainant in rape when it is usually women who are the victims.

Language often perpetuates hidden values, and a conscious effort has to be made to make professional language include women. Studies have shown that when women read job advertisements which use the male pronoun they do not see themselves as applicants. In the United States, Canada and Australia there is now a commitment to ensuring that legislation is drafted in neutral language, while existing legislation is being updated and revised. Judges in all these jurisdictions are coming to accept the symbolic effect of language. We have yet to win the argument.

It is also hard for men who have been used to male-only

environments to stop addressing people by their surname. I have a personal abhorrence of people in the dock being referred to by surname alone, and refuse to do so for men or women, even when it is the procedure adopted by the court. I was once corrected by a judge for always referring to my client by her full name. It may not feel demeaning to men, who refer to each other in that way from school, and do so even to professional colleagues, but it is not a normal form of address for women, and most hate it.

One of the main pockets of change in the courtroom is in the composition of the jury. Until the 1960s women made up a comparatively small proportion of jurors because there was a requirement that the 12 persons good and true should be 'householders', and few women were registered as such because it was usually the male who was designated head of the household. Now the jury panel is taken from the electoral register and women are called for service as readily and randomly as men. While some women excuse themselves because of young children and the difficulty in making provision for them, far fewer women excuse themselves because of important professional commitments. Unlike their male counterparts, few seem to believe their work-place will collapse without them. Changes to the rules of jury service, which now compel attendance save in exceptional circumstances, are designed to increase the numbers of professionals – even judges and lawyers – and corporate men on juries but, even so, women will remain well represented. It is difficult to know whether the increase in women's presence has made any significant change in the decisions of juries, since women are not necessarily easier on their own sex. I am convinced that articles about rape and domestic violence, for example, in the pages of women's magazines, raise understanding about the nature of these offences, and I am sure this has affected the discussions which take place in jury rooms. However, I was recently in a taxi and the cab driver recognised me as the barrister who had defended in a case in which he had been a juror. My client, who was a battered woman, had been acquitted of murder on the grounds that she had been acting in self-defence but the jury had deliberated over two days. The driver volunteered that it had been the women on the jury who had been most reluctant to acquit. Many women still believe that the female of the species should stoically accept her lot. Women, just like men, absorb all the prevailing myths about appropriate female behaviour and can be hard on those women who appear to break the rules.

Almost 30 years ago I was a co-author of a book about the profession, the title of which, because of a typographical error on the spine, read *The Baron Trial* (rather than *The Bar on Trial*). People who thought they were buying a thriller were in for a serious disappointment, but they would at least have been enlightened as to the inner workings of the Bar. It makes very interesting reading now, because our agenda for change could be seen as the ground-plan of so many reforms which have now taken place. But perhaps it says something about the law that gestation takes so long.

My chapter in the book was about discrimination in the profession, and it documented the very real problems that faced women then. I interviewed countless women about their experiences, most of which were pretty ghastly, but, as is still the case, few wanted to be identified. They knew that it is not possible to talk about prejudice from a position of weakness, either as someone who has not ridden it out or who is herself at the receiving end. It is one of the reasons why women who have made it in professions and men who understand the problems have such a responsibility. The women who told me their stories were fearful that, if it were known they had complained, they would never get on, the Bar being too small a place to be saddled with a reputation for having a grouse. A lot has changed: young women corner me now in robing rooms to talk about balancing practice with a family or when to apply to become Queen's Counsel but there are fewer tales of blatant discrimination. Sexual harassment is still an issue at the Bar but at least it is recognised as one. I explained to an audience recently that in my youth we just accepted that we would have our backsides groped by old men and a brave male voice shouted 'Those were the days.' Women no longer face unacceptable questions in interviews about whether they have marriage plans and intend having children. They can no longer expect to be the only woman in counsels' benches at court.

*

One of the significant drivers of women's advance has been structural change in the running of sets of chambers. Chambers administration depends on the clerks system, which functions on a good day like a theatrical agency and on a bad one like a Job Centre. The clerks are supposed to organise your practice, make sure you are in the right court at the right time, and generally sell your skills to the solicitor client. They also have to manage your books and financial relationships and get your money in from errant solicitors. Unfortunately, few people combine these skills, and those who succeed on the public relations side are rarely any good at the administration.

Clerks used to talk about themselves as if they were successful bookmakers. They referred to their 'guvnors' as if they were about to run the next race at Newmarket, and used expressions like 'horses for courses', 'my stable of barristers' and 'backing a particular young gentleman'. Women did not get too high a rating against those odds until they had already proved themselves.

Traditionally, clerks earned 10% of their barristers' earnings. Over the years this was slowly eroded to 7% or even 5%, but very high sums were involved. Others earned a percentage of their chambers's turnover, which still meant they could make as much as Queen's Counsel, often in excess of £200,000. Not surprisingly, they held on to their sinecures with an iron grip.

Reconstructing clerks has not been easy, but the cold wind of the marketplace has been the eventual undoing of the old breed. They had always operated a strange sort of Masonic closed shop, which bitterly opposed entry to anyone from outside their ranks. The 1990s saw an end to all that. To survive the removal of monopoly rights, with accountants and solicitors and in-house corporate lawyers increasingly taking on areas of work traditionally handled by the Bar, chambers realised they had to be more competitive and businesslike. They were being forced away from the quill pen and into intimacy with new technology. They needed a different infrastructure and most chambers identified the old clerking system as ripe for modernisation. Clerks were increasingly replaced by salaried practice managers and chief administrators, often women, who came from experience in the City and marketing and who were only too willing to realise the potential of women in the law so long as it was a money-spinner. A new generation of clerks has emerged which sees women as a resource not to be wasted.

Changing attitudes is a hard and slow process. It is now 80 years since the first woman was called to the Bar. When I was researching the history of women's arrival on the scene I could scarcely credit the intellectual somersaults the judiciary went through to keep them out. The myth of judicial neutrality was certainly exploded in the 'person cases' which came before the courts at the beginning of the twentieth century.

A series of nineteenth-century statutes provided that access to public office, entry to the professions and entitlement to vote should be granted to any 'person' who possessed the right qualifications. The judges bent over backwards to uphold the male monopoly by deciding that women could not be included, even if they were qualified, because they were not 'persons'. All the previous case law interpreted 'persons' as being male, and naturally our courts bound by precedent could do no more than follow suit. What else could a poor chap do?

The idea that women had anything positive to offer the justice system had always been a hard pill for men of law to swallow. As early as the thirteenth century legal commentators were holding forth on the inappropriateness of women on the Bench. According to Andrew Horn in his thirteenth-century treatise, *The Mirror of Justices,* 'Women . . . serfs . . . those under the age of twenty-one, open lepers, idiots, attorneys [i.e. solicitors], lunatics, deaf mutes, those excommunicated by a bishop [and] criminal persons' were ineligible for appointment to the Bench. In 1915 all the judges were members of the Athenaeum, a gentleman's club which until 2000 excluded women. The then Master of the Rolls wrote to a new Lord Chancellor suggesting it would make sense for him to join. Membership of the judicial club is exclusive and remains so, although it is no longer confined to a particular leather-bound watering hole. In the United States judges cannot belong to gentlemen's clubs because they would be asked to recuse themselves from sitting on gender equality cases; no such stricture applies here.

Bertha Cave, by some mistake, was allowed to join Gray's Inn in 1902. This should have been the first step in her legal career, but when the Benchers who ran the Inn realised their error they called a special meeting to make sure it was the last, rescinding the decision on the grounds that there was no 'precedent' for letting women in. An appeal before the Lord Chancellor and a tribunal of eight other judges confirmed her ejection.

In 1913 Miss Beeb, a brilliant Oxford scholar, applied for admission to the Law Society with a view to entering articles, the vocational training course for solicitors, but the courts denied her the right. Christabel Pankhurst tried to join an Inn but was excluded. The arguments presented by the judges were internally inconsistent, confused, and a disturbing resort to discriminatory practices in the application of the law.

By 1919, following the First World War, the tide of public opinion had changed and male exclusiveness was beginning to seem absurd but the only way to force change upon the legal profession and the judges was by statute, and the Sex Disqualification (Removal) Act 1919 was passed accordingly. There were already women practising law in other common-law jurisdictions like the United States, Australia and New Zealand; in Britain, Ivy Williams was at last called to the Bar by Inner Temple in 1922. The first woman solicitor also qualified in that year.

It was another 40 years before we saw a woman on the Bench, however, when Elizabeth Lane was appointed a County Court judge. A few years later, in 1965, she became the first woman to sit on a High Court bench. Trumpets sounded heralding a new era. It has taken another forty years to add seven more to her one. In Scotland, albeit a smaller jurisdiction, there are only two women sitting in the higher courts.

Dame Elizabeth Butler Sloss, now one of two women judges in the Court of Appeal and head of the Family Division, was not a practising barrister when appointed to the High Court bench either. She was one of the registrars of the Family Division – the 'back-room' judges that keep the procedural wheels turning – when her considerable judicial skills were recognised. It was almost as though the leap of imagination required in recognising judicial potential in women was particularly difficult. As in other professions, there is a glass ceiling for women which means that getting to the top floor often involves a detour out through the window and up the drainpipe, rather than a direct route along the charted corridors of power.

In the scramble up the professional ladder, becoming a Queen's Counsel is an important milestone. A successful barrister will consider applying after about twenty years, but the transition is not automatic and only a small proportion of practising barristers 'take silk', as donning the new robe is called. The procedure, like everything in the law, has been wrapped in secrecy and involves applying to the Lord Chancellor to be considered by him for appointment. As with judicial appointments, soundings are taken from the judges to assess your standing – and the sound might be a raspberry if you are a rocker of boats or a person not fitting the mould. No reasons are given for refusal; some barristers may wait several years before being appointed.

Applicants are very secretive about whether they have applied, considering a refusal a vote of no confidence. I was open about being refused on my first application, and spoke about it when asked on *Woman's Hour* in 1990 because I believe that furtiveness feeds into unacceptable practices and secrecy is far too rife in the law. I suspect the powers that be feared I would go on to make an annual announcement over the airwaves about being turned down, which is why they relented in 1991.

If you are successful in your application, it does not mean that you, in fact, sup tea with the Queen and advise her on her legal affairs. (My own children used to think I would be the person who would represent the Queen if she was arrested.) The silk system is a way of singling out for solicitors and lay clients those who are deemed to be the cream of the profession, at the height of their powers. It has considerable cachet and does wonders for your earning potential, as well as being a recognition of expertise. However, it involves secretive and therefore questionable assessments of a barrister's ability, and these days, where chambers are allowed to publish professional brochures and the professions exchange information readily, there is little need to signal to the solicitor or client who is any good. If the market is to be extolled, then why not let excellence find its own level and abandon the QC system altogether? At the time of writing a new system for appointing QCs is being devised which it is hoped will be more transparent and will identify not only senior advocates with skill and experience but senior lawyers in both branches of the profession.

Having more women on the top rung of the practitioners' ladder is as significant for women as increasing the number of judges. This is because lawyers in silk take on the most demanding and important cases, many of which have real social reverberations.

The old chestnut is that people must only be appointed on merit, a notion which on its face is unobjectionable. It is the old question of who defines excellence. Who are the gatekeepers? How many women are involved in the vetting procedures? Since the head of every circuit, every specialist Bar association except one, and every division of the courts is a man, there cannot be many women involved in any formal consultation. Women will not figure in the high table gossip much either.

Merit is presented as another of those neutral concepts, an apolitical criterion of personal worth, when in fact it involves subjective judgements made by a very narrow band of people. Like other institutions, the law uses the meritocracy argument to immunise itself against any challenge about how it makes its appointments. The merit test is rarely mentioned for jobs of low status. Merit is a concept designed to regulate the allocation of highly paid, prestigious positions, and the grander the appointment the more elusive and invisible the evaluative process becomes.

Ironically, as soon as any attempt is made to introduce awareness of the ways women and black people have been disfavoured in this process, there is an assumption that the merit principle will be violated. The port will be diluted. There is far more whispering about the rationale for the appointment of women and blacks than there ever is about white men. Sadly, the beneficiaries of any merit system, male and female, usually support that system simply because of the personal endorsement it affords them; thus they will defend the grossest interpretations of merit on the basis that *they* themselves got there because of outstanding ability.

In the studies of Dr R.M. Kanter, reported in the *Harvard Women's Lawyer*, whenever people of any social type are proportionally scarce (i.e. less than 20 per cent of the total), the dynamics of tokenism are set in motion. Token appointees are more visible and worry about being seen to fail. They are also faced with the choice of accepting comparative isolation or becoming a member of the dominant group at the price of denying their own identity and accepting a definition of themselves as 'exceptional'. The flattery of being labelled in that way can be quite intoxicating for women – the 'queen bee' syndrome – but it also creates a pressure which means that while in that role, she is not able to fight for her rights as a woman or to stand up for her sex, but is inclined to turn her back on other women, either literally or figuratively, in order to protect her place. It is perhaps not surprising that many senior women lawyers have not championed younger women. At the time when *Eve Was Framed* was first published a female High Court judge, Joyanne Bracewell, dismissed the idea of taking positive steps to promote women, arguing that it would reduce the quality of judges, and asserted that it was irremediably difficult to combine a family with a career at the Bar. This was 'a fact of life'. The idea that it was the institution which should change was not considered.

Even Dame Elizabeth Butler Sloss, a woman of considerable talent who outshines most of her male colleagues because of her ability and humanity, felt it was necessary to advise us all when we set up the Association of Women Barristers not to rock the professional boat too strenuously. Stealth was the old way forward and when she was appointed to the Appeal Court she made a conscious choice to keep the title Lord Justice like the men.

It is important to recognise the extent to which male values and perceptions are adopted by women. In 1985 an American experiment was reported in the *Harvard Law Review*. In it an essay was randomly assigned to 150 male and 150 female academics with the author's name indicated variably as John T. McKay, J.T. McKay and Joan T. McKay. The subjects were asked to rate the essays on such qualities as persuasiveness, intellectual depth and style. Although the essays were identical, those believed to be written by Joan consistently received lower ratings from male and female readers than those believed to have been written by John or J.T. Recent reports on comments made about women applying for silk or judgeships echo these findings. Women can be very negative about other women.

Some women say they have never experienced discrimination: they may be the lucky few or they may only find it kicks in when they have families or hit the glass ceiling. Yet there are women who sail through the process having made a conscious decision to identify with their male colleagues and become 'one of the chaps', albeit a feminine version. They see the world through male eyes and remain happily blind to the inequities of the system. These women can be a drawback to progress.

More and more women understandably ask whether their skills are undervalued in a system where merit is defined by men. They question whether account is taken of the differences in the career patterns of women, especially if they have had children and have tailored their practices accordingly. Is there any recognition of the considerable skills involved in running a home, caring for children and having a career at the same time? Few women with young children will travel away from home for extended periods to conduct cases, or will take on such a quantity of advice work that they cannot spend some time in the evening with their children, and these factors inevitably affect their earnings, one of the criteria for evaluating success and 'standing'.

Women also participate less in the interstices of the law – the circuit dinners, the cricket matches, the golf, the wine committees, the Bar Council and specialist Bar associations. If they have children, they certainly do not stay around for the drinks in Fleet Street wine bars, where solicitors and clerks are wooed for briefs by male members of chambers and where career-advancing gossip is exchanged. They know fewer judges socially and, given the male ethos of the profession, will not be championed in their career rise in the same way that men are. Legal cultures are premised on notions which are themselves exclusive. A woman MP, acknowledging similar problems in the House of Commons, described it as men 'talking-up' an aspirant male colleague in a way that would rarely be done for a woman. The lubrication of patronage is not as readily available to facilitate the rise of women. Male judges also invoke the decisions of their own wives who have withdrawn from careers, either permanently or for substantial periods, and who would never dream of expecting special consideration.

In 1990 I stood for election to the Bar Council specifically on the platform that I wanted to raise issues affecting women. Once I was a member of the Council I argued for the creation of a women's committee, like the one which existed on race discrimination. I wanted to see a survey conducted on women similar to that produced the previous year showing the failure of the Bar to embrace ethnic minorities. I was accused of political correctness – an argument invariably made by those who want to maintain the old order. The male leader of the North East Circuit – the grouping of barristers practising in the Newcastle and York area – berated me for having the audacity to speak for women and insisted that the women of his circuit were perfectly happy, thank you, and did not need me to complain on their behalf. I would have preferred to have heard it from them, and in private.

With the support of the new Association of Women Barristers, and Anthony Scrivener QC, who was then Chairman of the Bar, we secured the creation of a committee in 1992 under Sir Stephen Sedley, an enlightened judge. Research was commissioned and undertaken by Pamela Bhalla and Kathryn Hamylton. It was published in 1994 and added more flesh to the arguments made in the original edition of this book. Women experienced discrimination when they applied for pupillage, when they applied for tenancies, when they applied for silk and when it came to the appointment of judges. The research was conclusive and confirmed what many of us knew.

Since then a head of steam has developed around the way in which judicial appointments are made. In 2000 a Commission for Judicial Appointments was created whose remit was to audit the selection procedures and act as an ombudsman for the judicial and silk appointments process but not to make appointments. The Commission, chaired by Sir Colin Campbell, found that the criteria for making silk appointments was so unsystematic as to be subjective and that some consultees' comments appeared to be influenced by a perception of a 'silk mould', which meant that 'successful applicants had to conform to expectations as to appearance, dress, educational or social background and other irrelevant factors'. These consultees were all judges and grandees at the Bar who like some self-perpetuating oligarchy were clearly only endorsing people like themselves. It is a form of cloning. Ninety-seven per cent of those consulted about suitability are male, white and from a narrow social group. A small number of barristers' chambers have a stranglehold on influence: effectively seen as silk and judge incubators. The result of belonging to those chambers is that the judges and practitioners regularly mingle and the grooming for appointments starts early. Close study shows that a hard core of chambers monopolise the appointment process and their idea of what constitutes excellence is immutable. The numbers of women are low, and black faces are rare. In his first annual report in 2002 Sir Colin showed the system to be a real scandal, with unsupported and sometimes unattributable tittle-tattle and comment recorded against people to their detriment: 'Too primly spinsterish, though her other qualities are self evident.' 'She's off-puttingly headmistressy.' 'She does not always dress appropriately.' 'Down and out scruffy.' The eight commissioners, who have wide experience in industry, academia and the Civil Service, 'had not in twenty years of experience come across comments like them'. As can be imagined, the disclosures did nothing to dispel concern about the whole process of taking 'soundings' as a method for advancing careers. In any other profession people apply for jobs and produce references.

The report and the one which followed in 2003 reinforced for me how criteria like 'authority' and 'decisiveness' need unpacking because perceptions of authority and decisiveness are likely to be perceptions of the male way of doing things. The ideal of the judge – anonymous, impartial, authoritative – is intrinsically male. So long as women conform to male expectations, they are more likely to succeed. In the old days women were expected to dress in heavy dark costumes with neat white blouses, hair off the face. Nowadays the demands are not taken so literally but women are expected to be unthreatening, charming and agreeable not pushy, insistent, aggressive or unyielding or any of the other qualities exhibited daily by male judges.

When my daughter was small she used to think that all lawyers were women, and did not understand why everyone laughed at her assumption. Now, more and more lawyers are women, women who should have the same opportunities as men to rise within the profession and ultimately become judges. The judiciary needs to reflect the community it serves in order to ensure public confidence in the work of the courts. The Commission for Judicial Appointments rejects 'the notion that the trickle up of women and ethnic minority practitioners from the lower ranks of the profession will redress the lack of diversity in the judiciary'.

The courtroom is still an arena where men, for the most part, play the dominant roles. Most of the women are ushers or clerks or solicitors' representatives, spear-carriers or extras in the drama. I am not claiming that women make better judges or that their decision-making is of a higher calibre but I do believe that a judiciary drawn from a wider background will improve the overall quality of the Bench by bringing a broader range of views and experiences into the courts. It is also the only way to change the legal culture. Having women at the top in significant numbers would change the nature of the discourse. When Baroness Hale, the first woman law lord, gave the Independent and Bar Law Reform Lecture in London in November 2004, she quoted Chief Justice Beverley McLachlan of the Supreme Court of Canada in giving a rationale for women 'as judges'. 'The most important reason why I believe we need women on our benches is because we need the perspectives that women can bring to judging. This is because jurists are human beings, and, as such, are informed and influenced by their backgrounds, community and experiences. For cultural, biological, social and historic reasons women do have different experiences than men.' With women at every level in the law it would function differently: men would ease up on many of their attitudes, and myths would be shattered. If judges during their luncheon recess were sitting round a table talking about their cases with many more women and being ribbed for their arcane views, they might start taking stock of a different kind of experience. Isolated women cannot challenge that culture.

It is essential for people to see women in positions of power. We have to stop sending out the message that only a special breed of person can get to be a lawyer or a judge, and that they all wear dark suits and talk with marbles in their mouths. We can only hope to gain the public's confidence if that kind of remoteness from the real world is addressed.

No doubt methods of male networking exist in other professions too, but the smell of the gentleman's club permeates every crevice of the Inns of Court. The odour of exclusiveness, like most personal smells, never offends its owners – indeed, they are usually quite impervious to it. Moves are now afoot to create a proper Judicial Appointments Commission but Sir Colin Campbell, the judicial 'ombudsman', has expressed serious concerns that the plans are flawed, as there will be no independent auditing of the new system, which will give the Lord Chancellor and senior judges a veto on appointments to the higher courts. As Sir Colin pointed out: 'Some people are worried that the new commission might just be a shell in which traditional practices might continue.'

The drive to recruit more women, ethnic minority and solicitor judges has meant looking again at the current rules. As a result of a new government consultation in 2004 called Increasing Diversity in the Judiciary, posts will be opened up to university law teachers, the age for getting on the lowest rungs will be lowered so that women can start early and still have some time out to have babies. There will be more accommodation of women's commitments. Having to travel around circuits when you have young children is impossible. Rules requiring candidates to spend years sitting first as part-time judges while practising law – which solicitors find hard to comply with – could be altered to allow for intensive periods of part-time sitting. To remove candidates' fears of taking an irrevocable step by accepting a judicial post, judges in more junior posts could be allowed to return to work as lawyers, which is currently forbidden, should they have a change of heart. The proposal would radically alter the existing arrangements whereby judicial appointments are for life. This would help women who are deterred from taking a full-time appointment if it represents a final career choice; they may not wish to close the door too early on other career options. The other problem is that women 'don't ask'. It is a phenomenon I encounter all the time, that women too often wait to be invited to consider an option – and it is not confined to the law. They have greater inhibition about appearing pushy or ambitious or self-aggrandising.

It is hard to find evidence to satisfy those who have no interest in change. It is also hard to untangle the web of very fine biases which are insinuated into the system. As we have seen, most discrimination does not happen at visible levels. As Mary Robinson, the former President of Ireland and an eminent human rights lawyer, has said:

> Every society maintains an invisible life where attitudes and assumptions are formed. Every society is hostage to this unseen place, where fear conquers reason and old attitudes remain entrenched. It is here that the chance phrases and small asides are made which say so little and reveal so much.
>
> If we are to go forward we need to look at attitudes and the language which expresses attitude ... If we are to strike a balance, if we are to readjust participation and enrich our society with dialogue, we have to revise this way of thinking.

3

The Fragrant Woman

There was a little girl, who had a little curl
Right in the middle of her forehead.
When she was good, she was very, very good
But when she was bad she was horrid.

When Jeffrey Archer, the former Conservative Party Chairman, sued the *Star* for libel in 1987 over his alleged association with a prostitute, his wife gave evidence on his behalf. She indicated discreetly that she and her husband enjoyed a full married life, speaking with delicacy about the indelicate. She was the exemplar of the Good Wife, standing by her husband as the wives of John Profumo and Cecil Parkinson had done before her. She was dressed unassumingly but with great care, attractive without being striking.

Mr Justice Caulfield was moved to lyricism when he dealt with Mary Archer's evidence in his direction to the jury. He suggested to them that their vision of her in the witness box would never disappear. Indeed, His Lordship became quite rapturous. 'Has she fragrance? Would she have, without the strain of this, radiance?' His personal view that Mrs Archer's scent could expunge any whiff of scandal was undisguised. Here was the flower of womanhood, whose moral worth shone like a flame in the murky world of tabloid newspapers, sex and call-girls.

Monica Coghlan, the prostitute, was Magdalene to Mrs Archer's Mary in this morality play. Her evidence did not evoke much sympathy and in the view of judge and jury was probably untruthful.

Here was a woman who sold her body to the next buyer and who might lie for the right price.

Polar examples of the female sex, these two women created a contrast which was orchestrated by the press and which enabled Jeffrey Archer to recede from the centre of the courtroom drama. But in 2001, Jeffrey Archer was back before the courts charged with perjury. It transpired that he had lied in the libel action, having presented a false account of his movements on the night he had allegedly been with Monica. This time Mary had a tougher ride when she strode confidently into the witness box. No less fragrant, she was now portrayed as steely, calculating and manipulative. The stereotyping of women is an extraordinary phenomenon to behold and the lightning changes in how women are received can be the result of almost subliminal codes.

The good wife features regularly in our courts, though usually as the other half of a male offender. For, as the songs and stories tell us, the love of a good woman can be the making of a man, and any hope of redemption is often deemed to lie with a criminal's wife. Wives are also brought forth as a measure of whether the man has reason to mend his ways. Hidden victims of the criminal justice system, they and their children, as well as their spouses, have sentences passed upon them. Every year of a term of imprisonment means for them the loneliness of separation, bringing up a family without support, suffering financial hardship and the misery of long journeys and unfulfilling visits to remote prisons.

The Home Office decision to remove the right of remand prisoners to have food brought to them daily from outside was greatly criticised by many of us as an additional hardship for those who were still not convicted of a crime. Yet the wife of one client sighed with relief. Having to get up every day to cook the *boeuf bourguignon* that was her man's favourite dish (professional criminals often have a special interest in gastronomy, acquired from reading James Bond novels in the long waits), ensuring that she had prepared enough to feed everyone else on A wing as well (status-enhancing within the prison population, like standing the whole pub a round), then blow-drying herself into a *Hello!* magazine lookalike and getting down to Brixton prison with the smaller children in tow all before 11 a.m. would be a burden to the most devoted wife. Enough was enough, and the removal of this particular liberty seemed perfectly civil to a whole body of women whose views are rarely canvassed.

On the rare occasion when 'the good wife' does appear in the dock it is usually because she has allowed her love for her husband to 'seduce' her into crime, helping him to escape custody, harbouring him from the forces of law or concealing stolen items. If a woman can show that her will has been suborned by her husband it provides potent mitigation. The time taken off her sentence will be added to his. Wives are rarely indicted for being passive beneficiaries. If a husband indulges in unconventional means of bringing home the bacon, it is accepted as unlikely that his wife will be able to prevent it. She usually has to play an active role before the police will charge her, though her safe passage can often be the bargaining counter used effectively by the police to get the husband to 'cough'. Wives and womenfolk are the subject of frequent deals, where she goes home to the kids if the main contender sees sense and takes the rap.

Judges and juries alike have a soft spot for the good wife; when she is in the dock charged with playing some ancillary role she is often acquitted. This is what gives rise to claims that women benefit from chivalry, but it works only if she fulfils the stereotype. In the 2004 case of *Regina* v. *Sharif* and others, family members of a man who had committed a suicide bombing in Tel Aviv were put on trial, including his wife Tahira Tabassum. The allegation was that as his wife, intimately involved with him, she must have known that he was going off to kill himself and others in an act of terrorism. A new law had been introduced after September 11, 2001 which places a duty on people to inform on others if they suspect anything connected with terrorism. Failure to inform is now a criminal offence even for a wife. Wives of IRA men, who probably knew when their other half disappeared for weeks that they were part of an active service unit, were never prosecuted because it was accepted that to do so would be futile and counter-productive in the community. Expecting a woman who has the care of a family and profound emotional loyalties to pop down to the police station to 'grass' on her man was implausible. While 'tarring and feathering' of informants may have gone out of fashion, there are contemporary equivalents like kneecapping or worse. The Muslim community not surprisingly felt that the legal change with its new approach to wives was specially designed as an assault upon it and was affronted by the appearance of this devout, hijab-wearing, young mother bereft by her husband's death. The clincher in her acquittal was the irrefutable evidence that after the birth of her newest baby she had gone to her doctors to have a contraceptive coil fitted, not the act of a faithful wife who knew her young husband was on his way to his death.

Because the image of the faithful, supportive, if misguided, wife is so powerful, lawyers always try to turn a female client into just such a one. The use of the term 'common-law wife' is insinuated into proceedings precisely for this purpose. It is intended to communicate the positive aspects of wifeliness rather than the negative connotations of adulterous relationships: 'mistresses' do not fare so well in trials, though the smallness of their part may also be reflected in the sentences they receive. Bad wives are women who break the rules. They do so by being dissolute or unfaithful, or by not fulfilling their wifely functions. The courts do not like bad wives.

Wives who betray their husbands offend against the notion of women as keepers of the hearth. Fidelity was of course originally based on the need to secure the succession, to ensure that those who carry a family's name are entitled to do so – hardly pressing considerations today. Yet male indignation at betrayal is not paralleled when the shoe is on the other foot. In earlier times this female betrayal was exemplified by the women poisoners who, before the strict regulation of drugs, disposed of their tyrannical or inconvenient husbands by the subtle spicing of their food with arsenic or strychnine, obtained from pharmacists on the pretext of wanting to lighten their skin or get rid of vermin. Adelaide Bartlett's lover obtained the supply for her in 1896. That a wife who should nurture her husband and care for his domestic needs might abuse that very function, and on the pretext of ministering to him should feed him his own destruction, was an outrage which brought down the foulest condemnation. As a crime it was the perfect symbol of the deceitfulness of women. However, women who kill are rare. Women being killed is the common currency. It is women who are stalked and stabbed for no apparent reason in parks, women who are the prey of serial killers, female children who are the ones most often killed.

Half of all female murder victims are killed by a husband or lover. Two women a week die as a result of domestic violence. In the majority of these cases male defendants mount a defence of provocation: that their wives' conduct drove them to a sudden loss of control. Within the male stronghold of the court it is all too easy to create the feeling that a woman had it coming to her. Pictures of nagging, reproachful, bitter termagants who turn domestic life into hell on earth are painted before the jury. Man-haters skilled in the art of cruelty are summoned up to haunt the trials of men pushed to their limits. One dead wife who became known as the Lady in the Lake was described by defence counsel as 'an aberrant piece of humanity'. He meant that she had committed adultery and did not make the beds. In 2004 a man was freed by the court after killing his wife because her snoring had driven him over the edge.

On 3 December 2002 a number of cases were reconsidered by the Court of Appeal at the behest of the Solicitor-General, Harriet Harman, who argued that the sentences had been too low in the circumstances. Mark Paul Wilkinson and his partner had been in a relationship for approximately eight years and had two children. According to the victim's family, Mark was suspicious and jealous throughout their time together and had been violent to her. They separated, and shortly afterwards Mark lured his former partner to his flat on the pretext that they would be meeting a counsellor. Within half an hour of arriving the victim had been suffocated. According to the accused she told him that she wanted to settle with a new boyfriend and would like him to adopt the children. Mark saw red and pressed the life out of her. He was sentenced to four years' imprisonment for manslaughter on the grounds of provocation. Darren Suratan was sentenced to three years and six months for killing his partner, who died of a subdural haemorrhage after being repeatedly punched about the head. His story was that she kept falling over because of her drinking. Leslie Hume, a solicitor, stabbed and killed his wife Madeleine during the course of an argument at their family home. The event was witnessed by their four young children who will live with the horror for ever. He was given seven years after his plea to manslaughter was accepted without any resort to a trial, on the basis that a lawyer would only have done such a thing if severely provoked so a jury did not need to be troubled. None of the sentences were changed.

Families and friends listen in horror from the public galleries to descriptions of those they know and love that bear no relation to reality. Unless the groundwork has already been done, which is rare, prosecuting counsel is in no position adequately to cross-examine the defendant about the allegations, or to call evidence of rebuttal, challenging their truth. The very people who could give evidence are often sitting there in court, frustrated that they cannot be called to counter the stories being told against their dead friend or relative. Their confidence in the legal system is often shattered by what is seen as the collusion of weak prosecutors and ruthless defence lawyers.

It is almost inevitable in murder trials, regardless of sex, that the conduct of the deceased is called into question, but attacks upon the character of women victims often have a particular quality, and of course the denigration is not confined to homicide trials.

Even a fictional character, Lady Chatterley, came in for this kind of vilification when D.H. Lawrence's book was tried under the Obscene Publications Act in 1960. In this trial, counsel for the Crown famously asked the jury whether they felt the book was one they would allow their 'wives or servants' to read, displaying the outmoded attitudes of sections of the Bar at the start of the era of the Beatles and the swinging sixties.

Judges are not aware that they allow preconceived ideas about 'good' women to affect their decision-making. Few judges consciously subscribe to discriminatory practices: they all believe they are approaching the individual facts in a case in an individual way. However, hidden expectations creep in unawares. Judicial aberrations are always explained away as exceptional, maverick or isolated, but they are more likely a matter of the game being given away by the less sophisticated participants.

The sociologist Professor Pat Carlen has produced some wonderful work over several years (*Women's Imprisonment: Study in Social Control,* 1983; and *Criminal Women,* 1985) on the attitudes of Scottish magistrates and judges to the women who come before them charged with crime. In an attempt to discover why women were sent to prison when most of their crime was so trivial, she asked a representative selection of the judiciary the question, *'What affects your final decision when you are uncertain whether to send a woman to prison?'* The following are some of the answers she received:

'Women who live more ordered lives don't commit crime because with a husband and children to look after they don't have time.'

'It may not be necessary to send her to prison if she has a husband. He may tell her to stop it.'

'Women with steady husbands or cohabitees don't commit crime – they are kept occupied.'

'If she's a good mother we don't want to take her away. If she's not a good mother it doesn't really matter.'

'If you discover a woman has no children it clears the way to send her to prison. If she has children but they're in care then I take the view she is footloose and fancy-free and I treat her as a single woman.'

'If they have left their husbands and their children are already in care it may seem a very good idea to send them to prison for three months.'

Pat Carlen is still steadfastly working on women in prison and, as I worked on this update, I asked her if she thought these attitudes had substantially changed; her answer based on recent research was a resounding 'NO'.

When I first read Pat Carlen's material I found the endorsement of everything I had felt in my bones and witnessed in court. Here it was, from the very mouths of those who sat in judgment. There is nothing peculiarly Scottish about these attitudes: they have confronted me daily. Women whose children are in care, women who are divorced or separated, women who do not fulfil their appropriate role, all encounter unmatched prejudice. Men are never described as promiscuous unless they are homosexual. The work of criminologists like Frances Heidensohn, Susan Edwards or Russell and Rebecca Dobash added further texture and colour to my own picture of the criminal courts.

Magistrates and judges bemoan the limited range of possibilities when it comes to sentencing women. Yet another conditional discharge may seem too lenient a disposal, fines perpetuate the vicious circle of poverty, community service even today is inadequately developed and is insufficiently geared to women, especially if they have small children. In the trap of having to go down-tariff or up-tariff – the tariff being the mean sentence for the type of offence – because no really appropriate penalty is available, our judiciary plays the sugar and spice game of deciding what this little girl is made of. The tests are always the same, revolving around how our clients function as wives, daughters and mothers. Single women without those labels pose special problems. Here the issue is whether they lead orderly or disorderly lives, hold down jobs and have community or family ties. So long as they conform, they are dealt with in much the same way as men. But non-conformity draws down different judgments.

Good mothers get credit with the court. The equivalent for men used to be a good service record, a mention in dispatches or boxing for the regiment. Yet the principles applied in deciding whether or not someone is a good mother are essentially middle-class. The emphasis is less on how many hours women spend prattling with their children or rolling together on the floor than on cleanliness and homemaking skills. Pre-sentencing reports, written by people who know the market with which they are dealing, make references to the spick-and-span council flat, the well-kept home, the neatly arranged ornaments and the scrubbed children. If a woman's children are in care her failure is already established, and whatever circumstances led to the separation are largely ignored.

Transcripts of criminal proceedings abound with questions from the Bench which are in no way relevant to the issues but which are used as indicators of the kind of woman who is before the court. The men in our criminal courts, particularly the older generation, have a romantic view of motherhood. Perhaps the haze of time passing has affected their memories of parenting, so that they no longer recollect the penetrating cries of their own children – or perhaps *they* were protected from them by their wives and other domestic help. And, of course, the stereotyping of women extends to jurors, lawyers, experts and all the other participants in the process.

A male drug dealer or burglar, however, is rarely thought of in terms of fathering. The good father is unlikely to stir the compassion of a court by portraying himself in the bosom of his family. He should be out working, lawfully providing for them.

The compulsion to make women fulfil accepted criteria of decent womanhood is a great temptation to lawyers, who in colluding with it succumb to a paternalism which effectively marginalises women. I have very sharp antennae for the semiotics of the courtroom, those tiny signs and signals that a woman can emit which might alienate those who judge her: anything that makes her seem to put her career ahead of her family or which makes her appear flirtatious, which presents her as a 'slapper', a home-wrecker, a drinker, or a feckless parent. When Sally Clark stood trial for killing her baby sons the first question put to her in cross-examination was, 'You were not cut out to be a mother, were you?' It seemed that a woman who enjoyed her professional life as a lawyer would obviously find mothering deeply inconvenient.

A common feature in the three shocking cases where mothers were accused of killing their babies – Sally Clark, Angela Cannings and Trupti Patel – besides the fact that each of them had lost more than one baby in the circumstances that are commonly described as cot deaths, was that men in the police, medicine and the law jumped to conclusions about the capacity of these women as mothers. The burden of proof was reversed and there was an assumption of guilt rather than the presumption of innocence. In our system we start with the preferred truth that someone is innocent because it is so hard to prove a negative. Showing you have not done something can be extremely difficult if you have no alibi or witness to support your account. In addition these women failed to fit the straitjacket of 'natural' mothers according to some fantasy of how natural mothers conduct themselves. Asked about the commitment they had to their jobs, their drinking habits, their regret at losing their figure, the wrong answer could be fatal. They were questioned as to the frequency of the cuddles they administered and comments were made on the amount of tears shed. Perceived lack of emotion was read as callousness. Over and over again Sally Clark was described as a career woman who had a luxury, dream home as though there was clearly no place for babies in her world. Sally Clark and Angela Cannings were both convicted of murdering their babies and sentenced to life imprisonment until their convictions were overturned in 2003. Trupti Patel, a pharmacist, was acquitted by a jury in May 2003 despite prosecution claims that 'against nature or instinct' she too had smothered her children. At her trial she called her aged grandmother from India, who testified that she had lost five of her twelve children in early infancy, which suggested strongly that there could be some sort of genetic reason for the unexpected deaths. Our understanding of genetics is still in the earliest of stages and the future may hold answers to why some babies are unusually vulnerable.

In Angela Cannings's case, according to the expert micro-biologist, Dr David Drucker, her last baby to die had so few antibodies of a particular class that it was almost below the limit of detection of the tests that were being used. He remembered commenting to a colleague that he would have expected that baby to be dead or very seriously ill. Dr Drucker and his research colleagues take the view that some babies have a faulty switch – it fails to switch on the baby's defence system against killer bugs.

In Sally Clark's case, after one appeal had already been unsuccessful, her friends and lawyers still laboured away until they turned up a medical report which had never been made available at her trial; it showed that her second baby, Harry, had an infection at the time of his death. On seeing the test results which had mysteriously never been disclosed, two eminent British pathologists stated that in their view Harry died of natural causes. No one had ever doubted that the earlier death of Christopher was anything other than natural until doctors began to 'think dirty' because a second baby died. Sir Roy Meadow, the star witness for the prosecution had testified that two deaths were unnatural, telling the jury that there was a 'one in 73 million chance' that both deaths had occurred naturally, something that could only happen once in every hundred years. This statistic was the smoking gun that convicted

Sally. In one soundbite the jury had a compelling case against her. The jury, some of whom were openly weeping, convicted her by 10–2 after two days' deliberation. The statistic was grossly inaccurate. It is more rather than less likely that a mother who has suffered one cot death will suffer another. The true odds were not one in 73 million but one in 60. No one had challenged where Sir Roy Meadow had got his statistics, despite his wandering far outside of his field of expertise.

When Sally Clark's husband visited her in prison and told her that exculpatory evidence had been found, her first reaction was not 'Thank goodness, I'm coming home' but to burst into tears and ask whether Harry had suffered.

The Sudden Infant Death cases were cases where evidential gaps were filled with strange notions about how natural mothers should behave. Ideas about instinctive mothering floated through the courts. The fault did not just lie with doctors or lawyers; the police often fell from grace too. Chairing a recent working group for the Royal College of Pathology and the Royal College of Paediatrics and Child Health, I heard accounts from mothers who wakened to find their baby dead and were immediately the subject of suspicion – with crime-scene yellow tape being placed across the door almost as soon as the ambulance had taken the lifeless baby to hospital. Unlike other situations where a person is found dead and the body is left until professional help arrives, distraught parents lift and lay the baby, they try to breathe life into it, clean away vomit and mucus, pass the baby between them, splash it with water, put a finger into its mouth to see if something is blocking its airway. To policemen the removal of nightclothes and cleaning away of evidence may seem highly suspicious but parents do not want their baby in cold, wet clothes even if it is dead. They do not want its face crusted with detritus. Evidentially it may be unhelpful but to expect rationality is to lose connection with real lives.

Miscarriages of justice almost invariably take place when people play God and are confident that they *know* what happened. The miscarriages of justice which took place in the 1970s and '80s – the Guildford Four, the Birmingham Six, the Maguire Seven – were all as a result of experts, policemen, lawyers and judges feeling they knew who was guilty and cutting evidential corners or forcing confessions. In their daily practice when making a diagnosis, doctors will often use a sixth sense, a feeling in their bones that is based on a mixture of experience and hunch; many times they will be right. But the criminal courts which condemn people as criminals and remove liberty cannot work on such an unscientific evidential base. There are indeed women who suffocate their babies because they cannot cope, because they do not feel they can fulfil society's or their family's expectations of them as mothers. There are mothers who kill because they associate the baby with profound, negative feelings they have about the way they themselves were mothered. They may be crying out for help because of their own needs. Whatever the motivation for a killing, doctors cannot use guesswork in their role as expert and they must not confuse their function as an expert with their ordinary function in their professional capacity. Expertise has to come from a sound scientific base, with published research and peer review. It is not appropriate for people to use the courts to air a theory or fly a kite unsupported by a substantial body of work. Nor should authority and professional status be allowed to compensate for the absence of hard fact.

It should, however, be accepted that until comparatively recently there was an unwillingness to believe that women who were not witches might deliberately harm their babies. Our awareness about family abuse has alerted us to the alarming truth that some women do inflict harm, putting high levels of salt into their baby's bottle, pressing a hand over the baby's mouth and nose, holding it for prolonged periods under the bathwater, pushing pillows into its face. Unexplained breathing problems and other symptoms have put medical professionals on alert to what was described as Munchausen's by Proxy, where parents, usually mothers, take sustenance from being at the heart of a medical drama involving their child because of their own psychological needs. The numbers of women who behave in this way are few, but because of our heightened concerns about child abuse it is easy to fall into the trap of seeing abuse everywhere, even where it does not exist.

*

As I document the many cases I have conducted, representing women who have harmed themselves or their children or partners, it is hard to find one who was not herself a victim or an extremely vulnerable person with serious psychological problems. None of these women require traditional incarceration but they are squeezed into a system that was designed for male offenders.

Imprisonment is used as a means of social control, and that is particularly true in relation to women. For most people, prison is the end of a road paved with deprivation, disadvantage, abuse, discrimination and multiple social problems. Empty lives produce crime. In 30 years of practice at the Criminal Bar I have spent rather a lot of time in prisons. For those of us who have no experience of prison it is hard to imagine what it means to lose your liberty, to surrender to a regime where the rules are not your rules, where your autonomy dissolves, where your battered self-worth spirals into further decline. Small matters taken for granted in the outside world become complicated and strangely insurmountable because of the requirements of the authorities. Your timetable is directed by others, privacy disappears, petty resentments build into serious conflict and indignities are part of the daily round. It is my idea of hell.

In the early 1990s I was a regular visitor to Holloway Prison. Since that time I have served on the Health Advisory Board there and I am now involved with the Birth Partners Scheme to help pregnant prisoners through their pregnancy and the birth of their babies. The same issues arise repeatedly. Appalling family circumstances, histories of neglect, abuse and sexual exploitation, poor health, mental disorders, lack of support, inadequate housing or homelessness, poverty and debt, and little expectation of change. These are rarely women who make judges swoon over their metaphorical 'fragrance'. Many women in prison have themselves been the victims of crime, usually violence within the home or sexual violation when they were children. Poor, battered and abused they find themselves continually punished.

In the face of all this they often show remarkable resilience and courage and frequently do not fulfil the stereotype of victims, which can be why they end up in prison: because they are seen as 'bolshie' and in need of discipline. Of course there are some women who have had reasonably privileged lives who end up in jail, but they are few. However, virtually all women who go to prison come out damaged by the experience. The consequences of removal from their children, their families and their communities are immeasurable. They are overwhelmed with feelings of guilt.

Between 1993 and 2001 the female prison population for England and Wales increased by over 145%. As many as two-thirds of women in prison are now suffering from a mental disorder, with record numbers, as I have said, being driven to suicide because of a lack of adequate care. The majority of these women need psychiatric support and drug treatment in the community. They do not need to be locked up for hours on end in overcrowded prisons where self-harming, tearing into their own flesh with hairclips and bottle tops, is endemic. They do not need their medication to be pushed through the metal flap in the door as though they are lepers. Between 1990 and 1995 seven women took their lives in prison. In the first three months of 2003 the exact same number committed suicide. In 2003 a record number of 14 female inmates died. The mother of one, Pauline Campbell, has campaigned passionately on the subject after her daughter Sarah, who was only 18, took her own life. The chair of the Magistrates' Association has commented that there needs to be an increase in provision and improvement in the court-based diversion schemes for women with mental health problems. Although women make up only 6% of the prison population, they account for 11% of the self-inflicted deaths. Half of all women in prison are on prescribed medication such as anti-depressants or anti-psychotics. Most of the women who kill themselves take overdoses or hang themselves but one woman recently choked herself by swallowing toilet paper.

The Prison Service is under-staffed and under-trained. Officers have less opportunity to get to know prisoners individually and thus to spot the danger signs that a woman might take her life.

Most of the women enter prison vulnerable to breakdown because of their personal histories but not all. The *Independent* newspaper's 2003 campaign on mental health documented the experience of Wendy Kramer, who was imprisoned for two and a half years for conspiring to supply drugs. She left prison with severe mental health problems despite having no previous history of mental illness. She was never diagnosed or given therapy while inside but another inmate helped her find a counsellor.

> In prison I felt anxiety, panic, self-harm, suicide, depression – the unbelievable hurt inside your stomach which is what makes you bang your head against the wall. The main thing that gets to me is that there are a lot of women in there that shouldn't be. They aren't criminals; they are mentally ill.

Two-thirds of women who are imprisoned have children under the age of 16; an estimated 18,000 children are separated from their mother by imprisonment every year. Whereas many men serve their sentences knowing their partners are taking care of their children, according to the Prison Inspectorate only 25% of women stated that the father of their children was looking after them while the women were inside. Just 5% of those children stay in their own home once their mother is jailed. In our Family Courts the philosophy is that the child comes first in any dispute. Children need their parents, and only in the most extreme circumstances should we break that bond. Yet in the criminal courts officials wash their hands of responsibility by saying that if her children suffer it is the criminal woman who is to blame. The family is presented as the foundation of society, to be supported and preserved. Women who transgress accepted roles and fail 'the family' unleash punitive responses, yet a veil is drawn over the sacred institution when the ritual of sentencing takes place.

The work of Dr Dora Black, the eminent child psychiatrist, who conducted studies on the mother and baby unit at Holloway Prison, explains that the trauma of separation of young children from their mothers frequently leads to mental illness or at the least to profound emotional problems when they reach adolescence. In England and Wales a maximum of 102 mothers can keep their babies with them in prison; even then, children cannot stay beyond the age of 18 months. This limit on places means that keeping your baby is a privilege. Some states in the USA now recognise the right of every mother of an infant to have that child with her unless she has a history of child abuse or the child would suffer. It is extraordinary that this issue of children's rights has taken so long to be addressed. Babies should be with their mothers and unless a woman has committed an offence of violence which would carry a significant sentence, a mother should not be imprisoned. When I say this I am met with the retort that women would deliberately get themselves pregnant to avoid jail. The people who say this are also distraught at the idea of women using their pregnant status to get council houses. Yes, when we reach for principles to guide a civilised society there will always be those who cheat or play with the rules but against them there are the others who will be salvaged by more humane responses.

On one of my own recent visits to Holloway Prison's mother and baby unit, a young woman told me of the nightmare of being remanded in custody for report when there was no place on the unit to accommodate her baby. She was released after 24 hours on an application for bail to the High Court. In the meantime she was separated from the baby, which she was breastfeeding, and suffered the agony of engorged breasts and desperation at how the baby was coping without her. In the end she was sent down for nine months. Her offence was a cheque-card fraud valued at £700, and although this time she was able to bring the baby into prison with her, her other child, a toddler, was left in the care of her father and was seriously disturbed by the separation. Imprisoning mothers should be a last resort, but judges have different ideas as to what that means.

Where a parent, male or female, has primary care of a child, the criminal courts should be required to obtain social enquiry reports on the impact upon the family of imprisonment. The hypocrisy of lauding the family and motherhood on the one hand while refusing adequately to acknowledge the social and economic supports necessary to sustain women in their motherhood role is a shameful reflection on the values of the justice system. For men and women alike, separation from the family is the worst aspect of imprisonment, but for women the guilt of failing their children exacts a special burden. Their offence is seen as being against more than the criminal law, and that is how they themselves feel it.

The reason why it is worth looking so closely at the experience of women is that so few of them commit violent or serious crime.

Women in prison are more likely to be suffering from multiple problems of material deprivation than male prisoners, less likely to be career criminals or dangerous yet they are at the receiving end of a growing punitiveness. This has partly reflected the increased hostility to single mothers generally and the judicial inability to understand that they do not have to punish a woman exactly as they would a man if, for example, she has responsibility for dependent children.

Pat Carlen has examined what she brilliantly and sardonically describes as the 'carceral clawback', the way in which the arguments for reducing the imprisonment of women have been subverted and used as a rationale for locking women up. She sees the Jack Straw boast of 'making prison work' as the problem. The 'repairing gel', as she describes it, was to be the creation of programmes inside prisons to address the background problems of the women and indeed the men too. This has given sentencers a sense of justification and freedom to lock up women rather than find a community alternative: they persuade themselves that women will be helped when they are inside. In truth, provision of these programmes is very patchy because of overcrowding and can never be much use if the sentence is short. Even if they think a woman is troubled rather than troublesome courts adopt what they think is a welfare approach by imprisoning the woman so that she can be helped. Judges and magistrates sleep more easily at night if they think Styal Prison is like a short stay at the Priory, but they are deluding themselves.

Any review of sentences on women shows that women are now getting heavier sentences for less serious offences. There has been an overall explosion in prison numbers but the imprisonment of women far outstrips the growth in the male prison population. All the arguments women criminologists and lawyers made to persuade the courts and policy makers that the background of most women and their place in society explained their offending are now used, not to avoid prison, but to justify imprisonment. The very language we used in developing a feminist critique of offending has been appropriated and is used to legitimise the use of prison. There is talk of 'empowering' women prisoners and raising self-esteem. Yet as soon as a woman is assertive she is very quickly reminded she is a prisoner and that unquestioning compliance with the rules is the expectation.

The redoubtable Jackie Lowthian of Nacro – the National Association for the Care and Rehabilitation of Offenders – is well placed to provide an overview of prisons, particularly those incarcerating women. She points out that the need to accommodate ever increasing numbers along with budgetary constraints means that there is an overall sense of decline in many prisons. Because of the inexorable demand for places, prisoners are too often given inappropriate allocations in prisons so far away from their family that they receive few visits, or they are placed in prisons where the regime does not meet their needs. She has documented a deterioration in healthcare and hygiene. Staffing shortages mean that non-mandatory tasks such as help with housing and resettlement support have to be dropped in order to ensure that statutory functions like security and discipline are carried out. In turn, these inadequate standards of care increase the risk of bullying, self-harm and suicide. They also mean there is no cover, so prisoners' education or other activities are curtailed. Home probation officers have so little time or resources to spare that they cannot see women in prison or offer voluntary aftercare post-release. There is no help on offer on a statutory basis for people on short sentences.

One of our responsibilities must be to ensure that those who have to be in prison have opportunities to repair the black holes in their own experience which led to offending: many activities should be taking place in a more developed way. Government has been well-intentioned in trying to make some provision – therapeutic programmes have been created addressing violence or past abuse, and there are domestic violence projects for both victim and offender, therapy addressing childhood trauma, issues of sexuality or substance abuse. However, the schemes require Home Office accreditation and many of the best holistic services and programmes fail to get funding because they fall outside the narrow, prescriptive limitations required for accreditation, which are all about the current obsession with 'cognitive behavioural models'. Cognitive behavioural therapies are all the rage, getting women to have insight into their behaviour, the way their abuse as children leads them into adult relationships with abusive men, the way the violence they have experienced has led to low self-worth and addictions. The programmes available are sketchy, totally dependent on who is in charge or the special interests of certain professionals engaged with the prison or based locally. Whether a prisoner can access such a programme is more in the hands of the gods than based on any real assessment of need. Yet ministers talk about these initiatives as if they were available on tap.

It is of course right that psychological work with women in prison can be of real help, and may be crucial if they are to develop strategies for survival, but alone it will not address the main problems women face because it excludes the material conditions of their existence – poverty, racism and sexism. If politicians are going to talk about the causes of crime they cannot deny the reality of the women's existence in the communities in which they live. Much more has to be done about housing issues and training for work. Cathy Stancer of Women in Prison, an organisation which is in touch with more than 400 women prisoners, points out that the chaos caused by short terms of imprisonment and remand in custody before trial is huge. They have to help women sort out rent arrears, find accommodation for those rendered homeless, and help women retain contact with their children. Stancer points out again that most women in prison pose no threat to public safety.

I am not blind to the inhumanity some women wreak on others, nor to their criminality. Women can be ghastly, but the majority of those who are in prison should not be there. What is needed is the creation of real alternatives, such as appropriate community service, hostels and rehabilitation units. If the spirit of sentencing policy is truly that prisons are to be places for dealing with serious crime, particularly violence, then it should be translated into reality by the judges with support from politicians. Our female prisons could then virtually be emptied.

4

The Wife, the Mother and the Dutiful Daughter

Cases involving domestic violence are an important gauge of entrenched attitudes about the proper roles of men and women. Violence is still seen by many as a legitimate response to certain kinds of female behaviour. It may not be said openly but it lurks in the shadows of the campaigns for fathers' rights and the continuing characterisation of women campaigners against violence as miserable, men-hating feminists. Yet whenever I speak at events around the country, women of all kinds and all ages raise the ways in which women's lives are blighted by fear of male violence.

One of the problems for women has been the split between what is perceived as public, and therefore the law's business, and what is private, which shouldn't concern the law at all. Most of us are content that the law and the power of the state should be strictly limited so that their encroachment on individual freedom is kept to a minimum. The way in which people choose to conduct their private lives should be regulated as little as possible by the state and we have been happy to incorporate the ideas of liberal philosophy into our jurisprudence. Normally, it is only where private behaviour harms others that we condone the intervention of the law, and we use this as the basis of our argument for the legalisation of adult homosexual behaviour. Yet this separation of the private and public has worked against women, whose major sphere of activity is in the private domain. And so those who apply the law often fail women in the areas where they are most vulnerable.

The issue of domestic violence has gradually been tackled since the late 1970s after years of turning a blind eye, failing to prosecute and taking little action against its perpetrators. Marital behaviour behind closed doors was for a long time deemed a 'no go' area for law enforcement. This reluctance of the law to become involved accounts for much of the past difficulty in pursuing legal remedies for child abuse, both physical and sexual, and for rape, unless it involved being jumped on in an alleyway.

The arguments which are used to explain the failure of the criminal law in these areas always turn on the evidential problems, but in fact the private/public dichotomy is an essential element which has not been recognised because lawyers cannot see that not regulating is as significant as regulating. But finding remedies in law for the protection of women and their children poses a problem, because it inevitably involves greater intervention by the state and the possible erosion of defendants' rights. Policing the bedroom is not a course we should readily advocate, but there should never be any qualms when it is done at the behest of those who are being abused, or on their behalf by concerned parties. The whole point of human rights philosophy is that every human being be valued and respected and the state has a responsibility to ensure that some members of the community are not ill-using others. Modern rights discourse recognises that persecution is carried out not only by the state but by relatives and neighbours and that the failure of the state to prevent inhumane behaviour becomes a condonation. The police, who would have no problem entering premises believed to contain explosive substances, become very sensitive to the rights of man when the information relates to domestic violence; it has not been easy shifting the culture to acknowledge that human rights is not only about obscenities which take place in Kosovo or Sudan but also about the abuse of people closer to home.

But it is not fair to confine criticism to the police, who have made real strides in addressing domestic violence. Many forces have now established domestic violence units with specially trained officers conducting the investigations but the mindset that this kind of crime is not real crime is still present. American research has shown that when members of the public witnessed violence between two people they were more reluctant to report it if it was between a man and a woman. In answer to questionnaires, the majority of people felt that there were situations in which it was acceptable for a husband to hit his wife – and not necessarily when she was being violent to him. Since the 1970s, when the stone was lifted on this subject, there has been growing recognition of the problem and its social cost. New research commissioned by the Equalities Minister, Jacqui Smith, shows that time off work for injuries caused by domestic violence costs employers £3 billion a year. Research by Professor Sylvia Walby at Leeds University shows that domestic violence also costs the criminal justice system £1 billion, almost a quarter of the total budget for violent crime. It tells us a lot that women ministers who have done so much to get the issue on the agenda still have to focus on the economic costs to get through to male policy makers. Yes, there is spreading acceptance that something has to be done about domestic violence – it is a quarter of all violent crime and somewhere in the country every minute a woman is phoning the police because she is being beaten – but, for the media and for politicians seeking to grab headlines, domestic violence is drab and unsexy. It takes place beyond the reach of cameras, between people who, feeling shame, embarrassment, fear, even love, are unlikely to seek publicity. It is mundane and has very ordinary perpetrators – not sinister, stalking murderers, but simply boozed-up, angry, disappointed, ordinary men who would be unrecognisable in the pub or office as a wife-beater or control freak. The sheer scale of the problem is beyond comprehension.

The legal difficulties when offences take place in private are considerable. Usually there are no independent witnesses, deep and complicated emotional turmoil often surrounds the events, motives for making allegations are questioned and, if the allegations are of a sexual nature, there is a particular reluctance to convict. In the case of domestic violence, women are unsatisfactory complainants, fearful of, or ambivalent about, pursuing a prosecution because of the potential implications. Minimising is a coping device used by those who are abused, adult and child, but it is still too often misunderstood by those who investigate and by the courts.

According to Sandra Horley, the Chief Executive of Refuge, research shows that 90% of domestic violence incidents take place in the presence of children or with children in the next room. Both they and their mothers are at risk of depression, anxiety and post-traumatic stress. Sometimes worse. Think of the 14-year-old boy killed, only recently, trying unsuccessfully to save his mother; the two children killed alongside their mother; the four children who will grow up to learn they were asleep upstairs while their father malleted their mother to death in the sitting room. Being made to witness such events is another form of abuse.

In most cases it is quite understandably felt inappropriate to call the child to testify in court. In a 2003 case, Patricia Lawrence killed her husband with a kitchen knife because she was being strangled at the time; both her tiny children were in the room and witnessed the full horror. The older boy who was only six was interviewed on video by the police and described his mother being choked by his daddy and defending herself. There could be no claim that his account was influenced by speaking to his mother, as they had been separated at the scene of the events. Yet the Crown proceeded with a prosecution for murder and Patricia, desperate to prevent further damage to her children, did not want her son to be put into the witness box in her defence. (Hers was one of the few cases where self-defence has worked for a woman; she was acquitted of murder and walked free from the court.)

Many excuses given for failing to prosecute lack substance. Police officers still fail to look for evidence that would support the complaint, particularly of a forensic nature, once an assault has been labelled 'domestic'. The reluctance of victims to pursue a prosecution has to be understood. Harriet Harman the Solicitor-General told the *Independent* on 30 December 2002 that she had often come across cases where the woman was in hospital but begged the Crown prosecutor to drop the case. 'She knows she has got to get better to look after her children. The last thing she wants is the stress of having to give evidence. The prosecution then has to decide whether to witness summons her or drop the case.' As a result of this dilemma, ways are being sought to gather independent evidence so that prosecutions might be brought even if a woman does not testify herself. Any woman going through the court system to put a stop to domestic violence needs considerable support, and the proper resourcing of that support is imperative.

Women who are abused blame themselves, and on top of that they fear not being believed. They suffer in silence and cover up what is going on to doctors, family and neighbours. Their silence then becomes another stick with which they are beaten. Women are abused on average 35 times before seeking police support. Pressure not to use criminal sanctions is considerable. In the waiting areas of courts, ushers and court staff have frequently expressed the view to me that it is six of one and half a dozen of the other, despite the fact that in the majority of cases it is the women who bear the scars, literally, and who have called the police. The historical fallacy that women are usually equal and active participants in domestic violence lives on. The growing claim that men are just as much victims of domestic abuse as women has been exploded by the research of Dr David Gadd and others for the Scottish Executive (*Domestic Abuse against Men in Scotland* 2002). Their conclusion was that while some men did endure genuinely harrowing experiences, very few experienced prolonged forms of domestic abuse and very few lived in fear; it was therefore misleading to attribute victim status to these men. They add that some members of the group of men who are hit by partners are in fact more terrifying than terrified.

The alternative line taken by those who dismiss domestic violence is that many women invite beatings because of nagging, because they push their men to the edge or because they are masochists. The nagging wife is put on to the scales as a counter-weight to the violent husband, although few die in direct consequence of a tongue-lashing, and indeed most battered wives cannot afford the luxury of a grinding whinge because they know they will literally get it in the teeth. Sometimes they even instigate an assault to get it over; they know a beating is coming but the waiting in terror is even more excruciating than the blows.

Police, lawyers and judges often regard prosecution as inappropriate because it is likely to accelerate the disintegration of the relationship or damage the family unit; however inappropriate it may be, they often see their role as helping to preserve the marriage. In a *World in Action* programme shown on television in 1990, about rape as part of the pattern of domestic violence within marriage, Sir Frederick Lawton, a retired Appeal Court judge, explained that if it were open to wives to bring prosecutions for rape, even against a background of domestic violence, it would prohibit any chance of rehabilitation of the marriage and would have a deleterious effect on children – as though rape itself, rather than the prosecution, might not already have had that effect. Although such a view may seem dated, there are many who still feel that the criminal courts are not the right place for such issues because criminalising a partner has dire consequences for the whole family. Women themselves say that having a conviction will affect their husband's career and stigmatise their children so they do not want to go down that route and postpone taking the steps which so often in the end become inevitable. Their own security and sanity often take second place to concern for everyone else. Precisely these arguments about 'irreparable damage to the family' have been used to counter the introduction of every piece of reforming legislation for the benefit of women in the last hundred years, whether it was allowing a woman to divorce, hold property in her own name, gain the vote, or obtain the right to enter the professions and public life.

The musician, Bob Geldof, has highlighted the importance of positive fathering and the role men should play, even after separation, in the upbringing of their children but his campaign also provides shelter for men who have entrenched ideas about the role of the pater familias, who want contact in order to perpetuate control over the family. They argue that there should be a presumption in *all* cases of shared parenting. In *most* cases that should be so but we must not forget the significant number of children who depend on us for protection and emotional well-being. In New Zealand there is a rebuttable presumption of no-contact in cases where there has been domestic violence and it is for the violent partner to show that there is no risk to the family. This makes sense to me, given the evidence of continuing harassment and abuse in so many cases where violence has been part of the family dynamic.

In the majority of domestic murder cases, men kill women, and there is usually a history of abuse on the man's part. A recurring theme in research is of abusive men barred from contact with their partners stalking and finding them in refuges or hospitals, in the homes of relatives, even in a police station, and killing them.

*

93

On 18 November 2003 Alan Pemberton, a financial adviser, shot dead his wife Julie and his 17-year-old son William at their home. Mrs Pemberton had suffered years of abuse and became so afraid of her husband that she handed guns belonging to him to the police, and kitchen knives. She took out an injunction against him and agreed to have a panic button installed. On the night of the attack Alan Pemberton arrived at the house with a shotgun and shot William five times in the chest when he tried to protect his mother. Julie Pemberton hid in a cupboard where she dialled 999. During the harrowing 16-minute call the operator told her the police were on their way. Mrs Pemberton could be heard on top saying she had 'about a minute before I die'. The operator heard her say 'he's coming now' and a man's voice say 'You fucking whore'. She was found with four shotgun wounds to the chest and lower back. After killing his son and wife Mr Pemberton turned the gun on himself. In a letter found in his care he made it clear that he was taking revenge for her daring to end the marriage. The police did not turn up at the farmhouse for 40 minutes after the call and then waited a further five hours before entering the premises because they were waiting for an armed response unit. After an inquest, Julie's brother Frank Mullane said that Thames Valley police seemed to have 'a somewhat limited understanding of domestic violence'. He said that his sister had received 'next to nothing, if not nothing' in terms of support from the police and that the way police kept records of abuse was so disorganised that no one looking at the case could take an overall view.

On 6 June 2004 Stuart Horgan, who had a long history of domestic violence, pursued his estranged wife, Vicky, and shot her in the head with a shotgun after bursting into a barbecue at her family's home in Henley-on-Thames. Her sister, Emma, was also killed and her mother was in a coma for two weeks.

A study of 300 cases carried out by Napo, the probation officers' union, revealed that 61% of the fathers involved in the family court system had allegations of domestic violence made against them. According to the assistant general secretary Harry Fletcher, 'The true rate could be higher because of under-reporting of domestic violence.' In the eight years up to 2004, 22 children have been killed by their fathers who had been given visiting rights. They include the four children of Claude Mubiangata, the youngest of whom was three years old. Mubiangata locked himself and the children in his car and set it alight. In February 2002, Stuart Wilson took his sons to a golf course near Handsworth and slit the throat of Brad who was seven, then plunged a screwdriver into the neck of eight-year-old Brett. It happened shortly after he had met with his wife, beaten her up and made off with his children saying he would teach her 'a lesson she would never forget'. Wilson was put on trial but killed himself before its conclusion. Like Othello, these men are victims of their own pathological jealousy and make victims of the people they love. Mark Bradley, from Dorset, killed his wife, his children and himself on hearing that she had had an affair and wanted a separation. In London, José Pimenta pushed his two young sons off a fourth-floor balcony and then jumped himself when his estranged wife told him she had begun a new relationship. Their thinking is: 'If I can't have the children, you can't either.'

Time and again following an assault men are given a 'talking to' rather than being arrested. It used to be that when the police were called out to these situations they did not even record the incident, so that if a prosecution did proceed a history of previous violence was not available. Now there is a requirement to record everything but it will be noted as 'Male and female involved in dispute. No visible injuries. No action requested', making it unclear who is coming off worst. The 2004 report of the *Fawcett Society's Commission on Women and the Criminal Justice System* found that lack of communication between the police and other agencies and the victim was a significant problem. A Ms W. told the Commission, 'There is a huge problem with lack of continuity with the police – each time there is a new officer. You have to start again and it is so complicated to tell the whole story . . . We despaired and almost gave up.'

Supporting evidence is key in securing convictions both in domestic violence where a complainant may withdraw her evidence out of fear and in rape where the trial tends to focus on the complainant's credibility. The Criminal Justice Act 2003 allows hearsay and reported evidence into trials, which means that a much broader swathe of evidence will become usable. However, evidence-gathering by the police does remain central to successful outcomes but it is often carried out in different ways by different forces. There are 43 police forces in England and Wales, with different ways of operating and different priorities for responding to crime; training does not conform to a common minimum standard. Police and Crown Prosecution Service inspections have found inconsistencies throughout the country and even within police areas. Domestic violence is not a specific criminal offence; it is a range of behaviours which may constitute any number of offences depending upon the perceptions of the police. As a result, domestic violence is often charged as a minor common assault, even where there are visible injuries which would amount to actual bodily harm. This means that the cases are assigned to Magistrates' Courts, processed quickly, and treated less seriously than other types of assault, all in the spirit that such a course is more likely to lead to the couple making it up. In the few cases where they do go for trial, acquittal rates are high. Fining is still by far the most common outcome; imprisonment the least frequent. At a time when judges are being called upon to treat violent offences with severity, those labelled as domestic violence still seem to attract ambivalence.

A woman testifying to the Fawcett Commission in April 2003 described three years of violence and intimidation she had suffered from her former partner, during which time she had used both criminal and civil procedures. She said, 'The last time he breached the injunction was when he tried to kill me. It took the police three weeks to arrest him. Three weeks. So by the time it got to the courts, they thought, if the police aren't taking this seriously why should we?'

Women's fears of being killed have to be taken seriously because they are often right. In July 2000, Rob Mochrie bludgeoned his wife and four children to death before taking his own life. That same month Phillip Austin murdered his wife Claire and his children Kieren and Jade, because their mother 'started hassling him and arguing'. Claire's parents were aware of his aggression but thought he was seeking help for it. In August 2001, Karl Bluestone a police officer in Kent, murdered his wife and two of his four children before taking his own life. He too had been violent in the run-up to the killings.

Women at Magistrates' Courts can meet a hostile environment. At one time if the husband was on bail, he would often sit in the hallway feet away from her, harassing his wife and coercing her into dropping the charges. Now the courts are much more aware of the problems and victims' support groups will provide companionship and a special room for the woman. But the same pressure may be exercised by the man's family or mates before she ever gets to court. The initial questioning of the woman sometimes feels clinical, justified by those who are supposed to be on her side as testing the strength of any case they could bring and letting her see what is going to come from those who will represent her husband. Many victims internalise the blame implied by authority figures and, naturally enough, often decide not to go through with a court case. Such failure to proceed can be met with irritation from the authorities. If a woman does steel herself to go through with it, it is precisely then that she needs support. This is when further violence might occur, because involving the police and the courts is a declaration of the right to control her own life, and if there is one thing that upsets a wife-beater it is a wife who asserts herself.

Police lawyers and judges still have difficulties in abandoning their stereotype of the abused woman as someone who is submissive and cowed. When the woman appears competent or has a bit of gumption or if she seems to be materially well-off, there is a failure of the imagination as to how she could be victimised. Lawyers still say of a battered woman, 'She is a middle-class woman. It is not as though she could not afford alternative accommodation.' What are still not understood are the psychological effects of the experience – effects which are often so severe as to render women incapable of taking the necessary steps to end the relationship. In the early stages women believe the violent incidents are isolated events. The male partners are remorseful and the women believe everything will improve. They usually rationalise the abuse as the result of excess alcohol or the effects of stress on their partner because of overwork, no work, a new baby (30% of domestic violence starts in or is exacerbated by pregnancy). Eventually the excuses are no longer convincing but by that time the cycle is so established it is impossible to break. In almost every case in which I have been involved the woman presents herself in a very flat, unemotional way which can fail to arouse, in a judge or a jury, a full appreciation of her partner's behaviour towards her. Psychologists describe it as lack of 'affect'. Women are also often so filled with shame at the public exposure of what they see as their private failure that they may minimise the extent of their suffering.

Women with children often stay in such a relationship in the interests of their children: they fear that if they leave they will set up a situation which might result in the children being taken into care. If they leave their children they will fail as a mother; if they take them, they may face homelessness. It becomes a monumental step. In court even today few reasons are good enough to justify a woman leaving her children. The hostility towards a mother who contemplates doing this, even where she can no longer survive her husband's cruelty and has nowhere to bring children if she takes them with her, can annihilate her cause in a trial by jury.

When the playwright Peter Flannery and I were working on the television drama *Blind Justice* we were posed with a similar dilemma in the creation of the character Katherine Hughes, a radical woman barrister. We had to create a scandal in her past which the press could dig up and use in an attempt to discredit her. Peter was keen to invent a child left behind with a previous husband but I balked at that because the character of Katherine ran in the face of most stereotypes of women, and I felt that to have her abandon a child, however good her reasons, would completely lose her the audience sympathy we needed in order to lend credibility to her arguments. I won the day, but I know I was pandering to a negative reaction.

Now thanks to women ministers in the government, legal reform is being introduced in the Domestic Violence, Crime and Victims Act 2004 which will give greater powers to the police and the courts to protect victims and prosecute abusers with a power of arrest for breach of a non-molestation order or for common assault.

There are clearly cases such as child battering in which the quality of a woman's care for her children moves to centre stage. The evidence can make sickening reading and I am not without my own rage at the child's pain. Feeding children heroin or turning adolescent daughters on to the streets for prostitution can rarely be viewed in a sympathetic light.

In some cases, however, class divisions as well as gender expectations are at the root of the court's inability to understand how the offences were committed. A mother of four children was convicted of cutting her son with a breadknife. The woman's children had different fathers, none of whom was around, and two of the children were of mixed race. The family were living on the breadline and the oldest boy, who was eight, was already showing signs of problem behaviour. Social services confirmed that a change of personnel had resulted in a period with no social work support. The family was living in a flat without electricity. A doctor testified that the injury to the boy's head was not serious and would have involved little force. A schoolteacher wrote to the court to describe the effort the woman was putting into helping her children to read. She had minimal previous history of offending. She was sentenced to 18 months' imprisonment.

There is a chasm of misunderstanding between the privileged professionals who work the system and the offender bringing up children alone without financial and emotional resources. The misery of that existence and the toll it can take is rarely appreciated.

With horrifying regularity, cases of child-killing come before the courts. The components have surprisingly few variables. The couple are usually young. In the majority of cases the child is a girl and the male partner is a stepfather. The death is usually preceded by protracted neglect and abuse before a final brutal assault. The cases which stand out in our minds are, of course, those where social service departments, underfunded and under pressure, are severely criticised and formal inquiries follow. Among these are the cases of Jasmine Beckford, whose stepfather, Maurice, was jailed in March 1985 for ten years for her manslaughter, and whose mother, Beverly Lorrington, received 18 months for wilful neglect; Heidi Koseda, whose stepfather, Nicholas Price, was sentenced to life imprisonment in September 1985 with a recommendation that he serve a minimum of 15 years and whose mother, Rosemarie Koseda, pleaded guilty to manslaughter and was detained under the

Mental Health Act; and Kimberly Carlile, whose stepfather, Nigel Hall, and mother, Pauline, were both charged with murder. On 15 May 1987 Nigel Hall was convicted and sentenced to life imprisonment for Kimberly's killing, whilst Pauline Carlile was not held responsible for her death but was jailed for 12 years for cruelty. The wicked stepmother is the spectre that has haunted us all since childhood. Yet in the courts it is the male equivalent who appears with greater regularity. However, natural fathers appear in the dock with frequency too. In December 1999, two-year-old Chelsea Brown was murdered by her father, having been battered by him throughout her short life.

Public anger towards the men who commit these crimes against defenceless children is matched by bewilderment and disgust at the role of the women. The questions which spring into the minds of us all are repeatedly asked in court. Why didn't you protect the child? Why didn't you leave? Why didn't you seek the help of police, doctors, health visitors, social workers or even just a friend? Why did you cover up your partner's behaviour? Why did you protect him rather than your own baby? How could you allow him to harm repeatedly the child you had borne?

The women themselves do not know the answers to these questions. They have usually been beaten or emotionally battered by their men and are the passive partners in volatile relationships. Often they are grateful for the attention of the men in their lives, however abusive that attention might be. Their low sense of their own worth often emanates from childhood experiences. The children they bear become extensions of themselves, and I suspect this is particularly the case with female children. The apparent collusion in violence towards their offspring has often seemed to me to be a consolidation of what they have come to expect for themselves. The whole cycle is a paradigm of the worst kind of power imbalance.

Others have become incapable of taking action. The effect of long-term abuse, physical and mental, on otherwise capable, strong women is devastating. The abuser's control can become so absolute that he no longer has to use physical violence. The threat is ever present: even when women go out of doors or go to work the spell is not broken. In the pattern of abuse it is a common feature that the women are isolated, forbidden to have visitors or friendships or much contact with members of their families. Possessiveness and jealousy, which had been flattering at the commencement of the relationship, become oppressive and controlling. A psychological freezing means they lose their ability to take the protective steps that another mother could initiate. Their partners are perceived by them to be omnipotent, so that any move out of line will invoke punishment and avoidance becomes paramount, even if it means failing to protect a child. They learn to be helpless and hopeless, convinced that any attempt to escape will mean the infliction of more torture on them all.

Not only is it misunderstood that the woman's own reality becomes so distorted that she believes nothing will prevail upon her husband to stop, and that any challenge to him will destroy her, but it should also not be forgotten that in very many cases nothing does stop abusive men, and battered women *do* end up dead.

Understanding domestic violence is a challenge to the courts. To onlookers the response of the battered woman seems abnormal, but to her it is a rational response to her abnormal circumstances. Misconceptions litter the court and are reflected in the verdicts of juries: women have ample opportunities to leave; in some perverse way they like the pain; no real woman becomes so crushed by her abusive partner that her maternal instinct is extinguished.

Cross-examining of women in such cases frequently operates on the premiss that a certain level of violence is acceptable. One prosecutor's recent questioning of a man who battered his wife and child began with the assertion, 'Whatever your relationship with your girlfriend, the one person who did not deserve to be hit was the baby.' In another, where the woman had agreed that she was only ever slapped, it was suggested that the physical violence could, therefore, be put on one side.

In their lives with battering husbands, women themselves invariably minimise the extent of the violence to which they are subjected because of self-blaming and their own sense of shame. Or they cover up their man's behaviour because they fear the consequences of exposing him. They avoid going to the doctor, and cover their bruises. They provide innocent explanations to outsiders for injuries and concoct elaborate stories to distract attention from the abuse. They cannot face up to the horror of what is happening, and part of the pretence is to delude themselves.

Finding physical evidence of the abuse is difficult when the matter becomes material in a court, with lawyers for the other side claiming recent fabrication or exaggeration. In every contested criminal case I have conducted over the years involving the battering of a woman she is accused of inflating her account and exaggerating the extent of any violence. Corroboration of less than a handful of assaults is par for the course, and those often become the only instances of violence which are accepted.

The constant theme in the accounts of battered women who come before the courts is that they had lived in hope that everything would come all right, that if they had a proper home, or a baby, or the baby was older, or the man had a job, or his job had fewer pressures, or they had more money, then the relationship would return to the romantic idyll of the courtship. This is the sustaining factor in the early stages of the abuse, and thereafter the control is too well established for them to feel able to challenge it. However, continuing to live with the tormentor is seen as a testament to the acceptability of his behaviour.

A constant refrain in the questioning is 'Why did you not leave?', something the mother herself can never answer coherently. Because cumulative abuse can induce responses which are counter to common sense, I think it is crucial to call expert testimony in these cases as to the effects of it on its victims. The test for admissibility of expert testimony is whether the matters into which the testimony goes are outside the experience of the jury:

> It is aimed at an area where the purported common knowledge of the jury may be very much mistaken, an area where jurors' logic drawn from their own experience may lead to a wholly incorrect conclusion, an area where expert knowledge would enable the jurors to disregard their prior conclusions as being common myths rather than common knowledge. (*State* v. *Kelly*, New Jersey Supreme Court)

There was a tendency in the courts to think that everyone knew the effects of a hard clout and there was no call for expertise. But that has now changed. The question 'Why don't they leave?' is proof of our failure to understand the problem.

In the cases where experts are called, it is not their function to usurp the jury's role in the trial. They are able to state what effect the abuse would have if the history given by the woman were true. It is then for the jury to determine the truth or otherwise of the account. Ideally a situation will develop where the effects of cumulative violence will be so widely understood that courts will need no assistance. It will not be necessary for psychiatrists and psychologists to 'loan their experience' to the jury. We have yet to reach that stage.

In the United States a pattern of behaviour exhibited by abused women is labelled battered woman's syndrome and is a sub-category of post-traumatic stress disorder, recognised by the World Health Organisation in its classifications of mental disorders. It can be a useful part of the armoury in defending women who have killed their partner after years of abuse. However, it has its limitations because not all women will fulfil the criteria of the syndrome. A woman who comes before a judge and jury with the claim that she has been battered and suggests this may be a relevant factor in evaluating her subsequent actions still faces the prospect of being condemned by popular mythology about domestic violence: either she has invented her account of her husband's behaviour and indeed she was the violent partner, or she was not as badly beaten as she claims, or she drove her husband to violence with her own volatile behaviour. Although society has abandoned its formal approval of spousal abuse, tolerance of it continues in some circles today.

The leading case for the role of expert testimony, with a superb judgment by the Canadian Supreme Court judge, Bertha Wilson, is that of *Lavallee* v. *Regina*, which was decided in May 1990. It is now an authority cited internationally, and must be the finest legal exposition on domestic violence. The court of seven judges had three women on it:

If it strains credulity to imagine what the ordinary man would do in the position of the battered spouse, it is probably because men do not typically find themselves in that situation. Some women do, however. The definition of what is reasonable must be adapted to circumstances which are, by and large, foreign to the world inhabited by the hypothetical reasonable man . . . Where evidence exists that an accused is in a battering relationship, expert testimony can assist the jury in determining whether the accused had a reasonable apprehension of death when she acted by explaining the heightened sensitivity of a battered woman to her partner's acts. Without such testimony I am sceptical that the average fact-finder would be capable of appreciating why her subjective fear may have been reasonable in the context of the relationship. After all, the hypothetical reasonable man observing only the final incident may have been unlikely to recognise the batterer's threat as potentially lethal.

Frequently, the judgment refers to the work of the pioneering clinical psychologist Dr Lenore Walker, author of *The Battered Woman Syndrome* (1984). She describes in her research the recurring theme of abusive behaviour as intermittent, alternating with normal acceptable conduct, and argues that this inconsistency is the means by which the traumatic bond is established.

The designation 'battered woman's syndrome' is one that causes me some disquiet. It seems more sensible to avoid gender-specific labels like this because of the pathological cul-de-sac they create for women and also because of the hostility a special defence engenders in men. Furthermore, the features are also present in other relationships where there is a power imbalance: hostage and captor; battered child and abusive parent; cult follower and leader; prisoner and guard. I have acted for a homosexual man who was physically and emotionally abused in his relationship with his male partner, and, hard as it is to imagine, there might occasionally be men who manifest the same surrender of control in response to abuse from women. It also concerns me that acceptance of a rigidly defined syndrome can exclude those who do not completely conform to the criteria. There is a constellation of symptoms which are usually present but some psychiatrists take a mechanistic approach and if a woman does not squeeze herself neatly into the fit of the syndrome it is inferred that she was not battered. No such conclusion is justified but the psychiatric evaluation of the woman will often depend upon the world view and philosophy of the individual psychiatrist. There are hawks and doves amongst psychiatrists too. Sometimes a woman who has been severely abused is not suffering from battered woman's syndrome but depression. It can still be a sufficient abnormality of mind to diminish her responsibility for murder so that she is guilty of the lesser crime of manslaughter.

Women find such varied ways of surviving that behavioural checklists do not always work. What is clear from the now extensive research is that all sorts of women are subjected to abuse, deal with it in a multiplicity of ways and put up with it because complicated dynamics are set in motion. However, putting the name to one side, it is crucial that the principles of 'battered woman's syndrome' should be acknowledged by the courts in Britain, as part of the educational process to dispel myths about domestic violence. Women who are battered have highly developed antennae for when violence is going to erupt and know when it is truly serious. They can become hyper-aroused, which is nothing to do with sexual arousal but is all about fear and a terror of being killed. It is then that they sometimes take fatal steps to defend themselves.

The impact of Mme Justice Wilson's appointment to Canada's highest court should not go unnoticed. The Lavallee judgment and many other leading judgments affecting women illustrate the value of having women in senior judicial positions. Bertha Wilson – a Scot, incidentally – set the ball rolling. Four of the nine judges in the Canadian Supreme Court are now women including the Chief Justice. It can and does make a difference to have judges who are receptive to a female analysis of violence, who demand that legal doctrine is sensitive to its context and who render their judgments accordingly. What the women on the court now say is that it is not necessary for the women to guard women's rights any more; the men do it just as effectively!

Violence against men does take place but to pretend it is an equivalent problem is a denial of the underlying issues. It is hardly surprising that the battering, real battering, of men is rare, given the history of heterosexual relationships, the power disparity which has existed between men and women, the socialisation of the sexes and the physical disadvantages of women. But I am frequently informed by indignant males that men are battered too. Even men who would not dream of using violence against their own wives are very defensive about male violence. Dealing with it as isolated aberration rather than as a problem rooted in sexual imbalance is the easier route, and women are made to take their share of the blame. Blaming the victim is a constant experience for women in the courts.

In January 1992 Sally Emery stood trial with her boyfriend Brian Hedman charged with ill-treatment of their child Chanel, who died as a result of a ruptured bowel. The baby bore the signs of terrible abuse: fractured ribs, old and fresh injuries. Sally Emery initially lied to the police, covering up for Hedman, but at her trial she gave a classic and horrifying history of being battered herself and described how this was extended to the baby within months of her birth. The fact that Emery had two O levels was used in comparison with Hedman's low IQ to suggest that she would be the more in control within the relationship. It is frequently assumed that only women with low intelligence are dominated. Her frozen demeanour and failure to cry in police interview, so characteristic of those who are abused, was invoked to show her hardness. Her lying to cover for her abuser, of whom she was so terrified, indicated her proficiency at deceit. With the assistance of expert testimony, it was accepted that she was not the perpetrator of the assaults on her child. In fact Brian Hedman had punched Chanel in the gut because the baby had not shown enough appreciation of the Christmas present he had bought and seemed more interested in the paper. She was ten months old. Sally was sentenced to four years' imprisonment for failing to protect her child. Battering, it seems, would have to be of the most extreme kind to absolve women from their maternal responsibility. While I accept that the protection of children must be one of the clearest priorities in society, and that parental duty must be enforced by law, I think it is crucial that we also acknowledge the full impact of extreme violence on mothers.

The mothers in child abuse cases such as these spend the weeks and months after the child's death immersed in a legal process that is directed towards assessing the extent of criminal responsibility; little room is left to deal with their grief and personal guilt. Sally Emery cried out from the witness box, 'I feel guilty. I want to be punished.'

There was a serious loophole in the law of homicide where a child was killed and neither parent took responsibility. If neither testified against the other, both could end up being acquitted because of the absence of direct evidence. A change in the law in 2004 now makes it a crime carrying 14 years to allow a child to die while in your care and custody. However, the concern is that a battered woman who remains in terror of her partner will be convicted rather than tell the truth about his culpability.

This same background of low self-esteem and battering is usually present in those cases where women are accessories to child sexual abuse, but here the sexual violation and exploitation of children produces an even rawer response. Lifting the lid off the incest taboo has sent highly charged waves of panic through the criminal justice system. Statistically, women are rarely protagonists in sexual offences, and it is important that the reasons for this are fully appreciated. Sexual offences are deeply connected with the power structure in our society and closely related to sexual inequality and the different upbringing of men and women. Occasionally we see cases of an adult female being accused of committing sexual indecency with an adolescent boy, and there was the rare instance of the headmistress, Ruth Hartley, who was found guilty of indecently assaulting an 11-year-old girl with whom she slept naked. However, such cases have been unusual, probably reflecting society's denial of women's sexuality and a conviction that women are less prone to this type of abuse of power.

According to Dr E. Carol Sheldrick, Consultant Psychiatrist at the Maudsley Hospital, the sudden discovery that child sexual abuse is more prevalent than was ever believed has brought in its wake the revelation that 20 per cent of abused boys and 5 per cent of abused girls are assaulted by women, though it must be emphasised that this is still overall a very small percentage. Work here and in the United States has shown that girls are more frequently abused than boys, that perpetrators are more often male than female, and that whilst male victims are likely to become perpetrators, females are more likely to continue as victims. Of those who go on to commit crimes of sexual abuse the majority have themselves been abused.

Cases are now coming before the courts where women are charged with playing supporting roles, aiding and abetting the sexual exploitation of their children by husbands, lovers and other male relatives. The children are used directly for sexual gratification or in pornographic displays. Sometimes the women themselves actively participate in the degradation of their own children, and this has been a claim in recent allegations of ritual abuse. The whole process beggars belief and throws into confusion all the shibboleths about the sacred nature of motherhood. Few of us, on the other hand, had any problem understanding the gut response of the mother who poured boiling water in the crotch of the man who had assaulted her little girl: this was 'nature', outraged, protective mothering.

The taboo surrounding child sexual abuse still distorts the legal process. Mothers so often are held ultimately responsible for a number of reasons: failing to provide conjugal fulfilment; failing to protect their children; condoning abusive behaviour. Furthermore, with little statistical support it is claimed that large numbers of women invent allegations of sexual abuse to get their own back on their menfolk or to inflame prejudice against them. When June Scotland was tried for the murder of her husband in March 1992, the allegation that her abusive husband had also sexually interfered with their daughter was not only dismissed by the Crown as invention but used to measure Mrs Scotland's credibility in relation to the whole history of events. The girl's aggressive behaviour towards her father during adolescence, her suicide attempts and assaults on her own appearance, which psychiatrists saw as consistent with a history of sexual abuse, were described as rebellious teenage behaviour. Of course, there are occasional false accusations by mendacious wives. But the generalising of such notions requires examination. A new myth that all former wives are embittered is in the making.

In the handling of sexual abuse cases, social workers, predominantly female, are accused of hysteria, lack of professionalism and distortion of evidence.

Most people wish to see incest as very rare, occurring in families which are obviously socially maladjusted. In fact, although the sexual boundaries in such families have become confused and ill-defined, the incestuous family looks very much like any 'normal' family.

It is this very proximity to normality which discomfits people. We want our rapists, wife batterers and child abusers to have mean mouths and eyebrows that meet. If the men in the dock do not conform sufficiently to the stereotype of the deviant, or if incestuous families do not behave abnormally, they are better able to resist allegations.

While some are anxious to promote sexual abuse as aberrant behaviour, just as prevalent amongst women as men, others cannot accept the possibility that women are abusive at all. In her book *Mother, Madonna, Whore* (1988), Dr Estela Welldon explores the perversion of motherhood and provides an insight into the way women's own powerlessness can manifest itself in abuse of the one relationship where they do feel in control. She suspects that, by placing motherhood on a pedestal, we have refused to believe in the possibility of woman transgressing the purity of her maternal role. Dr Welldon met with resistance from some feminists because her conclusions were seen as blaming women, but her work provides one route to understanding this area of crime, which until now has been conveniently labelled as the ultimate in wickedness.

As yet there is little appreciation in the criminal justice system of why women become involved, and the main response is an intensified revulsion. Like other sexual offenders, women often exacerbate their position by slipping into denial or justification. It is a familiar view of both men and women involved in these cases that if a child doesn't physically resist an adult's sexual advances, this indicates a willingness by the child to have sex. The women in these cases often maintain that having intercourse with a child is not such a bad way for the adult to teach the child about sex, or express the view that it is better to have sex with a child in the family than to have an affair. Collusion by wives in the abuse of their children is despised almost as much as the actual assaults. In fact, collusion is greatly exaggerated, and most mothers becoming aware of sexual abuse take steps to protect the child or genuinely never know, but a commonly expressed view at trial is that the wife's frigidity or rejection was the root cause of the male abuse and that she subcontracted her sexual obligations.

The women who are convicted of sexual offences end up segregated from the general prison population for their own protection. Distributed throughout the women's prisons, they form tiny leper colonies in the institutions. The psychiatric facilities in the prison system are wholly inadequate and their problems can never be adequately addressed.

An attempt was made to break new ground in a special unit at Styal Prison in the late 1980s, where Fran Corder, a senior social worker, and Sharon Barnett, a probation officer, established a group project. All six women with whom they worked had abused children with co-defendants, such as husbands, boyfriends or neighbours. Five probably would not have abused if they had not been initiated into it by their partners. The sample is low, and any conclusions should be drawn with caution, but all the women lacked confidence and were introverted and nervous. All were heavily dependent on their partners. The idea of women's passive role in sex was entrenched in their relationships with males, as was the view that a woman's place was in the home. Unfortunately, the therapeutic scheme at Styal has been discontinued. There is no facility for women like Grendon Underwood, a male prison where intensive psychotherapeutic work is undertaken.

The method for ordering psychiatric treatment in the community is to make it a condition of probation. This means that the courts rely upon the probation officer informing on a woman who gives up on treatment. But in the eyes of the world a probation order seems like a very soft option, in no way reflecting the seriousness of offences towards children. Yet very often it would be of greater benefit to the well-being of a child if therapeutic work were undertaken, enabling a mother to confront her abusive behaviour. In reality, prison is the soft option for the courts.

It should be possible to mark the gravity of offences with a prison sentence which is then suspended while a period of psychiatric treatment is undertaken. The breach of this type of suspended sentence need not involve the commission of a further offence, as is currently the case: instead, the sentence could be activated where the offender refuses to go on with the therapy. This suggestion always alarms some psychiatrists, who insist that voluntariness is an essential feature of progress for those being treated, but the majority of those whose practices involve child sexual abuse are less inhibited and welcome any innovation which will surmount the present sentencing impasse.

There is a strange dichotomy in our criminal justice system which treats psychiatry with suspicion and at times derision while at the same time leaping to the conclusion that women who commit crime are mad rather than bad. However, while women whose behaviour is 'inappropriate' are subjected to a misplaced psychiatric labelling, which must be challenged, the criminal justice system is misused as a dumping ground for women who should be patients rather than prisoners. A significant majority of the women who go through the system have been subjected to more criminal behaviour than they have been responsible for. In a five-year review undertaken by the Chief Medical Officer at Holloway Prison between 1987–92, levels of childhood and marital abuse were found to be extraordinarily high. In a review of fire-setting, 72% of the women who did this had been subjected to serious sexual abuse. When preparing court reports, those working in Holloway believe that as many as 90% of the women have a history of battering or sexual abuse of some degree; according to a Home Office study in 2003, 66% of women in prison abused drugs – 70% if alcohol is included – and the work indicates a strong link between opiate abuse by the women and their experience of abuse. A recent Department of Health report suggested that 56% of the inmates serving more than six months' imprisonment might be suffering from 'a medically identifiable psychiatric disorder'. Women are twice as likely as men to have received help for a mental/emotional problem in the twelve months prior to custody, have symptoms associated with post-traumatic stress disorder and are more likely to have serious mental illness. Many women in prison harm themselves, using sharp objects to hack their own flesh. Such self-mutilation directly relates to the women's low self-worth, exacerbated by the impossibly high expectations of society and the claustrophobia of the regime.

Psychiatric disorders are often occasioned by this failure to fulfil expectations. The level of female suicides in prison has soared. Ann Owers, the Chief Inspector of Prisons has pointed out that 'Women's prisons are holding women who should not be there. They include those who are seriously mentally ill, as well as some women and girls with high levels of self harm, linked to substance abuse' (report in the *Guardian*, 14 October 2004).

The idea that women can be subject to their hormones was the traditional way of explaining otherwise inexplicable behaviour in women. The special crime of infanticide, available only to a woman who is responsible for the death of her newly born baby, recognises that 'at the time of the act or omission she had not fully recovered from the effect of giving birth or the effect of lactation and for this reason the balance of her mind was disturbed'. The offence was introduced earlier this century because it was appreciated that a charge of murder was wholly inappropriate, but the charge is confined to the first 12 months of a baby's life.

Historically, women had been treated with terrible harshness if they killed their child. There was an automatic inference if a baby was found dead that the mother was responsible, and undoubtedly many were executed where there had been no deliberate killing by the mother at all. Those who suffered most were poor single women, often maidservants, who tried to conceal their pregnancies because of the desperate consequences that flowed from having a bastard. Frequently the master of the household was the father. Disposal of the newborn meant the death penalty, and this was often carried out even where there was evidence that the infant was stillborn. The instances of men being indicted for killing babies or being accessories were negligible. It was not until the nineteenth century that the terrible injustice and cruelty of these decisions became accepted.

The availability of contraception and abortion, as well as a change in attitude to the whole issue of illegitimacy, has meant a reduction in the cases of infanticide. Girls and young women are less ridden with shame and fear of parental response. It makes all the more poignant the Irish case of 15-year-old Anne Lovett, who died in a churchyard in Granard, County Longford, where she had furtively gone to give birth, or the 16-year-old girl who was desperate to hide her pregnancy from her parents and, after giving birth in the bathroom of their home, choked the baby boy to death. In the last few years I have represented a number of young girls who have kept their state of pregnancy secret, almost deluding themselves into believing that they were not carrying a child. They have then killed their baby after giving birth in lonely, desperate circumstances in their bedrooms, or in the bathrooms or kitchens of the family home, silently enduring the trauma and pain of labour. In two cases the girls felt unable to tell their parents of their condition because the parents were going through an emotionally fraught divorce. In one the girl was in such a state of shock after the birth that she stuffed the baby in her hockey bag and when the bag moved, in her crazed state she hit it with the hockey stick. When I appeared in court, the judge spoke to me after the case and murmured that in the old days the family doctor would just have buried the baby at the bottom of his garden and the family could have got on with their lives. But those were not the good old days: the secrecy would probably have damaged the girl permanently and lived in the secret recesses of her heart, suffocating her self-worth. Shame at pregnancy outside marriage has largely disappeared in many communities and we should relish the fact. But in some the stigma of dishonour is still so strong that women's suffering is unbearable. In one recent case, the accused was a Bangladeshi girl, 14 years old and terrified of telling anyone she had been raped by an uncle. She threw the baby from the bathroom window of a multi-storey flat in the seconds after giving birth.

But if moral disdain has waned in most communities, the pressure of living up to the ideal is ever present. It is this pressure to be the perfect mother that is responsible for much postnatal depression. In 1989 Christine Annesley locked herself in a toilet of the maternity hospital where she had given birth to her baby son and killed him with her bare hands. She had been readmitted into hospital within weeks of giving birth because of stress, fatigue and lack of family support. In court she was described as 'not a callous mother or an uncaring mother. She set herself unattainable ideals and was concerned in case she fell short.' Pleading guilty to infanticide, she was placed on probation for two years on condition that she had psychiatric treatment.

The death of a baby is highly emotive. As a society we have a duty to protect the most vulnerable amongst us especially if they have no voice and cannot complain of their suffering. In nine out of ten cases where a baby dies it is as a result of natural causes. In most cases where a baby has been killed the mother is suffering from postnatal depression and has spiralled into a nadir of hopelessness. Usually the mother is overwhelmed with guilt and just wants to die herself. In one of my cases a perfectly wonderful teacher had phoned her husband at work in a catatonic state to tell him what she had done and he had to phone the police and break a door down to prevent her killing herself.

The young woman who stole baby Abby Humphreys from a maternity ward in 1995 became a hate figure to the public because of the terrible pain and anguish she inflicted on the baby's parents but she was a sad, mentally unwell girl whose own miscarriage and failure to produce a healthy baby had propelled her into a serious delusional disorder. Instead of telling her family and that of her boyfriend that she had lost her baby, she acted out an extraordinary fantasy pregnancy, filling her knickers with old clothing to simulate a swelling stomach and decorating a nursery for her expected child. The stoning of the prison van which brought her to the court may have assuaged primitive feelings amongst fellow citizens but courts have to reach beyond atavistic impulses to punish in order to deliver justice. This was a terrible crime but it was the product of mental illness and the judge's response – making a probation order and sending her as a condition to a place where she could have psychiatric treatment – was wholly appropriate.

The pressure to fulfil society's expectation weighs heavily on women. I have represented two very different women who had undergone years of *in vitro* fertilisation without success and finally adopted children whom they subsequently harmed. One child died; the other is permanently brain damaged. In each case the years of pursuing motherhood led to heightened expectations and an idealised notion of what it would be like to mother a child. Their personal sense of failure when confronted with the reality of parenting stimulated a mental breakdown in both cases. In another case I acted for a young woman who pleaded guilty to the attempted murder of her baby daughter. My client had been so violently abused by her boyfriend that she was demented with terror and could not take any more. She wanted a way out for both of them, took an overdose and tried to smother the sleeping baby. When the baby vomited she was stricken by what she was doing and phoned the police. She ended up in the dock while he was appearing on *Top of the Pops* in a music video but his behaviour was never exposed: he was covered with anonymity because to name him would have identified the child.

Since the creation of the special female crime of infanticide, the law has come to a greater understanding of mental impairment. The 1957 Homicide Act created a special defence to murder, reducing it to manslaughter where the offender's criminal responsibility was diminished because of such impairment. The infanticide law reflects a paternalistic and generalised approach to women's psychology and physiology, and it is probably time that it is removed from the statute books and absorbed into a reformed Homicide Act. Childbirth and lactation do not dissolve all women's brains, but severe postnatal depression is a recognised disorder and would fulfil the criteria for diminished responsibility in appropriate cases.

Research into postnatal depression has now developed, and in the right case it can reduce murder to manslaughter where the victim is other than the newborn baby, e.g. another child of the family, a spouse or friend. In 1986 a young woman of 19 called Ann Reynolds killed her mother shortly after giving birth to a baby whom she had surrendered for adoption. The girl had concealed her pregnancy and taken herself off to a hospital in a nearby town to give birth secretly. In the period that followed, she clearly suffered puerperal depression, and one night, after a confrontation with her mother, she killed her as she slept. She was convicted of murder, the jury having rejected her defence of diminished responsibility, but released on appeal after a campaign by local women had led to the involvement of experts, who testified as to her hormonal imbalance, with the emphasis on a chronic premenstrual condition.

Premenstrual tension (PMT) has figured a number of times in the last twenty years as a defence or mitigation to crime, and in two well-publicised cases has successfully reduced a charge of murder to manslaughter. Christine English crushed her former lover against a telegraph pole with her car, and Sandra Craddock was charged with killing another barmaid at the place where she worked. Both pleas to manslaughter were accepted on the grounds of diminished responsibility due to PMT. Christine English received a conditional discharge and driving ban. At first Sandra Craddock's sentence was deferred for a period, during which she received progesterone therapy. The success of the treatment eventually resulted in her receiving a probation order. At a later stage, after a further conviction, her counsel sought in the Court of Appeal to establish PMT as a special defence in its own right, but the judges were having none of it – quite rightly, in my view.

The issue has created unrest amongst many men and women, the former seeing it as a 'get-out' and the latter as a reinforcement of the 'slaves to hormones' view of women. The point which has to be emphasised is that these cases of a profoundly disturbed hormonal balance, in which women's physiology affects their mental state, are extremely rare. In my own practice I have used the condition in relation to my client's mental state only twice. In murder cases it can be raised only where evidence is strong that the hormonal imbalance is so extreme that the tests for diminished responsibility are fulfilled. There are probably just as many cases where exceedingly high testosterone levels in the male might account for outbursts of violence. It is just that, as usual, we are more predisposed to explore psychiatric explanations in women.

The workings of the female body and its potential for child-bearing are sometimes justifiably used in special pleading for women, but it does have the double bind of being used to shackle women to very confining roles. Biology is commonly assumed to determine women's lives, and there are times when it feels as though it does. Women are rendered much more vulnerable by virtue of their physiology, and the real evidence for this is in the extent to which they are the victims rather than the perpetrators of violence. Most of the violence women experience is in the domestic setting and not on the street. The home is by far the most dangerous place for women.

5

Asking for It

The core stereotype for women in the courts is that of victim, and blaming the victim is the classic courtroom response to crime in the private arena. Nowhere is this more clearly visible than in the handling of rape cases.

The word 'no' is at the core of a rape trial. A 'no' may be taken for granted when a respectable woman is attacked by a total stranger in a dimly lit street, but since the vast majority of rapes are committed by men known to the victim, consent in rape trials has always been an issue which makes men very nervous. Where does seduction end and rape begin? It is the subject of the old lawyer's joke about how to tread the fine line between tax evasion, which is criminal, and tax avoidance, which is every reasonable man's goal in life. As with rape and seduction, it is all supposed to be a matter of technique. Getting a woman to submit is an acceptable part of the sexual game plan, and straying across the line a ready peril for any man with a healthy sexual appetite. The notion that women, having been pressed into submission, will melt into the experience and find pleasure in it often erases responsibility for violence, fear and humiliation.

When I first started practising at the Bar attitudes were much more stark than they are now. A lot has changed and there is agreement that sexual activity should be based on mutuality, with no coercion acceptable. Despite advice from their brethren that they should watch out for mantraps containing snarling feminists, judges used to take on the furies like demented lemmings. They would say extraordinary things – that women who dressed sexily were 'contributory negligent' or that women who did not want sex 'just had to keep their legs shut'. After every outrageous statement made by a judge in a rape trial there would be calls for sackings and questions in the House. The judge in question would be publicly silent but privately bewildered, asking colleagues where he went wrong. Now judges are much more savvy and circumspect about their utterances. Judges now know that women's anger about the handling of rape cases is not confined to wild feminists but is an indignation shared by most women, including their own wives and daughters. However, myths and stereotypes still plague the process.

In the view of some men, a woman's 'no' is covered in ambiguity, not to be taken seriously if she is vivacious, friendly and seems to be 'up for it'; if she dresses provocatively; if she goes out late at night or has had sex with others before. There is an irrational theorem that if a woman has sex with Tom and Dick she is more likely to have sex with Harry. Having a lot of sex apparently does something to a woman's capacity for truth. In fact, the real problem is that it is an exercise of male power to subject a woman to sex and when women say 'no', they challenge that power.

At legal dinners, rape jokes used to be constant, although there seems to be a bit more restraint now because women in the audience make their displeasure heard. I am told that they are still a favourite in the male robing rooms. Did you hear the one about the woman who claimed she was raped and ran from a house clutching a doormat to cover her nakedness? Counsel for the defence asked if there was a 'Welcome' on her mat. Or the old chestnut about the woman who was describing the act of penetration by her attacker. 'He put his penis into me,' she says. 'Well, let's leave it there until after lunch,' suggests His Lordship.

The shared belief underlying the humour is that deep down women want sex but do not always know their own minds. It is not enough to say 'no'. Men hear a challenge to their masculinity in the sound. Sometimes, according to the *Boy's Own* theories about women, it is a female ploy to play hard to get in case men think they are easy or cheap. The signposts are hard to read and the perils engage the fellow-feeling of every man who has ever pressed his attentions, as well as parts of his anatomy, on a less than enthusiastic woman.

Rape summons up long-learned fears whispered into the ears of boys about the fickleness and deceit of women – fears that women are vindictive and bitter, that they will stop at nothing to trap a man and stoop to anything to make him pay; fears that the line which separates rape from seduction is easily crossed, and any decent fellow is at the mercy of an unscrupulous female. A speaker from Fathers 4 Justice told the boys at my daughter's school that they should prepare their defences now for false allegations of rape because a woman could make up a claim of sexual assault and the law is now so skewed towards the female of the species that men are being falsely imprisoned.

Until as recently as 1991 a married woman's 'no' was meaningless, since a wife was not supposed to deny her husband his conjugal rights. There was deemed to be no such thing as rape within marriage. It took long campaigns to convince the judges that married women were entitled to the same protection as any other woman.

Even in the last ten years attitudes to sex have shifted. Television programmes are more explicit, with sex treated increasingly like every other commodity, something to which you are entitled. Children are sexualised at ever earlier ages. While oral sex was once an addition to the sexual repertoire that came with greater sexual experience, it is now often the sexual activity that comes first for young people. Adolescent girls are performing oral sex on boys almost as casually as kissing, though some of these girls would be much more hesitant about having full intercourse. Changes in sexual behaviour are not always known to an older generation of juror, for whom the contemporary protocols of sex are shocking. Despite girls seeming more confident and sassy, their own desires can often be submerged in what they think is expected of them. The way they are socialised not to offend also helps keep the lines blurred. Girls are still told to be sensitive to the feelings of young men, to avoid telling them they are not fancied. Excuses are supposed to be better than rejection and confused messages can be communicated. 'I can't, I'm having my period' – 'I have to go home' – 'I already have a boyfriend.' The recitation is endless: all to avoid saying the hurtful 'no'.

For the most part, problems of men identifying with the male accused do not arise in the trial of the stranger-rape, happening at knifepoint in the dark of night. Everyone, male and female alike, is united in their sense of outrage. Yet even in these cases, distinctions drawn between worthy and unworthy women affect the strength of that outrage, as we saw in the investigation and media coverage of the Yorkshire Ripper case in 1981. The whole tone of the police appeals to the public changed once it became clear that the victims were not 'only' prostitutes and that all women were at risk.

However, most rapes are committed by someone known to the victim – an acquaintance, friend, partner or former partner. Myths are pervasive and enduring and they still influence the outcome of rape trials; even women succumb to them. As I have already indicated, women on juries can be as unforgiving of unconventional female behaviour as any man. Only one in 13 women who report a rape in Britain will see the attacker convicted. Rape still has the lowest conviction rate of any serious crime. Just 7.35% of reported rapes end in a conviction. Most cases never get to court. Only 30% of those pleading not guilty are convicted by a jury. One reading of the low conviction rate is that rapes where there has been a relationship are now more readily reported and there is more willingness to prosecute, but then the traditional evidential difficulties arise.

Professor Liz Kelly was commissioned by the Crown Prosecution Service inspectorate to review research into rape in Britain and abroad so that we might have some understanding of why so many alleged rapists go unprosecuted and unconvicted. Her review was included in the report of the Prosecution and Police Inspectorates published in 2002 and it suggested 'that at each stage of the legal process, stereotypes and prejudices play a part in decision making'. When police and prosecutors are swayed by pervasive beliefs, it is hardly surprising that juries, judges and defence lawyers are infected with them too. In deciding whether to forward a rape complaint to the Crown Prosecution Service, police express subjective, critical views about the complainant's character as a witness. Prosecutors review cases looking for weaknesses, not for ways of strengthening the case. The recommendations for specially trained prosecutors and for more sympathetic and expert treatment from the outset by the police ought to improve practice and may send out a message to women that their complaints will be treated more seriously. But the real problem is that from start to finish, the approach generally taken by the police and prosecutors is based on what they believe will happen at the trial. There is anticipation of the kind of cross-examination to which the woman will be subjected and a judgement is made as to whether she will survive the test.

The complainant in a rape case is required to be the ideal victim, preferably sexually inexperienced or at least respectable. Respectability is becoming more and more difficult to characterise as women go clubbing, drink in 'unladylike' quantities and, in the newly coined phrase of the tabloid newspapers, are part of a 'ladette' culture. They are also more prepared to have uncommitted sex than previous generations. However, none of those behaviours should prevent a woman saying 'no' when she does not want to have intercourse. Yet increasingly that seems to be the price paid for women choosing to be as independent as men. Women are asked questions which are never put to men about why they were out alone in the street or in a pub or at a disco. They are asked about their clothing: the tightness of the fit, the absence of a bra. They are asked about their use of contraception. And this is before we even get to sexual history. When *Regina* v. *A* was heard in the Court of Appeal in 2003, Judges Rose and Hooper both maintained that it was common sense that if a woman had had sex with a man before, she was more likely to have consented to sex on the disputed occasion. The possibility that, having tried it with a particular man, a woman might have decided 'never again' was incomprehensible to them. Just being on nodding acquaintance with a particular penis meant forfeiting the right to say 'no'. If a woman is middle-aged and perhaps divorced, frustration and loneliness are presented as motives for her consenting to sex with an unlikely partner.

There has been extensive debate about women being cross-examined about previous sexual relationships and legislation has now been passed to limit this (section 41 of the Youth Justice and

Criminal Evidence Act 1999) but much of the cross-examination which does not fall under that heading is almost as objectionable. The new picture to summon up, which is fatal to a rape prosecution, is that of the 'ladette' out on the town, scantily dressed and high on Bacardi Breezers. Getting blitzed and binge drinking set the stage for an acquittal. Few women escape the inquisition and possible humiliation of cross-examination by the barrister of an inventive defendant. Sometimes the questions themselves are enormously damaging. 'Is it not the case that you were smoking cannabis earlier that evening?' 'You took Ecstasy at the club, didn't you?' 'You are a user of cocaine, are you not?' Juries assume the lawyer knows something they don't; the denial still leaves a lurking doubt about the kind of woman she is.

In October 2004 two Surrey policemen stood trial for rape. They had been called out to help a woman who had been assaulted in a fracas in the street as she came out of a nightclub. On her own account she was very drunk, and one of her friends had wanted to accompany her when the police asked her to get in their car so that they could drive around to find her assailant. They refused to let the friend come. When the policemen, PC Mark Witcher and PC Andrew Lang, took her back to her flat, she thought they were going to take a statement but instead, according to the woman, they both raped and sexually assaulted her, pulling her around like a rag doll and shouting obscenities at her, telling her she was a slag. The men left laughing and afterwards boasted to colleagues in the police force that they had 'spit roast' her, both penetrating her at the same time, one orally, one vaginally. It speaks volumes about the police culture that they felt uninhibited about recounting their behaviour.

Despite being on duty at the time, both officers contested the case on the basis that the woman consented. This was because their DNA was found on her skirt and they would have been in difficulties suggesting that nothing had happened. In cross-examination, the woman was subjected to the usual litany about her clothing and her drunkenness: 'Why didn't you shout to waken the babysitter? Why didn't you go to the doctor? You were ashamed of what you had done, weren't you? You made this up because you were concerned that you would lose custody of your children, concerned about the new relationship you were enjoying at the time. You decided to turn this tale of consensual sex into one of rape, didn't you?'

Defence counsel's words highlight the new twist in the nailing of women: 'You are not a true victim. You are the victim of your own behaviour that evening,' he said. True victimhood has very demanding standards.

In Australia and Canada, judges are charged with ensuring that no questioning of the complainant is carried out in an unduly harassing or degrading manner, and in our own courts progress will be made only if judges recognise the hidden judgements secreted in these questions. Gender training for judges has now been introduced and legislative changes have tightened the circumstances in which cross-examination of sexual history can take place but the ways that women can be denigrated in the eyes of a jury are not confined to how they like their sex.

A woman is asked whether her vagina naturally lubricated to enable penetration, thereby encouraging the jury to infer that some gratification was being found in the sexual contact. Her reliability as a witness is challenged on the basis that her true sexual nature and desires are so repressed that she has now reconstructed events and believes them herself. Her credibility is thus being challenged, not on the basis of her lying, but of her not even knowing that she is lying!

To explain away multiple acts of rape, a gang-bang or physical injury, defence lawyers may even suggest to the jury that many women are turned on by violence and enjoy kinky sex or a 'bit of rough'. There is no winning. Without the physical signs of resistance, such as bruising, it is (automatically) assumed that the victim consented or is subject to female rape fantasies; where she does bear the signs of attack she is challenged as a masochist. Crude populist psychology is used in courtrooms to suggest subconscious desires that are not even acknowledged by the woman herself.

On the one hand psychiatry is mistrusted in the courtroom as hocus pocus which distracts jurors from the main issues, but on the other it can prove very useful in undermining the value of testimony. The slightest hint of anything that might affect the mind, particularly of a female witness, can jeopardise a case.

I have heard it suggested to a woman in a rape case that she had a history of mental illness which, as it turned out, was a breakdown under the pressure of taking her university finals, from which she rapidly recovered. The suggestion was used to undermine her as someone whose mental stability was questionable and might lead to her making irrational allegations. The leaps involved in such innuendo are never examined, and the damage can be irreparable unless the woman is given time to explain at length whole areas of her life which have no relevance to the proceedings.

A woman magistrate described a foraging exercise she witnessed at a committal proceedings, where a woman was asked whether she had ever taken medication such as tranquillisers. Her truthful answer unravelled an account of depression after the death of her father. This in turn was used to suggest that she had sought solace in the arms of her assailant, over which she had later felt guilt.

Suggestions of instability cling to women much more readily than to men, and even a mention of going to psychotherapy in search of self-enlightenment is confused with mental illness. There are no dividing lines for many people. 'Psycho' means mad, and barristers know the mileage that can be made with juries at the merest hint of any problem when credibility of the complainant is so vital.

Decisions about whether or not to bring a case to court are made by evaluating the quality of the evidence; prosecution authorities claim the measure is whether there is more than a 50% chance of success. Many rape cases founder on this test. Even so, I hear men justifying the low conviction rate in rape cases on the basis that the Crown is now being politically correct, pursuing cases which have no hope of success to satisfy policy demands.

Lawyers are past masters in the art of subtle discrimination. However, some disingenuous soul usually gives the game away, and in the case of the corroboration rule it was Judge Sutcliffe, who in 1976 reminded a jury that 'it is well known that women in particular and small boys are liable to be untruthful and invent stories'. It was interesting to speculate about when the moment of transition takes place and lying little boys become truthful male adults.

Because of the myth that women frequently invented allegations of sexual impropiety by men the law used to require corroboration in rape cases to support the woman's testimony. Her word alone was insufficient.

A ludicrous situation arose in cases where a man broke into a woman's house, burgled the premises and then raped her. The judge had the task of explaining to the jury that it could be dangerous to convict on the uncorroborated evidence of the woman in respect of the rape, but not dangerous so far as the burglary was concerned. An overhaul of the rules on corroboration has put an end to the judicial warning to juries that women can be untrustworthy. The judge's direction has now been reformulated, putting the emphasis on the jury's right to convict should they believe the woman's evidence and reminding them that all women are entitled to say 'no'.

A key issue at the heart of the rape case is credibility. Is the woman telling the truth about what happened? Can she be believed? But this is precisely the decision juries make daily in our courtrooms when they assess witnesses and facts. Are rape cases rendered special by the sexual component? Is rape different from other offences of violence because of the profound emotions and complicated psychological responses that men and women have to sex? Yes, it is different, but not so different as to invite a completely different set of values. In most cases juries can separate false from reliable evidence without judges or defence counsel wading in with half-baked theories about sexual neurosis and female fantasies and the need to approach a woman's evidence with special caution.

Of course, there are women who lie. There are a few misguided or malicious women who make false allegations of rape, and it is essential that the strong protections for defendants which exist within our system should be jealously maintained. Men who are in the public eye, such as sportsmen, musicians and television stars, may be especially vulnerable to invented claims; salacious sex means money in the media hunt for stories about the famous. However, male celebrities can also think sex is theirs for the taking. Pursued by battalions of young women they can swagger with the assumption that no one ever says 'no' to them. The alleged behaviour of professional footballers – from Leicester City footballers detained in Spain for their sexual conduct to Stan Collymore's sad, sexual escapades with strangers in car parks, to allegations of gang rape against Newcastle United players in a London hotel – all reinforce the sense of entitlement that men can have about taking women.

The change in social mores means few women now cover up their own indiscretions or pregnancies by laying a false allegation at the door of some innocent lover. The days of tyrannical fathers raging at the deflowering of their daughters have happily receded, and women do not feel under so much pressure to deny their willing participation in sexual acts (though it should be stressed that this is not true in all communities). The premium on virginity has largely disappeared and women feel freer to include sexual activity in their lives, but they want their sexual relationships to be based on consent and equality. The emphasis is on choice, and women are rightly indignant that they are viewed and tested according to outmoded assumptions. Few women expose themselves to the legal processes for the hell of it.

Juries gauge the truthfulness of witnesses in the way that we all do – by watching their demeanour and listening to their account, especially when it is being tested under cross-examination. Sometimes inconsistency counts against someone, sometimes it is utterly explicable given normal failure of memory or the trauma of events. Sometimes people lie about insignificant issues because of a misguided notion that the truth will count against them. There are times when this is fatal to a case, because juries then worry about what part of a witness's evidence they can believe. At other times the quality of detail and the sheer conviction with which the witness testifies on the crucial aspects of a case leave them in no doubt as to where the truth lies. Additional evidence from an independent source does make the task easier; the privacy within which intercourse usually occurs will always mean that the jury will feel anxious about whether the allegation has been proved beyond reasonable doubt. So convictions inevitably follow more readily if there is supportive evidence. But the police have to be trained to be more pro-active in securing it.

Discussions in courtrooms and barristers' chambers around the country expose the views still held by many lawyers and judges. Prosecution and defence lawyers frequently maintain that a rape took place because the guy was led on or was given a green light. 'Victim to his libido' is the recurring theme in the mitigation plea for a convicted rapist. If a woman has been in any way familiar, we are presented with the old idea of man, the overheated engine, incapable of switching off. We are to treat him as the functional equivalent of a handgun, something intrinsically dangerous.

To ensure a fair trial for men who may be wrongly accused, it is essential that only proper admissible evidence goes before a jury, and that a jury is reminded of the high standard of proof which must exist before convicting. However, there are other important facts which juries should know and be able to place on the scales of justice. This requires direction from a judge who truly understands the offence of rape.

The very nature of rape tends to locate the crime in the privacy of a closed room, in dimly lit streets, in the shadow of darkness. There are rarely eyewitnesses. Forensic evidence may prove that intercourse took place or, with the new genetic testing of semen, confirm the identity of the assailant. But in the majority of cases the defendant is not denying that he performed the sexual act. The issue in 88% of cases is whether the woman consented. Judges and juries are more convinced if they can see torn knickers and proof that the victim was beaten, but even the signs of resistance have to be more than the odd bruise, which defendants explain away as the result of vigorous sex-play and playful pinching. The paradox is that the requirement to show that they put up a fight flies in the face of everything we are told about self-protection. As one victim said when interviewed about her experience, 'Everything I did right to save my life is exactly wrong in terms of proving I was telling the truth.'

Most rape-prevention education advises women not to invite greater harm by fighting the assailant, who may have a weapon. The extensive reporting of cases where women have been raped and then killed confirms that the violence may not stop at the act of rape, and it may be better not to antagonise the attacker. The persistent cross-examination ploy of defence counsel is to deny that fear might paralyse the victim and to insist that a woman guarding her virtue would fight like a lioness. We are still haunted by powerful cultural images of what good women do in the face of ravishment. In a long literary tradition which begins with Livy and Ovid, Lucretia fights off her attacker and refuses to yield to his threats. The deed done, she takes her own life. In Lorenzo Lotto's famous painting in the National Gallery, there is a note on the table by the victim's side which declares: 'NEC ULLA IMPUDICA LUCRETIA EXEMPLO VIVET' – we would have no immoral women if Lucretia's example were followed.

What all this means is that, since there is rarely much independent evidence of the complainant's account, the jury and the judge are thrown back on the impression made by the victim in the witness box. It is as though *she* were the person on trial. Although the law has changed to protect women against being questioned unfairly about their past sexual conduct, it still happens more often than it should. I have always accepted that there cannot be a blanket ban on all such questioning because there could be circumstances where the fair trial of an accused might be jeopardised if relevant evidence were held back from the jury. A complete ban on questioning about sexual history hit the buffers in Canada when it was challenged on human rights grounds. Defendants have human rights too and when they collide with those of a complainant some very careful balancing has to be done. Some discretion has to be left with judges as to when questions about sexual activity may be relevant. I have myself acted in a case where a 13-year-old girl accused her stepfather of rape. She had been having sex with a stepbrother whom she loved and she feared would be prosecuted if their relationship came to light. After she had a miscarriage she was questioned about who had made her pregnant and named her stepfather. She may have been telling the truth about her stepfather's abuse but she may also have been covering for the stepbrother. The jury were entitled to know the full facts. However, Sue Lees's powerful research in her book, *Carnal Knowledge* (1996) showed that judges frequently misuse their discretion and allow unacceptable, invasive cross-examination. She also highlighted the questioning styles of barristers in her follow-up book, *Ruling Passions*.

In my own experience, judges too often confuse admissibility of evidence in rape cases with the similar fact rules, which allow the prosecution to introduce evidence of previous crimes against an accused where a pattern of behaviour is displayed. If an accused rapist always dresses up as Batman and trusses his victims like chickens, then his criminal leitmotif is relevant. But somewhere in the judicial brain this is the same as the situation where a woman says she has been raped by a seaman. If she has previously consented to sex with a sailor, then clearly she has a predisposition to sailors and will have sex with any man in a naval uniform. Sailor friends of the accused are then allowed to come and say they enjoyed nights of abandon with the complainant. If in the past a woman has had sex more than once in the back of a car, then clearly she only has to be steered into the back seat of a Vauxhall and she is a willing participant. The notion that we consent to individuals rather than sets of circumstance seemed hard for male judges to absorb.

Research in Canada showed that jurors who heard evidence of the woman's past sex life were less likely to convict the defendant, and the greater the amount of material they heard about her the greater their willingness to accept the account of the accused. It was by looking at work done in other jurisdictions that we embarked upon our own efforts at legislative change. An application under section 41 of the Youth Justice and Criminal Evidence Act 1999 now has to be made to cross-examine about sexual history. If the only object of such cross-examination is to show that this is the kind of woman who consents, it is not allowed. Because a woman has consented to sex either with the accused or with anyone else in the past does not mean she should be denied the right to be believed about her allegation. Unfortunately, applications to ask such questions are not being made early enough in the proceedings so that the Crown and the judge can carefully evaluate the relevance of such evidence. The evidence should not just impugn the credibility of the complainant, but it is often hard to separate out the two strands of relevance to an issue and prejudice.

Evidence which a judge rules admissible to assess the issue of consent almost invariably impugns the character of the woman. If there has been evidence about reddening and soreness of the victim's vagina, providing some corroboration of violent penetration, the defence may seek to introduce evidence of other recent sexual activity or practices which would account for the vaginal condition. By an alternative route an attack can, therefore, be mounted on the female witness which leaves the unspoken word 'slut' running around the courtroom. However, in some circumstances such evidence could be vital to the defence, and a blanket rule disallowing all cross-examination as to other sexual relations would be unjust. The simplification of the arguments as they are sometimes presented in public debate has not been helpful in addressing the complicated question of when such cross-examination is justified. Maintaining a proper balance between the rights of victims and those of defendants is fraught with difficulty.

Nowadays there is rarely cross-examination on a woman's past in total-stranger rape and judges are now wary of allowing defence lawyers to roam far and wide even in so-called 'date rape' cases. But the issues are rarely simple. The following cases, used in a judicial training course in the United States, show the problems which arise.

In one case the victim is a trained masseuse who normally works with female clients but accepts male clients on recommendation. One such was referred to her by a doctor friend who felt the defendant was suffering severe stress in his work as an executive. She testified that the defendant came to her by appointment a week before the alleged rape and that she performed her usual massage, which did not involve touching the sexual organs. There was no conversation beyond normal pleasantries. A week later, according to her evidence, the doorbell rang at 8 p.m. and the defendant asked to come in. He appeared somewhat intoxicated and she was reluctant to admit him as she was alone, but eventually did so because he was so insistent that he just wanted to talk to someone. He said he was feeling low and wanted a massage. She said it was too late, whereupon he became belligerent and loud in his tone. She asked him to leave and he calmed down, saying how depressed he was over work problems and all he needed was a massage. Reluctantly, she agreed.

After the defendant had undressed and covered himself with a towel the complainant began the massage. Within a short time the defendant started making inappropriate comments about her looks, and when he turned on to his back he grabbed her hands and forced them on to his penis. When she resisted he became violent, struck her to the floor, removed her pants and raped her. He then dressed, threw some money on the massage table and left.

Medical evidence showed a bruise on the side of the woman's head where she said it had struck the table in the struggle, and there was flesh under her nails which she said was a result of her scratching her assailant. A neighbour testified that the woman appeared at her door at 8.20 p.m., said she had been raped and asked that the police be called. The victim appeared in control and was not hysterical, but asked to wait in the neighbour's flat as she was afraid to go back to her own.

The defence applied to cross-examine the witness as to her sexual past, claiming that they had evidence that on a previous occasion a client had asked her to massage his penis until he ejaculated and that she had agreed to do so for an extra fee. They also wanted to produce evidence from the police files that some neighbours had complained to the police about her activities, alleging she was operating as a prostitute.

Should a judge allow such cross-examination and subsequently let such evidence be given? Few judges would allow the evidence of unsubstantiated complaint by neighbours to the police, but many would hesitate about her conduct with a past client and whether the woman had ever masturbated clients in the course of her work. She may deny this quite truthfully or may lie in her denial, but in either case the focus of the trial moves to the morality of the woman. There is no doubt such allegations would add to a jury's general suspicion that massage provides a cover for prostitution. But even if a woman had been prepared to masturbate a man on a previous occasion, does that make her more likely to have consented to full intercourse on this occasion? What prostitute fails to get her money in advance, and why the evidence of struggle and injury to her head?

In another case the victim was a young married woman whose husband frequently worked away from home. She testified that when he was away she sometimes went for a drink to a local pub on her way home from the office. This pub was frequented by old schoolfriends who still lived in the neighbourhood.

On the day in question she called in for a drink and met an old boyfriend whom she had known as a teenager. They had several drinks together and the defendant suggested he walk her home. She agreed, and when they got to her door he asked if he could use her telephone. She testified that she went to the bathroom while she believed he was making the phone call. As she came out he pulled her down on to the couch and told her he wanted her. When she resisted and told him to leave he ripped off her blouse and punched her in the jaw. He then pushed her on to the floor, pulled off her pants and had intercourse with her. At this moment, as in some Feydeau farce, her husband came through the door. The husband testified that he saw the two having intercourse on the floor and that the lights were on. The defendant immediately got up, said, 'Your wife isn't worth shit', and walked out before the husband could do anything. He gave evidence that his wife's blouse was torn and that her jaw was red and beginning to swell. She was crying and hysterical. The husband called the police immediately and the police doctor confirmed the swelling to the jaw and testified to reddening of the vulva. No sperm were present, as no doubt the spouse's timely arrival deflated enthusiasm, but ejaculation is not necessary to prove rape.

The defendant's counsel applied to cross-examine the complainant on her previous sexual conduct. The defence had statements from the barman in the pub who had seen the complainant drinking in the bar, often getting drunk. He had also seen her leave several times in the company of men. Another witness would testify that he had met the complainant in the bar some months earlier and had drunk with her a number of times. On one occasion he had invited her back to his flat, where they had had intercourse. A third would say that he, too, had known the complainant at school and that in recent months she had made a pass at him, telling him her husband was out of town and inviting him in. Judges vary in their approach to this kind of material and its admissibility but there should be no issue. Even if it is true that the complainant has filled her husband's absences with other sexual relations, it should not mean that any man can demand sex and obtain it by force. No doubt a man's expectation might be raised by what he hears in the pub about a woman but what should matter is what happens when he makes an advance. We are entitled to expect men to take steps to ensure that a woman is indeed consenting.

The real way through these conundrums is proper judicial training to address these and similar issues. The Judicial Studies Board has now introduced special seminars for judges who try serious sexual offences: the intention is to tease out the underlying attitudes which pervade the courts with the help of professionals from other disciplines who have long experience of these issues, as well as judges from other jurisdictions.

Another problem in rape cases is that not enough account is taken of the traumatic effect of the experience. Women who have been raped use different coping devices just to live with themselves after the assault, and some are able to draw upon reserves of composure and poise which can work against them with the judge and jury. Others manifest signs of rape trauma syndrome, including a strange distancing from the event, which makes them seem cool and unemotional. The very resources a woman uses to assuage the horror of the experience can be held against her by police officers, lawyers and judges at her trial. Dr Philip Sealy, a British psychologist, conducted research which showed that the law is more likely to protect the woman who makes a favourable impression. This is true in all crime but especially so for women in rape cases. In *The Fact of Rape*, Barbara Toner quotes a police officer and a barrister on the importance of a woman's performance. The police officer remarked, 'A good witness relives the experience in court. She doesn't hold back her emotions. If she wants to cry, she bloody well cries. If she wants a drink of water, she asks. She re-experiences the feelings she had at the time. A bad witness will frustrate the court.'

The barrister said:

When I say she was a good witness, I mean she was clearly telling the truth. There was a marvellous moment when she looked towards the dock and caught his eye. She totally broke down.

The defence counsel and I both agreed it was one of the most harrowing moments we had been through, because she was obviously reliving one of the worst moments of her life. A bad witness is one who will be dogmatic about something that she couldn't possibly be dogmatic about or doesn't answer the questions, or has a detached sort of manner.

Yet often the one thing a victim cannot bring herself to do is to relive the event before a courtroom of strangers. The reason for a rape victim's inability to 'emote' may be nothing to do with her credibility but a direct result of the rape itself. This is something the judiciary should learn about and be able to explain to a jury.

Women frequently describe their trauma in the courtroom as a further abuse. This may sound hysterical and exaggerated, but part of the problem is that a woman's powerlessness in the trial evokes all the feelings of powerlessness that were experienced in the original rape. In 2003 Ms M. told the Fawcett Commission, 'Six months ago I could not understand why a woman would not wish to bring her attacker to court. My own experience has taught me otherwise.' This is partly because the woman complainant has no lawyer and is no more than a witness being called by the Crown, subject to the same constraints as any other witness. American films like *The Accused* mislead British women into thinking they will have their own barrister who will talk them through the issues. In reality, counsel for the prosecution is constrained from spending too much time talking with a complainant under the Bar's professional rules. It used to be forbidden altogether but now counsel can introduce herself and explain the procedure; however, care has to be taken to avoid any question of coaching. The process seems remote and unconcerned with the woman's feelings. The Child, Woman and Abuse Studies Unit (CWASU) told the Fawcett Commission in 2003: 'Very few women understand the trial process in any depth, and find the process – especially the fact that they never get to "their story" – confusing and alienating.'

After the law was changed to restrict cross-examination, a challenge was mounted on behalf of a man who said that even if the woman had not consented, he genuinely believed that she had consented and this was because he knew of her sexual past.

Therefore, he argued, evidence of that history should be before the jury to explain his state of mind. This is called the Morgan defence and derives from a case involving the rape of a woman by a number of men who were told by her husband that she always screamed and resisted when having intercourse; that, he had said, was how she liked it. At appeal in the House of Lords in 1974, the judges decided that if a man acted in the honest but mistaken belief that the woman was consenting, he had a defence. Few men run the defence in the Morgan way – she was saying *no* but I thought she meant *yes* – but many accused men use it as a backstop. She did consent but even if I am wrong about that, I honestly believed she was consenting. Even if an accused does not say he was honestly mistaken judges tell juries that if they think he might have been honestly mistaken they can acquit.

I always remember a trial in Nottingham where an elderly woman was so paralysed by fear that she responded like an automaton when she was attacked by an acquaintance in her own home. The defendant maintained that she gave him no indication that his advances were unwelcome and put up no resistance whatsoever. The woman described with terrible poignancy getting into the bath after the assault and how, while lying in the water, she wanted to slip below the surface and die. Those in court felt it was the sheer power of her description that secured a conviction. Not all women have that facility. If a man can satisfy the jury that he might well have thought a woman was consenting, he is acquitted. And for juries who believe the woman did not want to have sex but worry about the effect of a conviction on the life of the man, or feel the woman may have given mixed signals by her own behaviour, the judge's direction is a let-out.

The landmark case of *R* v. *A* (No. 2) heard on appeal in the House of Lords in 2002 ran a coach and horses through the efforts to create a 'rape shield' law. The court decided that a woman could be cross-examined about her sexual history if the purpose was to support a man's claim that he *honestly believed* she consented. As long ago as 1991 I advocated that when a man claimed that he honestly thought a woman was consenting even if she was not, there should be an objective test – would a reasonable person have thought she was consenting (if she was saying 'no' or was asleep or was drugged)? In homicide cases murder can be reduced to manslaughter if the accused was provoked but there is an objective test: would a reasonable person have been provoked? The reason for this element of objectivity is to prevent people who fly off the handle at the slightest affront invoking the defence. It seems right to me that the same air of reality is introduced into rape cases. The case would still have to be proved by the Crown in the normal way, beyond reasonable doubt, with the presumption of innocence intact.

In the Sexual Offences Act 2003 the government has now changed the law to embrace my suggestion. The jury have to decide whether it was reasonable for the accused to think the woman was consenting. The change is very controversial and raises the question as to whether such a divergence from the normal criminal rules is justifiable. I think it is. In the second reading debate of that legislation in the House of Lords, Viscount Bledisloe chose an unfortunate but telling example from which to draw the principle: 'If I am accused of stealing your property, it is a defence if I show an honest belief that I had a claim of right to that property. That is the general test of the criminal law.'

The question is whether the protection of human beings, not property, from a profoundly damaging experience might justify higher expectations of human behaviour, a greater care and respect for the humanity of others. Is the principle drawing on the experience of women as well as men? In the same debate one of our retired judges Lord Lloyd, speaking about rape, very sensitively enunciated its kernel: 'the forcible penetration of the vagina is a corruption of the deepest and tenderest of emotions of which human beings are capable'. Homosexuals do not feel any differently even if the form of intimacy is different. Forcing inter-course or sexual acts upon someone, securing their engagement in sexual activity through fear, is a corruption of lovemaking. The fact that sometimes people do it casually and without any reference to love does not take away from the fact that it is the way we have found to express that profound emotion. That is why sexual offences are so lasting in the damage they do to lives, contaminating what is precious. It is why sexual offences are different, involving an 'abuse of intimacy', and it is why we may deal with them differently.

That does not mean reversing burdens of proof and forcing the accused to prove their innocence but it does mean prohibiting negligent disregard for the other. If human rights mean anything we are here walking on human rights terrain. The new law spells out a range of circumstances, not exhaustive, in which it will be presumed there is no consent. One example is if the woman is asleep, unconscious or too affected by alcohol or drugs to give free agreement. Some men claim that the reforms will place an impossible burden on them to show that the woman agreed to sex if she had had a few drinks beforehand. But this is wrong. It will not be for the man to show that the woman consented. The prosecution will still have to show that she didn't. Nor will it create a new hazard for women. The rule that a woman cannot agree to sex if she is too drunk is already well established in law and dates back to a case in 1845. It is a statement of the obvious. Rape is a denial of personal autonomy and a woman who is asleep, unconscious or in a state of extreme intoxication is in no position to say 'no'.

Suggestions that 'real rape' should be distinguished from 'date rape' are often floated, with proposals that a sub-category of the offence should be created with a less odious name, to encompass forced intercourse between acquaintances – as though it were inherently different. These proposals reflect not only a distrust of women but a misappreciation of the crime. There are degrees of seriousness in rape, but that does not alter the elements of the offence. Differentiating the degree of seriousness should continue to happen at the point of sentencing, and it should be done by assessing each case individually, within a sensible sentencing framework which recognises that rape psychologically damages its victims. Sentencing guidelines were revised in 2002 so that rape by a known defendant should be treated as seriously as stranger-rape because all the psychological research showed that it was just as traumatising. The Sexual Offences Act 2003 has also redefined rape to include penetration using objects and forced oral and anal sex.

The rape campaigns have tried to shift the perception of rape as being a crime about sex towards an understanding of it as an offence of violence and power. However, for many men violence equals force, a male threat which they understand. They fail to appreciate that there are many other, less explicit, ways in which men can cause women to fear them. It is the absence of actual force which often persuades people that something less than 'real rape' has taken place.

The professional code of conduct of the Bar requires that you accept any brief that comes your way. This is the already mentioned 'cab-rank' principle, based on the fiction that no taxi driver ever turns out his light when you ask to be taken to Brixton. Yet many women barristers declare an instinctive ambivalence about rape cases. The men immediately argue for the civil liberties of defendants who may be innocent of charges and deserve a rigorous defence. It is never our function as defence counsel to judge the guilt or innocence of our clients, and as women at the Bar we adhere to that principle just as men do. It is indeed essential that no defendant should go unrepresented because of an abhorrence felt about the charges laid against him. Otherwise there would be a large body of abandoned accused. In practice, some women rely upon the good will of the solicitors who brief them, and hope that rape cases will go somewhere else. Otherwise they grit their teeth and get on with the job, trying to conduct the case without the use of sexist innuendo. Others have no problem, because they will not entertain considerations of sexual politics. As in any other case, they see it as their duty to use every legitimate tactic to undermine the case for the other side, and if that means reducing the witness's moral value in the eyes of the jury, that is the course to be taken.

It is not difficult for most women at the Bar to understand why rape is so controversial: it invokes women's innermost fears, while for male colleagues it is just another of the outrages perpetrated by human beings upon each other. In the gamut of bombing, killing, stabbing and abuse, what is so special about rape, other than it usually happens to women? The apparent contradiction is hard to explain. Rape involves an invasion of the parts of a woman's body preserved for chosen intimacy, for communication of her deepest feelings, for pleasure of a deep and exquisite kind, for the creation of life. It is a violation which rages against women. Psychiatrists tell us it is perpetrated as a form of woman-hate committed by men with low self-esteem. Far from being an offence of overwhelming sexual passion and excess of ardour, as it has so often been presented, it is, as the campaigns have tried to show, indeed a crime of violence, intended to humiliate, debase, overpower, control. And so rape is a metaphor for the worst kind of oppression. I am sure many of the new generation of women lawyers feel that the aggressive maleness of the crime combines with the essentially male nature of the legal process to make the defence of a man charged with rape an undertaking that they would rather avoid. However, the pressure to do the job as well as men means that some women lawyers are still unwilling to admit a moment's hesitation.

The debate has engaged me as a woman and as a lawyer for many years. I have defended men charged with rape and secured their acquittal. I have felt ashamed as women I am cross-examining flash angry eyes at me for betraying them. Rape separates the girls from the boys. The fundamental difference in the way that men and women perceive rape has affected the conduct of cases, the nature of admissible evidence, and the pattern of sentencing by judges. If the criminal justice system were more even-handed in the way that rape is investigated and tried, women lawyers would feel less compromised by the role *they* are expected to play. Women should conduct rape cases, prosecuting and defending, because we should be setting the standards as to how cases should be conducted. I was sacked by a client in a sexual assault case because I said it was irrelevant that the complainant had on some previous occasion stood on a bar stool and performed a striptease. The accused was not even present at the time and had only heard about the incident after his arrest. I have no doubt that some other lawyer would have tried to find a way to get this piece of extraneous prejudice in by the back door but ask that same lawyer whether he thinks it is acceptable to use material to play on racial prejudice and he is unlikely to agree.

The forecast is not completely bleak. The Australian Chief Justice Bray said we have to dispel 'the absurd propositions that a willingness to have sex outside marriage with *someone* is equivalent to a willingness to have sexual intercourse with *anyone;* that the unchaste are also liable to be untruthful and that a woman who has sexual intercourse outside a stable relationship deserves any sexual fate that comes her way'. Newer members of our own higher courts are also expressing enlightened views, agreeing that women are entitled to dress attractively, even 'provocatively', be friendly with casual acquaintances and still say 'no' at the end of the evening without being brutally assaulted. That right to say 'no' is the more potent in the era of AIDS.

Since writing on this subject, I have been involved in endless discussions with colleagues at the Bar who regale me with stories of women who have indeed lied. In my view, the courts are right to imprison women for making a deliberate and calculated false allegation of rape. Nor was the issue helped by the 'kiss and tell' autobiography of Ulrike Jonsson in which she alleged rape by a well-known television presenter but refused to name him or to press charges. He was then outed by the media and his reputation left in tatters, but all the usual hares were running about women making easy allegations.

The cases where it can be shown that a woman has brought a charge maliciously are few. If women campaign for rape to be taken seriously, then on those rare occasions when a woman does make a false complaint she must bear the consequences.

In the rape debate it is very easy for the arguments to become so polarised that eyes are closed to the problems on both sides. In the early days of campaigning for fairer procedures I offered myself as a volunteer adviser to a group involved with the issue. My services were turned down because it was known that I defended men on rape charges and would not accept a rule against defending in such cases. As a lawyer concerned with civil liberties, you have only to be familiar with the travesties which took place in the American South, where black men were and still are regularly framed for the rape of white women, to appreciate the problems in a society filled with competing prejudices. Class also plays its role in rape: a middle-class woman making an allegation against a working-class man is more likely to be believed, and for a middle-class male accused the tables are turned if the woman is less socially acceptable.

Demands for justice are not necessarily the same as demands for law and order. So often discussions on rape descend into demands for punitive sentencing and fewer protections for the defendant, as though greater justice for victims requires a price to be paid by all accused. As with the campaigns on pornography, which bring together feminists and the moral majority, the making of a clear distinction between the different approaches to these issues is crucial. I want the inherent prejudices against women to be recognised in the courtroom and all steps taken to eliminate them without putting in jeopardy the person who stands trial.

After I spoke at a conference recently, a senior police officer sympathetically pointed out that there was anxiety about publishing a racial breakdown of conviction statistics in rape cases, because so many offenders were black. Such figures, however, reflect more upon the underlying attitudes which prevail in police stations and courtrooms, than upon any particular tendency of black males to rape. On racial grounds, black men probably lose much of the male solidarity which surrounds rape, especially if the complainant is white. Black men too have to deal with the weight of mythology about their sexual appetite, their lack of control, the size of their equipment and their desire to punish white men by taking their women, all of which tells against them in the courtroom. In the morass of prejudice, black women have the hardest time being heard and securing the protection of the courts. Black victims face both the rape myths that confront all women, and stereotypes of black women as more likely to consent to sex, more sexually experienced and less likely to be psychologically damaged.

When I ask women magistrates and lawyers who know the system what they would do if they were raped by an acquaintance, many say that they would think twice before exposing themselves to the legal process. Men in the law express the same reservations for their wives and daughters.

However, sexual assault referral centres have been set up by eight police forces. These units give victims access to women doctors, counsellors and specialist non-uniformed officers. There is evidence that specialist treatment by the police is more likely to end in conviction – but there are 43 police forces so we still have a long way to go. The Crown Prosecution Service should have its own teams of lawyers who are specially trained and charged with the task of properly preparing rape cases, and the steps to create such teams are under way. Barristers should also have specialist training.

Child witnesses would particularly benefit from better support in the courts.

Discussions about rape unearth profound feelings once you move beyond the trite condemnations. The subject of rape is complex because of the confusion with genuine intimacy which invades the emotions of everyone in the courtroom. It is never going to be simple, and women are often just as confused as men are. The singularity of the law of rape stems mainly from a deep distrust of the female accuser and from the fact that sexual relations are seen from a male perspective. Male lawyers and judges to this day say that rape is an easy allegation to make and a difficult one to defend. In my experience the reverse is true: the charge is hard to bring, but it is still easy for a guilty defendant to get an acquittal.

6

Sex and the Working Girl

The double standard in relation to sex is still invoked all the time in our courts. It is simmering beneath the surface in divorce, child custody and in every arena that women enter. Barristers have a strange shorthand for discussing cases back in their chambers. My first exposure to this was when I came upon a member of chambers confiding to my pupil-master that he lived in a block of flats and that his wife was having an affair with the man on the floor below. I coughed to indicate my presence, and then began to sidle towards the door to provide some privacy for these disclosures, until it dawned on me that he was talking about a divorce case in which he was acting.

The formula of talking about your client in the first person is accepted practice. 'I am a golden-hearted whore,' bellowed our head of chambers, a venerable and aged gentleman, seeking our views as to what sentence his client was likely to get for running a brothel.

Golden-hearted whores feature prominently in anecdotes, and Cynthia Payne, who was tried in 1987 for supplying sex for luncheon vouchers in her Streatham house, provided more than her fair share. Warm, welcoming women providing favours for men who succumb to the weakness of the flesh are a beloved subject in any predominantly male environment, and court cases that hinge on the subject are a wonderful source of titillation. In the heart of the serious business there is all this sex, and the chaps love it. Juries love it too, and you can always rely on them retiring for hours in a sex case, because it gives everyone a legitimate excuse for telling their most salacious stories.

A woman barrister tells of being junior counsel in a pornography trial. At the outset of the case the judge called counsel to his room backstage, but the clerk of the court whispered to her, the one woman in the line-up of lawyers, that the invitation was not extended to her: the judge wanted to speak privately with the men. She felt irritated, but duly waited outside, intrigued to hear what could be too delicate for her ears after she had ploughed through mountains of filth in preparation for the trial. According to the lawyers who emerged, the judge had said words to the effect, 'Come on, chaps, we're all men. The acid test for this stuff is our own reaction – did any of you get a rise out of it?' Apparently, if the material was so sordid that decent healthy men of law were revolted instead of being turned on, it had to be obscene.

It is very easy to call down judicial wrath by daring to suggest that our judges are guilty of anything more than the odd unguarded utterance or occasional lapse of judgement. Yet what we are talking about here is something much more pervasive, a cultural aura that excludes women and is so familiar to such men that they are oblivious of it. It is the oxygen of their mutuality. When you try to take it away panic sets in. They are in terror that they will never breathe again.

Tessa Sanderson, the Olympic gold medallist, suffered the consequences of the pervasive double standard in her libel action against Mirror Group Newspapers. She sued successfully over the published allegation that she had stolen the husband of Jewel Evans, by establishing that the marriage had already broken down before she embarked on a sexual relationship. But her damages were significantly reduced as a result of her being presented to the jury as someone whose reputation was not worth much because she was an adulteress. (There would be quite a few judges and cabinet ministers who would not pass the adultery test.) George Carman QC told the libel jury that Tessa Sanderson had fallen from her 'high moral pedestal'. She had tasted 'forbidden fruit' and her reputation was in 'shreds and tatters':

If a young lady chooses to get into bed with a married man she can't expect to be treated with the reverence of a mother superior of a convent. It is the first time I know in an English court that an adulteress wants a jury to order newspapers to pay her compensation for disclosing her adultery and their view as to the consequence of that adultery.

In cross-examination Mr Carman entertained the court by asking Ms Sanderson whether, on her visit to Buckingham Palace, she had mentioned her adultery to the Queen.

Sex almost invariably involves hypocrisy about standards and the law is rarely a corrective. There is something ridiculous about bringing the formality of the court to bear on the daily grind that is prostitution. Some of the funniest moments I have witnessed in court have been when female clients have been able to subvert the court's authority by poking fun at the well-rehearsed notion that men are victims of their sexual drive. This usually involves a scenario where the prostitute is in the witness box explaining an indecorous attempt to satisfy a customer's needs, and winks continuously at the judge, assuming that he will know what she means.

In the past the declared aim of laws against prostitution was the 'preservation of public decency', curbing the nuisance of soliciting on the streets and protecting the prostitute herself from violence and exploitation. Contracting to provide sex for money is still not in itself unlawful. This leaves women involved in prostitution in an ambiguous legal position. According to the famous Wolfenden Report in 1957: 'The simple fact is that prostitutes do parade themselves more habitually and openly than their prospective customers, and do by their continual presence affront the sense of decency of the ordinary citizen. In doing so they create a nuisance which in our view the law is entitled to recognise and deal with.' Therefore the law was invoked only to criminalise concomitant, 'nuisance' activity. This has helped sustain the fiction that the law is not concerned with morality. However, moral opprobrium is always present.

Selling sex as a commodity is perceived as depraved, but traditionally it was the seller, not the buyer, who bore the responsibility. The purchaser was seen as the victim of his own sexual needs; again the law has promoted the myth that men are ruled by their libido. Prostitution has been tolerated because of two sustaining concepts: the protection of the private sphere from the hand of the law and an acceptance of male promiscuity which is not afforded women.

The double standard is very evident in the cases where a woman is convicted of soliciting while her customer is guilty of no offence. Legislation was introduced to make the male behaviour of kerb-crawling a crime, but only because 'respectable women' had to be protected from persistent propositioning by a stranger. When it was introduced, lawyers and politicians expressed concern about innocent men being set up by the police, or innocent activity being misinterpreted, and it is for this reason that very strict evidential rules are applied. The police have to see two overt acts before they can make an arrest, which is frustrating to officers who watch a man driving around a red-light area for lengthy periods selecting his woman but making only one approach.

Prostitutes are not so fortunate; they could be charged for loitering simply because they were known to police and had been seen waiting around in a particular area. 'Loitering' is the charge selected by the police because it does not require repeated acts once a woman is on record.

Because of the evidential difficulties in securing convictions, the police policy on kerb-crawling was to move men on, reminding them that they could receive a rather embarrassing letter in the post if they continued their activity – 'Could create problems with the wife, sir.' The resulting problem for the prostitutes has been that they have to choose their 'john' at speed, getting into cars quickly before they can get a good look at him. Many of the women say they have antennae for identifying the real oddball, but the new policing methods reduce the chance to assess the customer. The English Collective of Prostitutes, a campaigning group, has been reluctant to see the law used because it makes life harder for the women. However, in 2000 the police were given powers of arrest for kerb crawlers to stiffen their resolve to deal with 'punters' and not just the prostitutes.

The harm which society sought to regulate by the laws around prostitution all largely revolved around the nuisance effects on the public caused by 'negative regulation'. Official discourse constituted it as a public nuisance and a matter of private morality. However, as a result of women's campaigns in the last 20 years there has been growing recognition of the harm to women themselves. Wolfenden had asserted that 'the association between prostitutes and ponces is voluntary and operates to mutual advantage' but women's groups have argued powerfully that prostitution is not always a victimless crime but one which victimises women, children, families and communities; that the men who run prostitutes often use coercion and violence to force women on to the streets. By 2003 the problem of prostitution had been reconstituted from one of private morality to one that threatened to destroy individuals and their families with great cost to society. The demands that the state afford protection to this most vulnerable group of women are totally understandable but in the rush to legislation there is often a failure to acknowledge that there is such a thing as adult consensual prostitution and to deny this infantilises women. While we are busy telling men in relation to rape to listen when a woman is saying 'no' to sex, it is counter-productive to claim that when women are saying 'yes' to claim they do not really mean it.

There was a great deal of media excitement in October 2003 when Margaret MacDonald, a British woman, was tried in France for running a high-class ring of more than 500 prostitutes and found guilty. She was sentenced to four years' imprisonment and given a substantial fine. What intrigued the public was that this was a highly educated, convent-schooled woman, who spoke French, Spanish, Italian, Arabic, Japanese and Greek, had worked for Médecins sans Frontières in El Salvador and also for a refugee agency in Nicaragua and who had then entered the world of business and marketing. She put the experience to use by setting up an agency 'run by women, for women'. She had started working as an escort herself when she had run up some debts and then spotted a niche market. 'It is the same skill, whether you sell computers or something else,' she told the judges. She charged up to 5,000 euros for an introduction and took 40% for herself, but explained that she produced the brochures and paid for upmarket advertising in journals and the *International Herald Tribune*.

There are women, operating on a less grand scale, who would vociferously endorse Margaret MacDonald's description of their activities as 'work' and they are quite indignant that all sex work is classed as exploitation. They do not want to be drawn into the all-embracing straitjacket of women as victims. They would say that sexual relations in the comfort of marital beds is often just as transactional but not subject to state interference unless there is duress or violence. They want the same rules to apply to them. This is difficult territory, as legal scholars have pointed out. There is always an avoidance of defining exploitation because vast tracts of the labour market might be deemed inherently exploitative.

The Sexual Offences Act which was introduced in 2003 is a mixed blessing because amongst the many positive sections of the Act, particularly those dealing with sex trafficking and child prostitution, there are those which could make life more dangerous for women sex workers. Because of the drafting, the role of the 'maid' will be criminalised; yet these are the women who see clients in and out of premises for prostitutes, provide a security system by screening out oddballs and offer company to a prostitute woman. Off-street work is always safer but the changes to the law will probably create a less safe environment.

The harassment of women on the street is legendary and always takes new forms. Putting 'Sexy Sadie' stickers with a telephone number on telephone boxes brought the self-promoters before the court for causing criminal damage. Ever inventive, the ladies shifted to calling cards, which involved no glue and, therefore, no damage. British Telecom, morally indignant, responded by cutting off the phones connected to the numbers (although they have maintained sex chat-lines, from which the company makes a lot of money). What has a girl to do but sue – only to find that litigants must come to the court 'with clean hands', a legal fiction used somewhat selectively. Their phones remained cut off. Then came the mobile phone which proved much more flexible. The placing of ads in telephone boxes was made an offence under the Criminal Justice and Police Act 2001, but the cards still go up.

In the summer of 1994 vigilante groups sprang up across Britain's cities to remove street prostitution from local neighbourhoods and zero tolerance zones were created. Their influence has spread up and down the country since then. The government's new Anti-Social Behaviour Orders are now being used to bar women from working certain streets or from associating with each other, although the public rationale for the orders was about protecting the public from gangs of boys or bad neighbours creating a nuisance. Breach of an order can attract a maximum sentence of five years, which means the reintroduction of imprisonment for prostitute women which had been removed in the Criminal Justice Act 1982. So while the rhetoric is all about helping women, England and Wales are fast becoming the most punitive countries in Europe.

Who are these men who pay for sex? At the higher end of the scale are businessmen, playing away. But according to police, the ordinary trade is maintained by the fellow next door who turns up on the car registration computer when they do a check on a vehicle number plate. There is no shortage of custom, and in our entrepreneurial times many women are taking to the streets, selling the one commodity they have which they know is in demand. The research of Dr Susan Edwards, an eminent feminist academic, has shown an alarming increase in the number of women forced into prostitution by poverty in Britain today. In addition, a significant proportion of these women are feeding a drug habit.

Men who use prostitutes may raise sniggers in court, but they are not despised in the same way. When the Duke of Devonshire appeared at the Old Bailey in 1991 to give evidence in a cheque-fraud case it came to light that he had been using the services of a call-girl and paying with cheques. Everyone smiled benignly and just thought how daft he was. There was no question of his not being able to show his face in the club.

When Allan Green, the Director of Public Prosecutions, resigned in 1991 having been seen at the back of King's Cross, allegedly looking for a prostitute, the sympathy for him was shared by most of us in the profession. He had been the fairest of prosecutors in his days at the Bar and was an exceptional director, of unquestioned integrity and courage, who had the unenviable task of dealing with the Irish miscarriages of justice. It was suggested by prostitutes in the red-light area that he was subjected to special police attention. Some lawyers and journalists believe this might not be unrelated to his sanctioning the prosecutions of police for malpractice: he was apparently detested in sections of the force. Whatever the truth, his judgement that it was impossible for him to remain at the head of a prosecution service which makes decisions about whether kerb crawlers should be prosecuted was right; but in well-meaning but misconceived allegiance, a number of senior members of the Bar publicly advocated that he remain in the job. Using prostitutes was not seen as a bar.

Even when Wayne Rooney, the footballer, was exposed in the tabloids as a young man who was known to the prostitutes of Liverpool, no one batted an eye.

In my own early practice, I appeared in court for a Glasgow woman who was facing prison because she had a suspended sentence for soliciting. Much to our delight, the magistrate, a deputy stipendiary (a professional magistrate) gave her another chance. A short time later he met a mutual friend and told him that he had succumbed to my plea because his own first sexual experience had been with a Scots prostitute. He is now a judge, his youthful peccadilloes no source of shame or handicap.

The legal treatment of prostitution reveals another prejudice – that of class. The British are famous for institutionalising social and moral hypocrisies. The well-bred unemployed are referred to as socialites; the poor on the dole are spongers. The upper-class divorcee is rarely included in the term 'single parent'. The prostitute who can afford the title call-girl and who has a flat in the expensive part of town does not face the indignities of the courts and runs few of the risks experienced by her poorer sister, who works on the street. The laws against brothel-keeping prevent two or three women sharing a flat for their work, which would reduce the risks of assault and provide companionship.

Prostitutes are regularly beaten up or raped by clients, but are inhibited from taking legal action because they know the problems they face once they go to court. Any excuse turns into a credible defence when the complainant is a 'tom', as prostitutes are called by police. The general yarn spun by defendants is that the prostitute tried to rob him and when accused became physically violent. The unlikelihood of a woman taking on a man in this way is forgotten when she is a whore.

In her book *Misogynies* (1990), Joan Smith highlights the contrasting attitudes to the murder of prostitutes as against that of 'innocent' women by the police investigating the Yorkshire Ripper killings. She recalls the words of a senior police officer at a press conference:

> He has made it clear that he hates prostitutes. Many people do. We, as a police force, will continue to arrest prostitutes. But the Ripper is now killing innocent girls. That indicates your mental state and that you are in urgent need of medical attention. Give yourself up before another innocent woman dies.

This distinction – between respectable women and the others, whose lives seem to have a different value – is made repeatedly in the press, by the police and in court. One of the most prevalent kinds of serial murder is indeed that of the prostitute; she especially represents the myth of Eve, of woman as responsible for male concupiscence and carnality. So entrenched is the idea that prostitutes have it coming to them that, in order to allay speculation and emphasise the seriousness of the risk to 'real' women, the police often feel obliged to stipulate that female victims are not prostitutes.

The risk of violence does not only come from the client. In June 1990, in a rare case, a notorious pimp called Colin Gayle stood trial at the Old Bailey on 18 counts of rape, threats to kill, actual bodily harm and living off immoral earnings. The victims of his appalling assaults were the young women prostitutes who became involved with him and who supplied him with money to pay for his cocaine habit. The evidence of brutal beatings with a metal rod and hammer sat uncomfortably with the love letters the women had written to him. Why would beaten, bruised and disfigured women return to their tormentor?

Love poems were written to Gayle by one young woman who had received terrible injuries at his hands, resulting in damage to her kidneys as well as extensive cuts and bruising, because he did not think she showed enough respect.

Amongst the prosecution evidence were letters written by Gayle promising that he would stop the relentless beatings: it was probably those careless pieces of self-incrimination which secured his conviction. Even so, he was acquitted of the charges in relation to one of the prostitutes because her evidence was confused. In the view of police she 'lost' the jury by swearing and being foul-mouthed. Many prostitutes cover their vulnerability with a carapace of steel.

The prosecution have a terrible problem in these cases because the women themselves are terrified of the consequences of giving evidence. The fear of reprisals from the accused or his friends is enormous and the women also know that they will be cross-examined in detail about their lifestyles in a way that will reinforce hostile views of them. Prostitutes who do give evidence for the Crown against their controller are enraged by the comparatively short sentences which are passed. Soon the pimps are back on the streets, seeking revenge.

By contrast, the courts are punitive to prostitutes who 'roll' or rob their clients. Sometimes a woman appears in the dock charged with complicity in a robbery in which she has acted as a foil, enticing a male into a hotel room or secluded place where he has subsequently been robbed. A 16-year-old girl was recently convicted and imprisoned for assuming this role and the judge made great play of her wickedness, which seemed to him to go beyond that of the older youths who committed the robbery and had put her up to it. More recently, women have been arrested for operating a 'sting' by persuading men to part with money for a hotel room and then disappearing into the blue. These sorts of offence are seen as taking advantage of men at their most vulnerable, because reporting the events to the police could have humiliating ramifications.

Prostitutes have come to expect poor treatment in the criminal courts, but they have problems in the civil courts too, particularly concerning the welfare of their children. Many prostitutes who appear before the courts say they do this work because it fits in well with their childcare arrangements: they can work during school hours, or in the evenings when they have a babysitter. Many are women living alone with children, with little prospect of any other kind of employment.

Charges of living off immoral earnings were introduced to reach the pimps who exploited women and forced them into sexual misery. However, many women complain that the law is too frequently used against boyfriends and husbands who exercise no control over them at all but who the courts think ought to be breadwinning and functioning in a conventional way. If the men have no obvious source of income they are readily convicted and are usually imprisoned. The new Sexual Offences Act will further entrench this problem.

The evidence offered to prove that the man knowingly lives wholly or in part on the earnings of prostitution is usually that the woman pays the rent or buys the food or gives the man money or buys him drinks. The defendant has to prove that he did not know the money came from prostitution or that he did not receive anything at all. The men who suffer most are black, because of the way the police choose to prosecute, assuming that predatory black men are more inclined to put women on the streets. The effect is to prevent these women having any semblance of a home life.

In 1987 the High Court upheld a refusal to include a former prostitute on an *in vitro* fertilisation programme because of her past history. She had also been rejected by an adoption agency, because like any man with a previous conviction she could be eliminated as unsuitable. Although she and her husband were desperate to have a baby and even braved the exposure of her previous convictions to challenge the decision, her past 'immorality' disqualified her. It is hard to imagine a man being disqualified because of his misspent youth as a womaniser.

One of the things we have learned about our world is that cataclysmic events like wars and social unrest create special burdens and risks for women. The end of the Cold War and the collapse of the Soviet Union, the disturbances in the Balkans, the unrest in whole tracts of Africa have all created vacuums in which organised crime has flourished. The underbelly of free markets in legitimate commodities is that the same developments which allow lawful trade to flourish also facilitate the trade in drugs, arms and human beings. Prostitution and people-trafficking is now considered the world's third most lucrative black market activity. Thousands of women and children are spirited into Britain every year to work against their will as prostitutes, domestic slaves or agricultural labour.

The scourge of sex-trafficking, which is now a billion-dollar trade, is one of the dirty secrets of the last decade which has yet to be properly exposed. It preys on the most vulnerable and is a heinous sustained violation of human rights. There are 730 flats, massage parlours and saunas selling sex in London alone, with 81% of the women in them from overseas. A survey by a charity called the Poppy Project concluded that a growing proportion of women 'on the game' were being coerced into prostitution through violence, repetitive rape and entrapment and found evidence of trafficking rings operating in all parts of Britain, from Cornwall to Glasgow. The most common sources of women are Albania, Romania, Moldova, Ukraine, Nigeria, Sierra Leone and Thailand.

The Sex Offences Act 2003 has introduced wide-ranging offences to tackle trafficking for sexual exploitation and further measures to break the links between prostitution and trafficking are now part of a government review of prostitution but as Mary Cuneen, director of Anti-Slavery International has said, passing laws is not sufficient. 'These laws must be accompanied by measures to protect and support trafficked people.' When the women come to police attention they face deportation as illegal immigrants unless they explain their circumstances fully and agree to testify against their traffickers. What they really need is time to regain a sense of trust and security after the trauma of their experiences rather than immediate expulsion. They need to be recognised as victims and not the perpetrators of crime. Some are anxious to return to families but others could be in danger in their home countries, particularly if they give information against organised criminals. Yet there is only one safe house caring for and assisting women, and no safe house for the protection of children.

A report by Nigel Morris in the *Independent* (14 October 2004) told the story of Stef, a 21-year-old Nigerian mother who was lured to Britain with the promise of a place at a college in London as a route out of poverty. She found herself trapped in a cycle of vice, imprisonment, abuse and the threat of violence to her family if she tried to break free.

'When I was young my parents died and there was a friend of my mother's who came to me and said she would help me out in getting my education in the UK, which is why I followed her. She never put me into college. Instead she taught me about prostitution.' She was told by the friend that she could only return if she raised £40,000 from working as a prostitute. 'She insisted that was what I was going to do and I must give her the money. I feel so terrible and disgraced. I knew of Aids, I knew HIV goes round, there were so many other diseases that I was scared of. But even with a condom I feel I am not safe. She threatened me that if I don't work for the money she will kill my grandmother and my son . . . she hit me anyway.'

Stef escaped with £200, which she lost when she was mugged. She was befriended by a prostitute who told her there was no other way to make money as she was in the country illegally; they worked in a south London brothel until it was raided by the police and she was arrested. She claimed asylum, which she eventually won, arguing that her life could be in danger if she returned home. She says: 'There are so many women and girls out there who need our help. It's not that they are making up stories. They need our help so much.' Sandra Dickson of the Poppy Project, who has counselled Stef, says her case is typical. 'Some women have been raped repeatedly . . . as a kind of breaking-in for prostitution. We don't have any women who haven't experienced sexual violence. They have been stabbed, burned, thrown out of cars, tortured, or watched other women being tortured.'

In the last few years I have represented several prostitutes who have been caught up in the trafficking of sex workers. Incapable of stepping out of the shadows, they are utterly controlled by the men who have bought them. Ill health and fear of pregnancy stalk them and they are forced to have illegal abortions because they are too frightened to go near doctors. This is the sort of inhumanity we collude in when we take away legitimate routes of surfacing and systems of support.

In one case I defended a young Croatian woman who became a pawn in a turf war between pimps arguing over ownership of different women. She was present when a pimp was murdered, her fingerprints found in the seedy hotel room that was the scene of his violent death. A terrible story of sexual grooming from the age of 14 came to light and a background of such horrifying cruelty that the court was stupefied. Even after she was given her freedom and her pimp was imprisoned, she was frightened out of her wits that he would have her killed.

An understanding of child abuse has led to intensive government action on child prostitution. The new approach redefines child prostitution as sexual abuse. The children's charity Barnardo's has led the front: 'there can be no such thing as a punter, or a customer or a kerb crawler when discussing children . . . a man who winds down his window and asks for sexual services from a child is a child sexual abuser.' The way in which child abuse can end in adult prostitution has also entered the official bloodstream:

> The prostitute is a commonly vilified figure. This is often based on a general assumption that those involved are in control of their situation. However, the evidence is clear that this can be far from true. High levels of childhood abuse, homelessness, problematic drug use and poverty experienced by those involved strongly suggest survival to be the overriding motivation. (*Paying the Price*, Home Office, 2004.)

In recognition of the high levels of coercion involved in prostitution, the government has adopted a two-pronged approach by using charities and other welfare-based organisations to deliver 'soft law' or social policy responses to divert women and children from prostitution, while reserving the full power of the criminal law for two categories of people: those who persistently return to prostitution and those who exploit individuals in prostitution.

The approach is at first glance a huge leap in the right direction. However, a very persuasive book by Joanna Phoenix and Sarah Oerton, *Illicit and Illegal: Sex Regulation and Social Control* (2005) analyses the hidden currents operating beneath the surface to the detriment of some women and girls. They point out that this significant policy shift has a flaw: that by basing the approach on the victimisation of women, any women who do not fit into the victim mould suffer disproportionately. Those who face the full rigour of the law are women who choose prostitution for economic reasons, women who are poor and who have few options, or women who are forced into the nether world of sex work but find it very hard to abandon when a new demand for rent or electricity payment arrives. Women who stay on the game after social work interventions move beyond the pale. The Home Office consultation paper, *Paying the Price*, neatly demarcates the problem of prostitution into two categories: the problem of 'victims' and the problem of 'offenders'. Victim status is conferred only under specific conditions – there has to be a third party coercer and the 'victim' must never return to prostitution after being offered help. They must co-operate with the NGOs and the authorities and behave like good women or they are sacrificed to the criminal justice system. Any sign of voluntarism or willing participation in prostitution brings down the weight of opprobrium.

On an initial reading of *Paying the Price*, the striking argument is the overwhelming level of victimisation experienced by women and children in prostitution and their need for support in their struggle with drug addiction and debt. However, as Joanna Phoenix and Sarah Oerton point out, 'the other story of prostitution is all but completely absent: the story of the individuals whose lives have been so violently fractured by the aggregate effects of poverty, by being without the traditional disciplines (and benefits) of family, education, employment, by being pilloried by press and communities and having so few options that involvement in prostitution is a plausible, if risky, choice'. But the prevailing thinking is that poverty is largely the fault of the impoverished, who do not pull themselves up by their bootstraps and the help of 'back to work' initiatives. Talk of poverty as a driver of human behaviour is out of favour. Victimisation is recognised as a valid excuse for prostitution. Poverty is not.

The double standards experienced by women in the courts are also prevalent in the youth justice system. The remit of the Youth Courts goes beyond that of adult courts because it is concerned about the well-being of children and young people. This means that sanctions can be brought into operation for behaviour that is not technically criminal but likely to affect a young person's development. Children can be brought there for truanting, for being neglected or in 'moral danger' or beyond parental control. Many girls are thus brought into the system for non-criminal offences or trivial misdemeanours simply because they are not conforming to notions of proper behaviour. Girls are often referred to the Youth Courts for different reasons from boys, and are dealt with differently. A son's overnight absence will earn him a knowing wink, and drunkenness will be seen as a natural part of his growing up – boys will be boys – but 'ladette' behaviour by a girl calls down very different responses. There is a clear preoccupation with the sexuality of teenage girls and an over-emphatic concern with their moral welfare. If she fails to come home on time, hangs around the wrong part of town or adopts dubious friends, a girl is far more likely to be declared in moral danger, for which, at the instigation of her parents, school, social worker or the police, she may be taken into the care of the local authority. These young women often start off in the penal system having committed no crime at all, but once it is on their record that they have been locked up, a cycle of imprisonment begins, and offending often follows.

Girls who have been sexually abused within the family are often rejected, even by their mothers, when they make the abuse public. They often absent themselves from school, run away, go on the streets and end up in care. They feel such self-loathing and lack of worth that abuse by other men follows or they prostitute themselves to survive. The police are now required to involve social services and avoid criminalising the girl if she is under age. But I frequently hear the police complain that for some of the 16- and 17-year-olds it is a lifestyle choice and they are 'getting away with it'. Young women who are on the game rarely have a happy story to tell about their home life. The majority of them become involved in drugs and end up before the courts anyway. Girls who need to be taken into custody – because they have committed violent offences – should be placed in the secure units run by local authorities but there are few places and custody orders are often made where there is no violence at all, just repetition of offending. Many girls who are arrested and have nowhere to go still end up in adult prisons despite proof that it is damaging to lock up the young with people who are older.

*

There are compelling arguments for and against the decriminalisation of street offences and the legalisation of brothels. Although the arguments are mainly articulated on the grounds of keeping neighbourhoods decent and avoiding offence to citizens, the core issue is the symbolic importance of punishing deviant sexuality. It would be quite possible to divert the police vice squads to more pressing crime problems by abolishing the soliciting laws and using in their place, where it is occasionally necessary, offensive-behaviour legislation. Where any passer-by is seriously affronted, public order charges of insulting words and behaviour can still be laid. At the same time, provisions protecting children from sexual exploitation and adults from coercion and fraud could be strengthened. It would be interesting to look closely at the reforms in the Australian state of Victoria and in the Netherlands to see whether legalisation has seen an improvement. The creation of legalised brothels there has not removed all street soliciting but has greatly reduced the numbers. Brothels are not run by the state but have to maintain health standards for permits to be obtained, and their location is controlled by town-planning laws. Local residents can make objections at planning hearings if nuisance is a serious problem – all of which shifts some of the problems associated with prostitution away from the criminal courts. Failure to have a permit or planning permission means premises are closed down. Inevitably, advertising has to be permitted for a legalised brothel system to work, and strict codes are established regulating where such information can appear.

Police claim that 'respectable clients' who use street prostitutes would never risk entering a brothel for fear of being seen, and that likewise some women with children who work on a casual basis would not want to chance being discovered. However, risk is half the excitement for many of the men, and since danger of criminal prosecution has not dampened enthusiasm it is unlikely that entering a brothel would. The majority of women on the street would welcome decriminalisation and might feel differently if they realised a brothel scheme would not be run by the government.

There might even be tax benefits for the Treasury if the law was reformed. Lindi St Clair, a prostitute who lost her High Court challenge to the Inland Revenue's taxation of her earnings from prostitution, wittily accused the government of living off immoral earnings. The outlawing of prostitution and then the application of fiscal regulations as if it were any old job is an indication of the double-think involved in the whole issue. The income from prostitution would probably write off the national debt if properly audited, but, as it stands, only women on the low end of the scale are 'taxed', in the form of regular fining. Women appearing in the central London courts describe the fine as their licence fee and get straight back on the job to pay it.

Saving women from prostitution must also mean removing sexual and economic inequalities, providing job opportunities, training and equal pay – in other words, recognising the economic realities which drive most women to the streets. Unfortunately, economic realities escape some members of the Bench and the chasm of class misunderstanding still exists.

The contradiction for the law is that it cannot contemplate abolition of prostitution because it sees the need for a class of women who will sell sexual services to men and because private transactions between people for sex would be impossible to police. Although the Sexual Offences Act 2003 uses gender-neutral language it is really men who buy sex. However, prostitution challenges traditional order, and raises fears that if the taboo were lifted even more women might see it as a means of securing financial independence. The established female role would be further eroded.

One of the effects of the change in women's status in society has been the greater confidence it has given them to express their sexuality freely, a factor which has highlighted many dichotomies in the law. The new confidence has enabled gay women openly to declare their sexuality. The fact that lesbianism has never even been acknowledged in the criminal law is an extreme expression of the way the law denies the existence of active female sexuality.

In a divorce case reported on 21 May 1954 in *The Times*, the judge was so wedded to Queen Victoria's disbelief in the very existence of lesbianism that he refused to grant the divorce. In his judgment he said:

At the highest the wife and Miss Purdon were seen hand in hand, used to call each other darling, kissed on the lips, spent a good number of holidays together, were constantly alone in the wife's bedroom at the vicarage and on two or three occasions occupied the same bedroom at night . . . It was a very odd business, two grown women spending all this time together often in the same room and often in bed together, but the court is quite satisfied that that is perfectly innocent.

Although in theory there are laws which can be used against lesbians such as 'Behaviour likely to cause a Breach of the Peace' or 'Indecent Assault on a Woman', in practice lesbians are rarely charged under these laws because there is little male interest in the punishment of female homosexuality. The law puts much more emphasis on protecting women from vaginal penetration by an unsanctioned male and on protecting men from homosexuality.

However, when a woman's lesbianism is before the court as part of the general evidence, another agenda operates, as in the case of the prostitute or the promiscuous woman. Women who have rejected heterosexuality and their prescribed role are perceived as threatening; some lesbians challenge the idea of passivity so strongly that the law is used symbolically for public condemnation. One woman who wounded her lesbian lover was imprisoned for seven years in circumstances where corresponding heterosexual domestic violence would have had a much less severe result.

Another scandal of the penal and justice systems is the inappropriate detention of people in prisons and special hospitals. This is partly because of the devastation of psychiatric facilities in ordinary hospitals through lack of funding. Many women are made the subject of Mental Health Act sections who should not be sectioned at all. They are left to spend indeterminate periods in the prison asylums that are euphemistically called Special Hospitals, places like Broadmoor and Rampton, largely because they have been aggressive and angry or generally acted inappropriately for their sex. Lesbian women are particularly susceptible to being labelled 'inappropriate'.

To get into these places, patients have to be diagnosed as

mentally ill and deemed to be a danger to society or themselves. For women it is very often the latter, because their desperation is so often turned inwards. Many of the female patients in Broadmoor are there for comparatively minor crimes, whereas the detained men have committed sex offences or sexually motivated murders.

Prue Stevenson of Women in Secure Hospitals (WISH) describes the attack on identity and sense of self that women, especially lesbians, experience in places like Broadmoor, where they are put under pressure to wear make-up and feminine clothing, grow their hair and have tattoos removed. Most women comply, since to refuse could go against them in assessing their readiness for discharge. However, the process of making women conform starts much earlier in the criminal justice process, and young lesbian women feel they are partially punished for non-compliance.

Lesbian women experience the criminal justice system, from policing onwards, as hostile, treating them as social outcasts and sometimes as freaks. As the victims of crime they are at a profound disadvantage, and have difficulty persuading the police to pursue complaints of sexual harassment, verbal abuse and assault by men. It is a particularly courageous gay woman who will brave the attack upon her character she knows will attend any trial such as rape. Some attacks are not confined to cases of sexual assault: in almost any case a gay woman's sexuality will be used against her. A gay policewoman told me that she has always had to be prepared for an attack in the witness box on the basis that her arrest of a male accused was based on hostility to men.

Sex is a potent force in most working environments. Hardly a woman exists who has not had to deal with unwelcome sexual attention. Yet the subject is met with collective denial by many men. A lot think sexual harassment has nothing to do with them, that it is an invention of militant feminism put forward in a spirit of prudery and puritanism by women 'who should be so lucky'. For these reasons, women who like men and enjoy sex often don't want to involve themselves in the issue.

Of course, sexual attraction is a component in many of the relationships which compose our daily round. The gentle flirtation of our social commerce is a harmless and pleasant aspect of life. Many of us know from experience that the positive exchange of sexual energy can be as creative at work as elsewhere, but sexual harassment is of a different order and both men and women know the difference. One involves mutuality; the other is unwelcome. It is not the product of the fevered feminist imagination. Most women can give plentiful accounts of dealing with groping and *risqué* remarks, and some women with a quick wit or a strong arm can handle anything. However, many women feel humiliated and demeaned by the experience. Those who complain are sometimes considered by confident women to be whingers, who have let it happen – what has been described as an extension of the 'good girls do not get raped' theory. Men groan that things have got so politically correct that they can't enter the office and say 'That's a nice dress, Doris,' without letting loose the furies. It is disingenuous nonsense but is designed to marginalise women's complaints.

The *combination* of sex and power is a destructive one. All things are not equal when someone in a superior position within an organisation presses attentions or constantly comments in a very suggestive way about the appearance or clothing of a more junior member of staff, or insists on talking about sex, or engineers intimate interludes. As women become more successful and powerful themselves, they experience less harassment.

Yet even today women find it hard to have a complaint taken seriously. They are frequently met with the response that 'Charlie is just like that. He's harmless.' Pressing ahead can be career suicide, alienating the boss and every other male, and sometimes female, in sight. The complainant is hardly likely to secure the patronage of the spurned office romancer in any bid for promotion. The perpetrator, for his part, usually feels confused and defensive, often unaware of the misery he has caused the woman. Alternatively, his ego is so bruised that he can no longer find a way of working effectively with the victim.

From time to time I have adjudicated in internal hearings within organisations on allegations of sexual harassment. Dispute resolution is a sensitive business and both parties must feel the justice of the outcome. In each case the male party has accepted that he perhaps 'went too far' but only with hindsight has he recognised the issue of power imbalance. In these cases the most important lesson for the man is an understanding of the responsibilities that go with power, and the recognition that it is an abuse of his position to leave a woman uncertain about her right to say 'no' to his familiarities without a career comeback.

Relationships within society are being renegotiated as a result of women's changing status. The new terrain is sometimes a hard place for men to travel when they are using an outdated map. The challenge now is to create a climate of mutual respect in which we can locate our human relationships.

7

And She was Black

The brutal murder of Stephen Lawrence in 1993 was an iconic event. His killing by a group of white thugs and the bungled investigation by the police sparked off a long period of soul-searching in British society. Stephen's mother Doreen Lawrence has been the keeper of the public conscience, constantly reminding the nation that in a civilised society there must be justice for all. The subsequent inquiry into the death of Stephen was led by a retired judge, Sir William Macpherson and the Macpherson Report in 1999 found that the police were institutionally racist. It was a moment of hope for black people and the government pledged to stamp out racism in the criminal justice system. The Race Relations Amendment Act which came into force in 2001 places a positive duty on all public services to promote equality in every area of work, although immigration is noticeably excluded from its provisions. Despite this genuine commitment to racial equality, the government often loses a sense of what the implications of new policy agendas will be for racial minorities and race relations. For all the rhetoric of anti-racism, immigration and asylum policies feed into hostile views about those who are seen as 'other' and the erosion of civil liberties invariably has a disproportionate effect on minority communities. Leaders of the black community, male and female, know that changes in legal protections and lowering of standards will have greatest impact on the most vulnerable. They know that black people will take the biggest hit. Public debates about racism implicitly refer to black men while similar debates about gender discrimination have white middle-class women in mind. The inability of policy makers to see the simultaneous interaction of multiple discriminations is a continuing problem for black women.

The issue of race is highly contentious in legal circles. Judges will not have it that the colour of a person's skin in any way affects their judgments, even if it is suggested that attitudes may be unconscious or that discrimination can be indirect. Many see racial disadvantage as rooted in society, requiring a political resolution, and as outside the province of the courts. They describe their function in a mechanistic way as the application of 'the law', an impartial set of rules, without fear or favour and regardless of sex, colour or creed.

Yet something does go wrong. Although black people constitute approximately 7% of the population Home Office statistics for 1992 show that they make up 22% of the prison population. Indeed, 29% of the female prison population is now black. Since social deprivation is linked to criminal behaviour it is not surprising that black people, who have experienced discrimination and disadvantage, should be over-represented. It is hard to accept that this alone accounts for the discrepancy. There are, of course, those who choose to interpret the statistics as proof of black criminality; such crude views defy contradiction or rational debate. However, it is always maintained by the preservers of the status quo that the research so far conducted into any sentencing disparity is still inconclusive.

The study by Roger Hood of the Cambridge Institute of Criminology for the Commission of Racial Equality in the early 1990s knocked squarely on the head the idea that there is no sentencing differential, yet there continues to be resistance to the idea of racial bias. Home Office research in the same period claimed little difference in outcomes for white and black accused, but when white Irish were taken out of the frame the picture changed. The prejudice faced by the Irish community particularly in the wake of Irish terrorism distorted any simple white/black comparison and created a more favourable impression than was the truth. Minus the Irish, the differences between what happened to black offenders and white offenders became quite stark.

The unwillingness to admit that the problem exists arises because those involved in the administration of justice know the courts must be above reproach – the one area of society which should be beyond doubt. The legal establishment can accept that people may be discriminated against in education or employment because of their colour, but insist that as far as the courts are concerned the problem is in the minds of defendants (which they consider unsurprising since recipients are rarely satisfied with the justice of their deserts). If something cannot be measured in empirical terms it does not exist. If there is no proof beyond reasonable doubt of discrimination, it must follow that the courts are colour blind.

The problem with conducting research is that different responses may be obtained in different regions and before different courts. Equally, the outcome may vary if the researcher asking the questions is white or black. It has also been shown that surface examination of the offence and the sentence may show no discernible difference in approach, because in such an assessment no account is given to the complicated process which has gone before.

When I started practice at the Bar I spent a large part of my time in courts representing young black men charged with being a 'suspected person'. The accused did not have to commit an offence; it was enough that the police saw him behaving in a way that led them to believe that he was up to no good. There was no right to jury trial. In court, the standard case involved two police officers corroborating each other, using their identical notes made back at the police station. They would describe seeing the suspect behaving suspiciously, looking around him to see if there were observers and then trying a car door handle or pushing against a gate or reaching into a shoulder bag. There were never any fingerprints or independent witnesses or stolen items. Large numbers of young black men acquired criminal convictions on this kind of evidence, with magistrates nodding the cases through. The scandal of discriminatory police practice around the 'sus' laws led to legal reform but 'stop and search' has become the new litmus test of police attitudes.

Home Office figures released in March 2003 show a leap in stop and search by 16% against Asian people and 6% against black people in the year 2001–2002. Those of white people fell by 2%. In London over the same period the Metropolitan Police stopped

40% more Asians and 30% more blacks but 8% fewer white people than they had done in the previous year. The disproportionate use of stop and search against the black community is the most alienating policing tool in contemporary use. The Macpherson Report agreed that stop and search was an important operational tool but said over-use against ethnic minorities had to be stamped out. Darcus Howe, the broadcaster and journalist, describes being stopped and searched ten times in the last 20 years. Once in the West End of London, an officer lied through his teeth and claimed he had seen him dipping into women's handbags with intent to steal. Even Neville Lawrence, the father of Stephen Lawrence, whose face was so familiar from television appearances, was stopped and searched after his son's death. As indeed was Bishop Sentamu, one of the Commissioners on the Macpherson Inquiry. The same story can be repeated by almost every black male, no matter how prominent.

Black people are also more likely to be arrested. Their sense of injustice often results in greater confrontation with police and consequent accusations by the police that they have been disorderly or violent. Black people, in their understandable distrust of the frequently all-white bench of magistrates, will elect trial by jury in the Crown Court more often than their white counterparts, and this means longer sentences on conviction because higher courts have greater sentencing powers. It is also noteworthy that a significantly greater number of black defendants are ultimately acquitted at trial, suggesting that the original arrests may well have been unwarranted or that there was overcharging. The whole process confirms a sense of unfairness.

The contact of black communities with the police is so often negative that it spills over into the courtroom. However, when some judges see part of their role as validating a pressurised police force, they are faced with an unpalatable choice and either side with the police or avoid criticising them in the way that an aggrieved defendant feels an impartial judge should. The judge's attitude may not actually affect sentencing, but it will affect the way the court process is experienced by the black defendant.

Black defendants face all the usual problems: fear, worry, confusion and concern for their families – but they also have especially low expectations of how they will be treated, anticipating hostility from court staff and the Bench. Authority is white, and the courtroom reinforces that message. Not only are the great majority of lawyers and almost all judges white (only 9 of the 632 circuit judges are black, and, as I have already mentioned, there is only one black judge in the High Court), but so too are the clerks, the probation officers, the press reporters, the ushers and the policemen. Increasingly, Group 4 security officers are black, which means that black faces in courts often seem to be confined to the dock. The Society of Black Lawyers states that 'the poor image which black people have of the courts leads to the sense that if one is black in court one has to prove one's innocence rather than the court prove one's guilt.'

Members of the Society comment that 'the sense of having to prove one's credibility is also felt by black lawyers. They feel they often have to spend the first five or ten minutes demonstrating their credibility to the court . . . before they can genuinely get on with the job of defending the client' (an experience echoed by some white female practitioners). They point to the fact that few black lawyers do work for the Crown because prosecution work tends to go to specific chambers where black lawyers are hardly to be found.

The experiences of African, Afro-Caribbean and Asian defendants within the criminal justice system are in some ways different, and whilst a sense of alienation is shared by all the groups, they face different forms of racial stereotyping. Asians, unlike other ethnic minorities, are considered industrious and family-minded, which means, for example, that they are more likely to obtain bail than West Indian or African defendants. However, like Africans they are seen as more dishonest and lacking in credibility than West Indians. The special burden carried by West Indians is that they are often assumed to be more violent. The ultimate albatross for all black men, of whatever race, is that they are believed to be sexually insatiable.

The experience of black women is the corollary of that of black men but the racism of police attitudes is often compounded by sexism. In addition, women need to use the police to investigate domestic violence and sexual assault but in those negotiations are distrustful because they have witnessed the abuse of police authority in relation to the men in their communities.

On a recent visit to Holloway to talk to women about separation from their children I was surprised at the numbers of black women and questioned the probation staff on the size of the ethnic population. That week the number of black women in Holloway had passed the 50% mark (counting both unconvicted prisoners awaiting trial on remand and those already sentenced). This is ten times the ratio of black to white in the population at large. I know that Holloway presents a very different picture from other prisons because of its wider catchment area and because it covers the metropolis and the major ports of entry. But the visual impact of so many black women kept incarcerated by so many white women (few of the officers are from ethnic minorities) was shocking.

Why should black women be deserving of prison sentences or refusal of bail where white women are not? A reasonable percentage can be accounted for by the high incidence of black women from abroad being convicted of importing drugs, but this does not provide a full explanation. In addition to the factors affecting the treatment of black men, many black women are penalised for failing to conform to 'appropriate' notions of womanhood. To some judges and policemen the lifestyles of many black women in Britain today, particularly Afro-Caribbeans, seem unorthodox. The set-up is often matriarchal, lacking the 'restraining male influence' for which judges tend to look. Fewer black women have a tidy domestic picture to present to the court. The fact that the family unit of four is no longer an accurate reflection of social organisation amongst the white population, and that the percentage of single-parent families is high regardless of race, does not help black women, because we are now also seeing a moral and political crusade against the 'lone parent'.

A recurring theme for young black men refused bail is that they have insufficient roots in the community to guarantee their staying around to stand trial. Often they will have children but live separately from the children's mother. The men are often just as deeply involved with their children as any white father, and the likelihood of their absconding is no greater than that of most, but their family attachment is minimised by the difference in lifestyle. The historical background to the different cultural attitudes to the family is rarely acknowledged by the courts. To ignore the role of slavery and the consequent separation of black families, with women bearing children and raising them separately, denies the experience of many black people. The old taboo on illegitimacy was hardly a concern to those who were denied any legal status whatsoever. These historical influences continue to impact on the shape of many black families today.

The courts still see single motherhood as a signal of an unstable background, regardless of family structure. Afro-Caribbean girls are often given independence at an earlier age than white girls and are allowed to be responsible for their own lives. They are assertive in a way that is not accepted in the dominant culture. The writer Ann Oakley has pointed out that the dividing line between what is masculine and what is criminal is at times a thin one; assertiveness and independence are seen as exclusively male characteristics, and when displayed by young black women are seen as indicative of 'trouble'.

Afro-Caribbean women are far more frequently refused bail, because they are more often seen as homeless, their domestic arrangements not conforming to name-on-the-rentbook requirements. There are also very few bail hostels for women, and there is a general assumption that ethnic women will disappear into a subculture which will be difficult for the police to penetrate. In addition, poverty within the black community often means that it is difficult to obtain financial sureties. Black women who should be on bail can thus have it refused, only to be acquitted at their trial several months later. The shocking revelation was made in September 2004 by the Prison Reform Trust that two-thirds (66%) of women who enter prison are on remand and under half are in the end sent to prison. Yet the conditions in which they await trial are often worse than those experienced by the convicted. Fewer than one in ten is facing charges for violent offences; more are there for shoplifting than for any other crime.

Another objection to bail frequently raised by the police is that they consider it likely that the accused will commit further offences. This objection, usually based on the existence of previous convictions, communicates the view that the woman is so undisciplined that appearing in court operates as no constraint on her behaviour. If the court sees a young woman who is affecting lack of concern they read her demeanour as supporting the police view, and off she goes into custody.

Black working-class women are often less submissive in the face of the legal system than their white counterparts. This is not to say they are unafraid of courts – they are as much in terror of them as any woman – but they see no reason for colluding in a system which discriminates against them. They arrive at court angry. Their anger is rarely understood: it is taken for aggression, and as an unwillingness to show deference. Even if they themselves have not gone through criminal proceedings before, they have often learned from the experience of male family members and friends not to have high expectations. The collective experience goes into court with them.

Young black women in particular are seen as 'lippy', often expressing their feelings with dagger-looks and with 'tchuking'. Nothing is more irritating to policemen, prison officers, judges and magistrates than this extraordinary sound of teeth-sucking, a hiss of insolence when it resounds in a courtroom. Even those unfamiliar with its use can tell that it combines the criticism of a 'tut' with the despair of a snort. There is always a danger that judges, threatened perhaps subconsciously by a woman's anger, will seek to quell it with incarceration.

One of the views firmly held by white defendants, which leapt from the Nacro report on the courts in 1991, was that black people did not know how to play the system, did not realise that passive, remorseful behaviour served you best. But for many black people the court appearance is their last stand. The whole process has been humiliating. Often until the moment before entering the court they have been addressed in terms of abuse. The women talk of feeling dirty, like scum; the relative calm of the courtroom is their last chance to say: I am not going to be crushed.

A classic story of a black woman's road to crime is told by a young woman who was first convicted at the age of 14. The family was celebrating her brother's marriage, and the wedding party was in full swing when the police raided the house, suspecting that drugs were being consumed. The festive spirit was immediately spoiled and the house was turned upside down in the presence of all the guests. No drugs were found, but the girl became involved in a struggle with the police and was arrested. Despite all the claims that girls are treated lightly and are cautioned for first offences, she was brought to court and given a two-year conditional discharge as well as a fine and compensation to the officer for a torn epaulette amounting to £82.

It took the schoolgirl a long time to pay off the money, and her deep sense of the unfairness of what happened lives on. The conviction counted against her when she left school and tried to get a job, and offences of dishonesty started to accumulate. In interview, this woman made the important point that even as a girl she had the physical appearance of a mature woman, and she was dealt with as such. She felt that this assumption was often made about black girls if they were physically well developed.

Another handicap for black women is that police consider their colour before their gender, and in situations of arrest they are often dealt with quite aggressively. The police assume, as they do with black men, that black women will be violent, and that perception informs the way they handle a situation. In turn, any altercation with the police is dealt with seriously by the courts; defendants on charges of assaulting police are invariably sent to prison.

Assumptions about the sexuality of black women are insidious. They are deemed to be inherently promiscuous, happy not only to have sex with anyone but to do so with rampant regularity and abandon. This belief, which excites both fascination and disgust, is often subtly present in courtroom exchanges and social enquiry reports, and affects the way they are sentenced.

In rape cases in particular, the black experience seems to represent an amplified version of the handicaps facing women generally, whether in the juvenile or the higher courts. When black women are raped they have problems having their allegations heard, because all the usual assumptions merge with those about black sexuality and aggression. Black Afro-Caribbean women are not readily seen as fragile creatures in need of protection, but as well able to look after themselves. It is also assumed that they are

173

much more open to casual sexual contact and that less commitment to formal marriage means promiscuity.

Black people are much more likely to be apprehended on the street than white people; they feel that there is an accepted belief that they are dishonest, criminal and possibly terrorist. A colleague of mine represented a hospital sister who was arrested at the Chelsea Flower Show. Not many black faces are to be seen at the Flower Show, a quintessentially English, middle-class affair, but the woman in question was in fact both English and middle-class, and also a lover of gardens and horticulture. To her amazement, she was pulled out of a group of women who were queuing to use the ladies' lavatory by two young police officers who maintained that they had seen her put her hand into the handbags of other women. She was aghast. No stolen article was found on her and no person in the queue had complained, but she was charged with attempted theft and trailed through the nightmare of a Crown Court trial before being acquitted.

Black mothers often feel that their bond with their children is perceived as less significant and that their views on a child's welfare are less valuable. One mother, sentenced to two months in prison for refusing access to her daughter's father, felt that she was viewed as bloody-minded and obstructive, when in fact she was trying to express deep concern for her child's well-being. Her ex-boyfriend was a drug user and the little girl returned from visits describing in detail his use of drugs and drug involvement with others. The mother feared that the influence of drugs would affect his ability to care for the child when she was with him, and wanted any access to be supervised. In court, her concerns were ignored. She explained:

> The judge thought I was a stubborn, determined person who was going out of my way to break a court order. I think had I not had two children by different fathers they would have viewed me as a different type of person. I think the judge was trying to say, 'You can't have your children and do what you like with them.' I think the colour factor comes into it, but it's something that can never be proved.

The heroism of 'mother figures' who bring up families in the face of hardship and poverty is part of the received wisdom. While young black women are often underestimated as committed mothers, older black women are almost invariably seen as over-committed matriarchs, who indulge their sons. The assumption is that black women protect their wild boys from the forces of law and order. The Brixton riots in 1985 were fired by the shooting of Mrs Cherry Groce when the police were looking for her son, Michael. The race riots which took place in Tottenham later that year were sparked off by the death of a black mother, Mrs Jarrett, who suffered a heart attack while her home was being raided by police.

The racism experienced by black women cannot be disconnected from what they see happening daily to their fathers, brothers and sons. When you unpack the stop and search figures, they suggest a greatly increased interest in young Asian men (including men from the Middle East), in the aftermath of September 11. Americans would call this racial profiling. The Asian communities feel very beleaguered, sensing a growing hostility and Islamophobia not just from the authorities but also from their neighbours. Statistics for 2001–2002 show that race hate crimes doubled in Lincolnshire, Staffordshire, West Midlands and North Wales. Nearly 9,000 people were cautioned or prosecuted for racially aggravated offences in the same period nationally, double the amount the year before. Most victims are Asian but many are middle eastern and include asylum seekers. So the communities feel they are getting a rough deal from all sides. Whilst it is mainly men who are targeted for stop and search, it feeds very negative feelings amongst women and undermines confidence in the police as a source of help when women need them. A report called *Policing for London* (2003) now describes relations between the police and the Pakistani and Bangladeshi communities as deteriorating so rapidly that the tensions are as bad as those existing between the police and young blacks. If handled insensitively the 'war on terrorism' could greatly exacerbate race relations, particularly in northern cities and towns with large Islamic communities. The sense of 'them' and 'us' has repercussions for women. Women's groups working with minorities feel that the community solidarity created to deal with this perceived targeting and Islamophobia makes it impossible for women who are being abused or forced into marriages to turn to the authorities for help.

Asian women's experience of the courts is different from that of other racial minority women so long as they are very traditional. An interesting paradox was presented to the courts during the Grunwick dispute in 1977, when assertive, politically organised Asian women picketed their place of work and were arrested for offences arising out of the dispute. Mrs Desai, the union leader, was charged a number of times and defended the cases successfully, and with great dignity, discarding the stereotype and earning herself an individualised hearing.

If black Afro-Caribbean women suffer from a female version of the myths about black male sexuality and violence, Asian women suffer from feminised versions of the 'untrustworthy oriental'. They are often given an even lower rating on the credibility scale than other black women, and there is a suspicion that behind the demure exterior lurks deceit and dishonesty. A recurring lapse is the misreading of Asian people's failure to make eye contact, which is a mark of respect and culturally inculcated from the earliest age but is seen in the courts as shiftiness.

Asian women on trial often have language difficulties and an interpreter has to be used. Conducting a defence through the medium of a translator is never satisfactory because the usual methods of measuring truthfulness are greatly reduced: questions and answers become mechanical and bland, and the emotion and subtlety in a person's intonation are lost. The delay before the answer is treated with suspicion: jurors imagine the witness understands more than she is letting on, and that she is using the time to consider her response. It is true that if you try to conduct cross-examinations in poor English, the risk of misunderstanding is considerable, but the accused is not as 'real' when she is distanced by language from those who try her and she suffers the consequences. The ultimate linguistic failure happened in the case of Mrs Begum, a battered wife who pleaded guilty to the murder of her husband in Birmingham Crown Court in April 1985 without understanding the language spoken to her by her lawyers or the court clerk.

*

As with white working-class women, it is assumed that violence is just part of black women's lives. Black women's organisations campaign vociferously about the neglect of black women's complaints when they are subjected to battering. They say there is an assumption that they can give as good as they get and the police avoid getting involved. In the trial of a Ugandan woman for grievous bodily harm to her husband by pouring hot cooking fat over him, it came to light that, although she had called the police repeatedly, her violent husband had never been arrested. Indeed, it was suggested to her that she was not telling the truth when she said in interview to the CID that she had made many previous complaints: there was no record of such complaints and the claim that she was exaggerating her husband's brutality was put to her again at her trial by prosecuting counsel. It was a prosecution witness, a neighbour, who inadvertently came to her aid. He complained in the witness box about the number of times he had been awakened, first by her screams and then by police mistakenly ringing his doorbell when they came in answer to her calls.

Women in the minority communities are particularly vulnerable to the effects of cultural relativism, where non-intervention is justified because certain behaviours are assumed to be cultural norms. 'They're not like us and we have to tread with care or we will be accused of racism by their community leaders,' was one of the explanations I was given by a prosecutor. Needless to say, most of the community leaders are men. If police do arrive on the scene, and the wife has poor English, the police tend to rely on the story being told by the men around. Repeatedly, Asian women report that by the time police turn up they are too distressed to be very coherent, and little effort is made to discover what they have suffered. Securing supportive evidence is difficult because connection with the authorities is mediated so often by male elders. One Asian woman testifying to the Fawcett Commission Inquiry into Criminal Justice in 2003 described being taken to the doctor's by her husband who had caused her injuries. He did the talking. 'The GP, who was an Asian friend of the family, did not pick up on the violence.' Another said that after ten years of domestic violence and reporting it to the police, the first real help came when she saw a domestic violence co-ordinator who took on all her cultural concerns. 'Until then the response of the police was very poor.'

It is true that the pressures on women in some minority communities are great, because it is considered an insult to the honour of the man's family if his wife should leave. A shocking number of Asian women have been killed in recent years by their husbands or a member of their husband's family because they have attempted to leave or seek help from the criminal justice system and been fobbed off. Balwant Kaur was killed by her husband inside Brent Asian Women's Refuge. Others are killed by their own families for bringing shame on them. Culture does have a bearing in terms of the strategies available for Asian women to escape violence. But there is a precarious tightrope to walk. While not wanting to construct Asian and particularly Muslim culture as some monolithic and static phenomenon, problematic and pathological, it has to be spelt out how women can be constrained by their families and communities.

In June 1995 Tasleem Begum was killed by her brother-in-law, Shabir Hussein. He ran her over with his car, reversed over her body and sped forward once more, crushing her three times. She had been married to an older cousin who lived in Pakistan and did not visit her for four years. In his absence, she met another Asian man at work and married him, an action which dishonoured the family in Hussein's eyes. He was sentenced to life imprisonment for murder but appealed and was eventually convicted of manslaughter on the grounds of provocation, receiving six and a half years. The result was attacked by women's groups, including Southall Black Sisters. Hannana Siddiqui, the co-ordinator, explained:

> For us, the concept of honour is being used as a justification or mitigation for violence. It can often be used to judge women's sexual conduct or just general behaviour like refusing to be obedient, regardless of the reasons why they might be refusing. The consequences for women can be anything from social ostracism and harassment to violence and, in a few cases, murder . . . Cultural defences which use notions of honour to justify murder or other offences of domestic violence have been

accepted by the courts, which has led to differential treatment of black and minority women and a system colluding with that justification.

In recent years the courts have had little truck with the plea that cultural difference can explain away murderous behaviour. In 1999, Rukhsana Naz was strangled by her mother and brother after she refused to have an abortion. When she was 15, Rukhsana had been forced into a marriage. Her husband lived in Pakistan and she had only seen him twice. Her family were incensed on discovering that Rukhsana was expecting an illegitimate child by a young man called Imran whom she had secretly dated since she was 12. He too had been forced into a marriage he did not want. Rukhsana's body was found five days after her death when a farmer stumbled across it in his field. She was eventually identified because scrawled on her hand was Imran's pager number. Both the accused were sentenced to life imprisonment but some members of the community believe that strangling was too good for an adulteress and she deserved to be stoned to death (see *From Homebreakers to Jailbreakers*, edited by Rahila Gupta, 2003).

Heshu Yones who was 16 and a student from west London had her throat cut by her father in October 2002, after she was discovered dating a man from outside the Kurdish Muslim culture. Abdalla Yones had become so 'disgusted and distressed' by his daughter's westernised ways that he stabbed her 11 times and left her to bleed to death before trying to kill himself. He was convicted of murder and sentenced to life.

Yasmin Akhtar was kidnapped, strangled and then set on fire in March 2002 after she filed for divorce. Her stepson hired three men to track her down and they strangled her with parcel tape when they tried to silence her. All were jailed for life. In September 2002 Badshu Miah suspected his estranged wife was having numerous affairs, including with white women, so he used a machete and a kitchen knife to slay her and her four-year-old daughter and her disabled brother. Faqir Mohammed stabbed his daughter 20 times when he found her with a boyfriend at their family home. Sahjda Bibi was stabbed 22 times on her wedding day in 2003 by her cousins Rafaqat and Tafarak Hussain because she dared to marry a man of her own choice, a divorcee and non-blood-relative. The men got life. In May 2004, a Sikh elder, Palwinder Dhillon, was jailed for life for strangling pregnant Anita Gindha, after she fled an arranged marriage.

The police insist that gathering evidence is rendered almost impossible in many cases because the value systems in some communities still legitimise domestic violence. They point to how families and groups close ranks to protect their menfolk. Communities are not always the cosy havens of warmth, security and comfort romanticised by politicians. Sometimes they are places with secrets and hierarchies and practices like female genital mutilation.

Nuziat Khan was found strangled to death in August 2001. She had asked for a divorce because she could take no more abuse. Her husband Iqbal Zafar remains on Scotland Yard's most wanted list in connection with her murder. He is believed to have fled to Pakistan, with whom we have no extradition treaty. Nuziat's relatives believe he is being protected by the community there. In 2001 I represented a young Bengali girl – 14 years old – who was charged with attempted murder having thrown her newborn baby out of a council flat window. The case is mentioned in an earlier chapter. She had been raped by her uncle, who disappeared into the Bangladeshi community, protected by a wall of silence. When I asked the prosecuting authorities to reconsider the charge I was told that it was important to send out a message to the community about the treatment of unwanted babies. The message about condoning sexual abuse of girls was the one that needed amplifying.

The Southall Black Sisters have been constant in challenging the underlying racism and sexism in official decision-making for over twenty years. Standing at the intersection of race, gender and class, they have changed the landscape of feminist activism and their doggedness is beginning to pay off. The Home Office, in conjunction with the Foreign Office, is now actively tackling the issue of forced marriages, providing support and return flights when young women are taken to South Asia, ostensibly for family holidays but forced to marry while there. There are also plans to make enforced marriage a specific criminal offence because the present charges of assault or kidnapping are so inadequate, especially when families trick a young woman into making a visit overseas and out of the British jurisdiction. The initiative is not seen as an assault on the custom of arranged marriages but is to prevent marriage where a party does not consent or only consents under duress. In 2002, SBS helped a young Asian woman secure the first annulment of marriage in England and Wales in a forced marriage case. The bad news is that throughout the nineties there was a year on year increase in the numbers of women seeking their help over dowry disputes, family violence and forced marriage.

Women's organisations say that the police are still insufficiently responsive to early signs that a woman is at risk. The very high suicide rate amongst young Asian women is one of the secrets in our society. Unsuccessful attempts at suicide often go unheeded. The tension of living in a Western developed nation, where the relationships between men and women are in the process of great change, and reconciling that reality with the mores and customs of another cultural tradition can be unbearable. The pressure to conform, combined with high expectations, can cause massive strain on young women, who are taught to hide any problems that bring shame on the family. This is not an experience confined to the Asian community. Domestic violence and pressures to marry people from the same background have operated in Catholic, Jewish and other communities too. Speaking publicly about the behaviour of your own people is an act of betrayal because minority communities feel that such exposure will further stigmatise them in the eyes of the majority. On the one hand are those who want the lid taken off the secrecy and call for a clear denouncement of unacceptable practices; others fear that focusing on 'honour and shame' may lead to the Asian community being stigmatised and stereotyped. Baroness Pola Uddin of Bethnal Green who co-chaired a commission on forced marriages has expressed concern that old and dangerous prejudices are reinforced by too much emphasis on *izzat* (honour). She points out that overall levels of domestic violence are actually lower in the Asian community and insists this is not just a consequence of under-reporting.

However, activists like Hannana Siddiqui are anxious that

multicultural sensitivity may lead to moral blindness and feel the government is still wary about taking on the leaders of ethnic minority communities over cultural traditions. Shamshad Hussain, a leading Bradford community worker, is concerned that abuse against women could grow. 'Unless we all unite to take an honest and strong, intelligent and open stance on this issue now, you are likely to see a backlash of traditionalism by young people, particularly young men, as a defence against Western values that threaten them and their traditional position.'

Police in London receive two calls a week from women and girls reporting so-called honour crimes, such as being forced into marriage or being threatened with murder by their families, but many incidents go unreported because of fear and cultural taboos. Sometimes the only 'offence' to family honour is that the woman wants to be a student or pursue a career. Between June 2003 and June 2004 there were more than 12 such murders in the UK but other women are missing after being taken abroad by relatives or have suffered suspicious injuries claimed to have been caused by road accidents or chip pan fires. There is currently a police review of murder cases going back ten years to see if any were 'honour' killings so that the police can learn from those investigations. They are difficult cases evidentially because of the collusion of whole families but the police are now being trained to listen to suspected victims, not to inform families and not to try to mediate. In 2000, a UN report estimated that worldwide 5,000 women a year – more than 13 a day – die because they are deemed to have brought shame on their families or communities. This is probably a gross underestimate. A secret refuge has been set up in Berlin for Turkish girls, and campaigners are pushing for Britain to adopt the idea. They believe that there is a need for special provision for women with distinctive cultural problems, which cannot always be provided by other refuges.

SBS raises the important issue that many immigrant women, who originally acquired entry to Britain through their marital status, feel obliged to stay in violent marriages because to leave may jeopardise their right to remain in this country. Such fears make women diffident about calling in the police or, if they do, about answering all their questions, which in turn is perceived as deceit. The One Year Rule in immigration law means that if a marriage fails within a year, a party who has come from abroad will lose their right to stay. Following campaigns by SBS, concessions to the rule have now been made for spouses and partners who are victims of domestic violence.

The case of Zoora Shah has become a *cause célèbre* amongst women campaigners, for it throws into stark relief the failings of the courts to understand women who challenge cultural stereotypes. Zoora came from Mirpur in rural Pakistan following an arranged marriage. Her husband, who had subjected her to violence, abandoned her and her young children when she was pregnant with her third child. She was totally destitute and isolated when she was befriended by Mohammed Azam, a drug dealer from the criminal underworld of Bradford. He helped her acquire a house and because of her indebtedness to him he began to make sexual demands. This sealed her reputation as a 'prostitute'. In the years that followed she became enslaved to him, used for sex as and when he pleased, and was threatened and tyrannised so that her home became a prison. She suffered from periods of depression and illness which were confirmed in medical records. Her efforts to get help from community leaders fell on deaf ears or they would themselves exploit her sexually. Eventually Zoora poisoned her persecutor when she thought he had sexual designs on her daughter and might ruin her life too.

At her trial Zoora Shah refused to give evidence. She was ashamed of what she had become in the eyes of the community and could not bring herself to reveal the full details of her debasement in public. Bound by all the powerful notions of honour and shame, she therefore chose to remain silent in the hope of saving the honour of her daughters. She was found guilty and sentenced to life with a tariff of 20 years. Her subsequent appeal also failed. In the words of the lawyer, Pragna Patel, 'she did not lead a "normal", "passive" existence as a "victim" of violence but tried to retain control in an impoverished world inhabited by male predators'. The conservative psychiatrist for the Crown had no experience of gender issues within Asian communities. He presented Zoora as a cold and calculating woman, especially because she chose to stay silent at her trial, acted in contradictory ways and had an ambivalent relationship with her abuser.

The judges were utterly confused and their judgment was littered with misconceptions about women's responses to violence and the cultural context in which this is experienced. They made sweeping assumptions about honour and shame which bordered on racially gendered stereotypes. They said:

'This appellant is an unusual woman. Her way of life has been such that there might not have been much left of her honour to salvage.'

As Pragna Patel points out: 'There was a complete absence of awareness of the intertwined issues of culture, gender and power within minority communities . . . Women face very real consequences when they find themselves transgressing the norms of their community and it is important for those sitting in judgement to understand why cultural values keep a woman silent and close down her options.' The sustained efforts of SBS meant that Zoora Shah's tariff was reduced to 12 years in 2000.

The abuse and violation of women is a human rights issue and there can be no hierarchies of human rights. Women from ethnic minorities deserve the same legal protections as any other women, and women deserve the same protection as men. As is said by my friend Claire L'Heureux-Dube, who recently retired as a Supreme Court judge in Canada, context is everything. But this is a lesson still to be learned here and until it is, equality at the hands of the law and before the law will not be secured.

Black women are given probation less often than others, and a review of social enquiry reports showed that recommendations as to sentence are less often made for black women. The inevitable consequence is that prison is a likelier option: two to three times more likely, according to the statistics. They are also assumed to be involved in drugs, and that cultural inference is hard to shift when they appear in the dock. However much they might deny involvement in drugs offences, there is a particular burden on the black defendant in challenging such charges.

Social enquiry reports are not scientific documents and are bound to be subjective. They are also, inevitably, directed at the middle-class magistrates and judges. In an increasingly punitive climate there is a temptation to pander to the expectations and prejudices of the Bench in ways which will secure a favourable outcome. (It is an approach to which we have all succumbed, lawyers and probation officers alike. We have all experienced the fear that our client will turn up with a mohican haircut, or with her tattoos showing, or with a ring in her nose or a jumper shot with Lurex, especially when the judge really is a conformist and is likely to draw adverse inferences.)

The Probation Service is now actively addressing the issue of racism and sexism, and their studies have identified stereotyping as a particular problem. The accepted image is an easy shorthand to fall back on when there is little time. When I was making a television programme on a similar subject I interviewed the BBC's head of comedy, who told me that reliance upon stereotypes in sitcoms was partly due to the need to impart information quickly and to create shared laughter in shared values. The problem is that these values are then reinforced, allowing prejudice to creep in. In the courtroom their use prevents important distinctions being made between each case and each person. Basic information is provided, responses are triggered, and the individual who is encased in this envelope of assumptions is never allowed to surface. For black women, emerging as special and different is especially tough.

Black women lawyers have well-tuned antennae and empathise with the problems faced by women clients of their race. As the barrister Tanoo Mylvaganam says, 'You cannot be a woman lawyer, experiencing discriminatory practice yourself as a professional, without being alerted to the way that the same attitudes affect women who do not even have our class advantage.' Black women lawyers complain that the problems of being taken seriously are exacerbated for them, as is the difficulty of securing authority within the courtroom. Those who are successful are constantly told by white colleagues that they do not 'seem' black, as though there were some special stamp of blackness which they had shrugged off. Such comments are proffered as compliments; it is often not understood why they are offensive.

Another black woman barrister, a rising criminal practitioner, describes defending a black client who was one of several defendants; the other lawyers were all white. She had the strong feeling that the trial judge, who is renowned for his rudeness, was particularly dismissive of her legal arguments. At one stage, when she sat down, he sent her a note asking her whether her accent was English, and if so where she had been to school. She ignored the note, uncertain what it meant, but felt very undermined, as though her fluency and education were being questioned. After this barrister had made her final speech to the jury, the judge summed up to the all-white jury with this remark: 'Members of the jury, we are British and this is a British court and British standards of behaviour are being protected.' She felt that the comment diminished her own address to the jury, as coming from someone with a different and less valid value system.

Elizabeth James, a British barrister of Nigerian descent, was defending a Nigerian woman charged with credit-card fraud when the judge opined that 'this type of crime is far too prevalent amongst the Nigerian community'. There is absolutely no support for his view, and she had the courage to challenge him in court and to say that she took personal exception to the remark.

It is not just the ethnic minority communities who suffer racial prejudice. Those who do not hold British passports have similar experiences. To be foreign is a handicap for *anyone* in British courts. Around 20% of the women imprisoned in England and Wales are women from overseas imprisoned for drug offences, usually importation, mainly from Nigeria, Ghana and Jamaica but also from India and Pakistan or Latin America. In Holloway Prison, the ratio is higher (26%), because of its London location and because it includes women awaiting trial. In Morton Hall, a female prison which is used to incarcerate women with longer sentences, there are times when the proportion of foreign inmates (usually black) is around 65%. (*The Times*, 6 August and 28 August 2003). The conviction rate is high because, even where the women claim they have been duped or pressured into carrying drugs, judges and juries are sceptical. The worlds they are hearing about are so alien to British people that the accounts often seem fantastic. A woman from Colombia, currently serving nine years, said that her trial judge suggested to her that she had read too many books about the Mafia or watched too many films. Yet the more we hear about the Latin American drug cartels, the more real seems her terror at what could be done to her family.

To people who lead impoverished lives in Third World countries, the financial rewards for importing and distributing drugs, though often not very substantial by Western standards, are considerable. The sums range from hundreds to a few thousand pounds, and for many these incentives outweigh the risks of arrest. The use of women as couriers or 'mules' is frequent and intentional. The belief that women travellers attract less attention from Customs and Excise officials was initially well founded, especially if they appeared respectable or had children with them, although nowadays the policing of our ports is so sensitive to illegal immigration, people trafficking and the ploys of drug importers that women can expect as much scrutiny as men.

The inventiveness of the importers knows no bounds, with drugs secreted inside toothpaste tubes and cosmetics, the heels of shoes, in dominoes, draught sets, artefacts and false-bottomed boxes of every variety. A ploy used for a while in some importations was for the courier to arrive at an Asian or African airport and check in perfectly ordinary luggage with no drug contents, and for the drugs organisers to pay off airline employees to put duplicate luggage directly into the hold. When the luggage arrived in London the courier would pick the cases containing the contraband off the carousel and take it through the green light. If stopped, they would be able to produce the luggage label attached to their tickets, showing that there was some mistake, point to the 'clean' original luggage still circling the carousel, and identify it as theirs. There is no end to criminal ingenuity.

The swallowing of condoms full of heroin and cocaine is a method that has been used for years, sometimes to lethal effect when the contents have begun to leak into the intestines of the courier.

In the streets of Jamaican, African, Colombian or Indian towns, an endless supply of extremely poor women can be persuaded to earn cash which will see their children through school, pay for medical bills or just secure their family's existence for the foreseeable future. Most are single parents and first-time offenders and usually coercion has played a part in their decision to act as a courier. They are the pawns of the drug gangs and they become the forgotten prisoners within our system. Few of the women are aware of the sentences they are likely to face, or of British sentencing policy, despite advertising campaigns back in their home countries, so the rationale of long sentences to discourage others is a nonsense; little publicity is given to the experience of these women in their communities.

The courts are anxious to show that no leniency will be extended, however heart-rending the personal circumstances of those caught bringing drugs into the country. They are obliged to follow the guidelines established by Lord Chief Justice Lane in the case of Aramah, a drugs appeal which was decided 20 years ago which set down the tariffs for drug-related crime. A strict equality principle operates, which has led to a large increase in women of all nationalities going through the criminal justice system and ending up with very long prison sentences. The 'one size fits all' type of sentencing always creates injustice. For these defendants there is no slow induction into the vagaries of the courts. The experience is usually new to them, and the implications of their foray into criminal activity come as the most profound shock. Many cannot speak a word of English, and court interpretation is often inadequate. Spanish-speaking Latin Americans explain that having a Spaniard to translate often distorts what they mean because of linguistic differences and nuances. They rarely have friends or family in this country to provide emotional support, and their lawyers become their only contact with the outside world. Often they have an innocent belief that their legal representatives have some special influence with the authorities.

I remember especially an elderly Indian woman who had been used by her son-in-law to bring in quantities of cannabis when she travelled to this country with her grandchildren, who had been to stay with her for the holidays. It was her first journey abroad apart from a pilgrimage to Mecca, and she had been so terrified of the moving escalator on her arrival at Heathrow that she was unable to stand upright on it, but simply crouched on one of its steps in a state of panic. She was sentenced to three years' imprisonment, with little account taken of what a nightmare prison would be for someone who spoke not a word of the language, who had never undressed even in front of her daughters, let alone strangers, and who was in purdah because of the recent death of her husband. In the cells she clung to me in abject terror, pleading like a little girl. The interpreter who was with us explained that she was saying that she did not want to die away from her home. As they peeled her away from me and took her to the prison van, a little trail of betel-nuts that she had been chewing fell and lay scattered on the ground. I wept for her as I made the miserable journey back into London.

Human rights principles require that there is equality before the law. This should embrace the concept of unequal impact when it comes to sentencing. If an offender is likely to suffer from the sentence to a significantly greater degree than most other people, there is a case for reducing the length.

An analysis undertaken by the Esmée Fairbairn Foundation in 2003, published as *A Bitter Pill to Swallow*, showed that drug 'mules' are rarely major players in the drugs trade and that if all the Jamaican women bringing in drugs were stopped it is unlikely it would have a noticeable impact on the availability or the price of drugs on the streets of Britain. A significant number of these women are serving well in excess of ten years, and many of those feel they are sentenced more harshly than British women who have committed the same offences. Cannabis is a class B drug and the sentences are usually shorter than for heroin or cocaine: two to four years.

The rhetoric in the courtroom is that drugs would not enter the country without the courier. The role is central to all the problems involved in drug abuse, and in my experience juries, ever sensitive to the effects of drugs, are understandably resistant to the arguments about whether the transporter actually knew herself to be in possession.

Juries are also unable to accept the gullibility of some women who unquestioningly carry items for friends and acquaintances. Maria Gonzales was convicted of bringing four kilos of cocaine into this country from Colombia and was sentenced to 14 years' imprisonment. The substance was pressed inside long-playing records and would in no way be detectable to the untrained eye.

However, she was a vivacious woman who had worked as an air hostess when she was younger. Clearly the jury had difficulty believing that she would not suspect the motives of a man friend asking her to bring some personal belongings to one of his friends in Europe.

Because the sentence on conviction for drugs couriers will automatically be imprisonment, pre-sentence reports have little impact on the judge. Most of the information inevitably has to come from the woman herself because there is little access to information from abroad: the assumption is that the woman could have made the account of circumstances up. In any event, this is one of the areas of crime where a respectable past and family responsibilities cut no ice. There is also a cynical belief that the couriers will invent handicapped children and dying mothers just for the day in court. These women, who are referred to inside prison as 'deportees', feel aggrieved that they have no adequate opportunity of presenting their background fully to the tribunal. Some of their circumstances could be better substantiated and allowances should, in their view, be made for the pressures on their lives.

Martha, whose daughter in Colombia is seriously ill with leukaemia, is currently serving nine years. The girl, along with Martha's other children, is being looked after by her elderly mother. She had lengthy letters showing the truth of her history, but the court showed little interest in them. It was clear, listening to her, that she was uncertain who was who in the courtroom or what function each person played in her trial. This is an experience shared by many people, white and black, but it is exacerbated when language is an additional problem:

> I explained my situation to the judge, explained it to the solicitor [prosecutor] the reason I was involved in this case and they didn't believe me. They didn't believe me so the result . . . nine years. I couldn't take it in my mind. It took me quite a few days to think: nine years away from home! I was just thinking of being in there. It was horrible, I wished to die.

Another courier is Stephanie, who is of Jamaican origin but whose home was New York:

> You are prejudged for the idea that you are from Colombia or Jamaica. Jamaica is a drug country, drug-orientated. Or you are from New York. It is a bad place. That is where the guns and the drugs are. All the bad things that happen, you are just a part of it. You should know what is happening and you have been doing it all your life. That's your lifestyle.
>
> Basically I think the judge looks at the stereotype. If you're a woman, you shouldn't even think of committing a crime in the first place. You should be home with your children. But then in most cases the reason they've done it is because of the children, which sounds horrible. But it is to send them to school, to feed them, to clothe them. Depending on which country they are from, there are probably no social services nor any help from the government. So it's looked on as, well, you shouldn't be in court in the first place. You expect some kind of punishment, but six, eight, ten, twelve years! It is a bit much, especially for women. We know that even though we scream equality, in the home the woman she's the backbone. In most cases she is both mother and father in the home.

Many of the women feel that they are dealt with as if by rote by both judges and lawyers. Stephanie saw her solicitor on only a few brief visits, and her barrister, whom she had never met before, arrived 15 minutes before the start of the case. The solicitor was away on holiday so there was no familiar face at court. Defendants in these cases have little power, and at times feel forced to accept a poor service from the legal profession.

At the time of her trial Martha's English was negligible and she too felt that she was never able to get her case across. She describes the experience as deeply traumatic. Like Stephanie, she felt dissatisfied with her representation because, although she had had a conference with a barrister at the prison, someone different turned up on the day. She could not believe that it was sufficient for someone to read the papers in the case and to talk with her for as little as half an hour. It is not unreasonable for clients to want the opportunity to talk to their lawyers at length if they are facing imprisonment of maybe ten years. But there is pressure in the court to get a move on, and the lawyer fears the judge's wrath. Since the solicitor Martha was familiar with was not present either, the trial was like a bad dream in which she felt like a powerless observer rather than a participant.

The problem of last-minute changes in counsel is an old chestnut for the courts. Complaints are myriad and resolution is difficult for those who are trying to administer the courts speedily. It can only be reduced as a problem if more and more cases are given fixed dates in advance and if the real seriousness of importation cases is recognised. Needless to say, foreign prisoners are not a vociferous or influential group of complainants.

For the women from outside Europe who are convicted of drugs charges there is no parole, and there are no home visits, and few visitors, because everyone they know is elsewhere. Prisoners can now buy phone-cards, but a call to Nigeria or Latin America is expensive, and few can afford to buy more than the occasional card out of their prison earnings. They are given one free five-minute phone call to their families every three months.

Some of the women arrive in this country pregnant, and because they will not be released by the time the child is 18 months old the baby is taken away soon after birth to be cared for in a British foster home, ultimately to be reunited with its mother in the years to come. A recent deportee faced the excruciating problem of her child not wanting to go to live in Africa when she herself was released and deported. The grief of most of these women is too terrible to describe, the damage caused out of all proportion to the crime, and their cries of pain reverberate throughout the prisons. Yet few can be returned home to serve sentences there, either because of the absence of reciprocal arrangements or because their own countries often do not recognise the criminality of what they have done. Some countries, such as Nigeria, are now introducing laws to charge them on their return with exporting the same drugs, so that they face a double punishment.

The number of couriers being imprisoned now represents one fifth of the female prison population. These women are often ruthlessly exploited by drug barons, but when they are caught they are too afraid to name names because they know that the consequences could be terrible for their families back home. Statistics relating only to Jamaican women show that as a result of their imprisonment over a thousand children are kept apart from their mothers. Since Jamaica has no social welfare system, children are left to fend for themselves and are vulnerable to abuse, rape and recruitment into crime. On the rare occasions when Mr Big is caught he faces a sentence of 15 to 20 years, whilst the tariff for others in the chain moves down from that. The Esmée Fairbairn Report suggests a fairer sentencing policy to reflect the low-level role of these women but also recommends that the UK government assist Jamaica to develop its community-based correctional services, with a view to women being able to serve non-custodial sentences at home after being deported.

Until our sentencing policy is revised and real distinctions between defendants are made based on the circumstances which drove them to offend, we are denying justice to these women. But when judges try to use their discretion to take account of personal circumstances, they are criticised by the press or politicians for leniency. Some women are ruthless exploiters of drug dependency, but many are themselves the exploited. A test case is currently being mounted by Hibiscus, the small charity which works with the women imprisoned as couriers, to change the Aramah guidelines. The Director, Olga Heaven, is an extraordinary woman whose long commitment to these women is inspirational.

Those who go through the criminal justice system rarely have much voice, but immigrants are one of the most silent groups. There are few votes in prisoners, and none in foreign men and women charged with crime. They are the most vulnerable of all the adults who appear in our courts.

This takes us to a sensitive issue in the courts: the potential racial imbalance of juries in cases with a racial component. In London it would be rare to have a jury that was not multi-racial. However, even in the metropolis it can happen that a jury is overwhelmingly white and if the accused is black it may create the feeling that white justice is being delivered on black people. The removal of the right of the defence to challenge jurors without cause has happened by salami-slicing the entitlements of those who stand accused. When I first came to the Bar it was possible to challenge up to seven jurors on behalf of each individual client. This right was reduced under a Labour administration to three challenges per defendant, and was finally removed altogether in 1988 because it was claimed that anyone who carried the *Daily Telegraph* or who looked as though he or she had half a brain was being dismissed by manipulative defence lawyers.

There was no doubt that efforts were made to second-guess the type of juror from all sorts of aspects of their appearance, a lot of the time to little avail. (I myself, for example, had a sneaking aversion to men who had badges on brass-buttoned blazers and women who looked like my old headmistress.) But there were occasions when the challenge had a valid and important use. In cases involving aspects of child-rearing, such as cases of baby-battering, it is helpful to have people who have not forgotten the demands of a newborn. Equally, age can be important in cases involving youths, where their lifestyles may be incomprehensible to jurors of an exclusively older generation. However, it is particularly worrying that in cases of a racial nature we can have all-white juries trying black defendants.

After the abolition of the defence right to challenge, it was thought that at least the judge had a residual right to affect the racial make-up of the jury in the interests of justice. However, Lord Justice Lane scuppered that in the case of Ford in 1989 by ruling that this was not an appropriate use of the judge's power, and that 'fairness' was achieved by random selection. A mechanism to secure a racially balanced jury has to be available if a trial is to be fair and it may be that appropriate test cases using the Human Rights Act should be mounted.

Some positive developments are taking place. Judges are consciously endeavouring to remove the spectre of cultural indifference from the courts. It is unheard of now for courts to insist, as they did until recently, that Rastafarians remove their hats, which their religion requires them to wear to cover their dread-locks, or for generalised statements about racial groups to be made. But before reaching the position where racism is completely ousted there has to be recognition that people do not start equal – that the old British playing field is not level. The baggage which comes with the defendant or complainant to the courtroom must be thrown into the scales. All the experiences of black people at the hands of the law have been absorbed into the collective consciousness of their communities: the black taxi-driver badly beaten for no reason by off-duty policemen; the middle-aged woman who suffered a dislocated shoulder when her £20 note was automatically suspect and she was wrongfully arrested with force by a detective; the young man whose head was stamped on in a police station; the unprotected Asian families burned out of their homes.

When the subject of racial and sexual awareness training was first raised in the legal profession it used to be greeted with sneers but judges now speak of the benefits of learning about cultural difference and recognise that judicial training has played an important role in securing confidence in the system. But the learning does not run deep enough. Until there is a clear appreciation of racism and the social factors which bring black people before the courts, as well as an understanding of the subtle dynamics which work in the courts to discriminate against them, those from minority ethnic communities will continue to be amongst the sections of the community least well served by the law.

8

Man – Slaughter

The idea of woman as a killer challenges popular beliefs about femininity. Women kill infrequently but the rarity of the occurrence often fuels the repugnance. There is still a shock value in women, the begetters of life, taking a life.

Murder is almost exclusively committed by men. Analysis of the crime figures shows that children are more likely to be killed by men and women are more likely to be killed by men than by other women. A woman is eight times more likely to be killed by a husband or male friend than by a stranger. Men, by contrast, are more likely to be killed by a stranger. (HMSO, 1998: 70). In 1997, just over half of male victims of murder (54%) and nearly four-fifths of female ones (79%) knew the suspect before the offence took place. While only 8% of men were killed by former partners or lovers, the figure was considerably higher for women (47%).

Women keep their killing within the family: usually they kill their children, mainly babies (40–45%), and about 35% kill their partner. All the same stereotypes blight the justice system, whether the women are in the dock or in the witness box or no longer live to tell the tale. They have to come across as appropriate victims to gain the court's sympathy.

For the defence of provocation to succeed in reducing murder to manslaughter, the victim's words or conduct have to render the defendant 'so subject to passion as to make him for the moment not master of his mind'. Inevitably the conduct of the deceased is called into question because the conduct is what is supposed to have triggered the killing. In so many cases the accused's account stands on its own, unchallenged because there is no admissible evidence and no victim to counter it.

There are a million variations of how the defence has been used by people who have killed, and it would be facile and untrue to suggest that only dead women are vilified in this way. However, there is a hidden agenda for women that makes the possibilities for attack even greater.

The trial in 1955 of Ruth Ellis, the last woman to be hanged in Britain, was over in one and a half days, a feat which would no doubt win the acclaim of many judges today, who bemoan the long duration of trials. In some cases the issues are so narrow that they can proceed at quite a lick, but these are rare. A murder trial, which involves exploring the psychological state of a defendant against a complicated background of emotion, violence, insecurity and abandonment, inevitably takes a good deal of time and is built upon a very full knowledge of the person represented.

In the years since Ruth Ellis stood trial psychiatry has come to play a much greater role in murder trials, and we as lawyers have become better versed in its language. There is also, as we have seen earlier, a growing understanding of domestic violence and the reasons why it is endured.

Ruth Ellis's case would have been conducted differently today and would very likely have led to her acquittal of murder. This is largely because of the changes in the law in 1957, which introduced a number of fresh concepts to homicide trials. Parliament established two statutory defences to murder, reducing the offence to manslaughter (a) where the accused was suffering from a mental disorder which diminished his or her criminal responsibility, or (b) where the killing was a response to provocation.

Provocation was available as a defence prior to the enactment, but because of concern that vengeful behaviour would escape just punishment, which for murder meant the death penalty at that time, it was narrowly interpreted in the case law. Provocation was interpreted for juries by the judges as conduct immediately preceding the killing. The archetypal case was that of the betrayed husband finding his faithless wife and her lover *in flagrante* and killing one or the other, or both. Words, for example, could not amount to provocation prior to the 1957 Homicide Act.

As for diminished responsibility, until the Act, the only debate about mental states was whether a defendant was sane or insane according to the 'M'Naghten rules'. There it had to be clearly proved that at the time of committing the alleged offence the party accused was labouring under such a defect of reason or disease of the mind that he did not know the nature and quality of the act he was doing, or that he did not know it was wrong. The defendant had to be so demented that he would think he was squeezing an orange when he was throttling his victim. The test derived from the case of a Scotsman who felt he was being persecuted by the Conservatives because he refused to vote for them; in delusion he murdered a Tory agent. (I used to wonder whether anyone who refused to vote Conservative in those days was readily considered mad by members of the judiciary.) By the 1950s the test had become seriously discredited as a method of determining the mental state of an accused. The verdict of not guilty to murder by reason of diminished responsibility, reducing an unlawful killing to manslaughter, does not require that someone is certifiably insane, just that he or she has a definable degree of mental disorder. The defence can include a difficulty in controlling one's actions, provided this arises from an abnormality of mind.

Even today, the issue of whether someone suffers from an abnormality of mind which diminished their responsibility for a killing is one which taxes juries. It used to be said that juries were reluctant to convict people of murder when they faced the death penalty, but even without the ultimate sanction there seems to be an unwillingness in jurors to declare someone guilty of wilful murder when they were in the grip of overwhelming emotional turmoil at the time. Equally, juries are reluctant to let a person who takes a life escape all sanction, which is why self-defence is rarely successful in murder. The moral conviction that the taking of a life cannot go unmarked is present in the court and there needs to be an overwhelming sense of justification – that one's own life was under immediate threat – before a jury will allow an accused to walk free with no conviction whatsoever. However, the willingness to accept manslaughter as the appropriate plea often depends on the sympathies evoked by the defendant. In mercy killings, where family members bring to an end the misery or pain of a terminally ill relative, judges and juries alike are usually prepared to stretch the definition of diminished responsibility.

There seems little doubt that the outcome of Ruth Ellis's trial was affected by a moral evaluation of her way of life – as a sexually active divorcee, the mother of an illegitimate child, and a club hostess. The tabloid press would still have a field day at her expense, but today's jury, furnished with as much information as has subsequently come to light, might take a more generous view.

Ruth Ellis's own leading counsel, Mr Melford Stevenson, later became a High Court judge and the scourge of the Old Bailey. When I started practising, in 1972, he had just conducted the trial of the students who had taken part in the Cambridge riot case, following a demonstration against the Greek colonels, and sentenced them all to imprisonment and Borstal. He was held in very low esteem by many of my generation as a judge of the old school, dogmatic and misogynist. Many senior members of the legal profession speak of his charm off the Bench, but that is hardly the essential test of a judge's ability.

My one particular memory of Sir Melford, as he had then become, dates from the time when I was junior counsel acting for Myra Hindley when she was charged with conspiring to escape from prison in 1974. She was indicted with a young woman prison warden who became emotionally involved with her at Holloway. Both pleaded guilty at the Old Bailey to this ludicrous conspiracy based on grandiose plans to flee together to South America, where they would work as missionaries. The woman had been a nun and had never lived outside the confines of rigid female institutions. Any careful examination of the evidence showed that the plot was fundamentally flawed, that it was essentially the fantasy of two people whose relationship was blighted from the start. For a wardress to become a prisoner carries a special burden of resentment from both staff and prisoners, but Sir Melford passed a sentence of six years.

When Melford Stevenson represented Ruth Ellis he was relatively inexperienced in the criminal courts: he was mainly a divorce practitioner, and had done few major criminal trials. He had none of the instinctive feel which the good jury advocate needs to overcome the unspoken prejudices that lie beneath the surface in any criminal case. Nor did he have the empathy which might have helped Ruth Ellis tell her story in a more compelling way. So many witnesses, particularly a woman who has gone through an emotional battering, disengage from events and give their evidence in a cool, remote way. Her own counsel has to break through that, or at least enable her to explain that detachment; otherwise a jury is left unpersuaded of the defence. At the time, the view was openly expressed that either of his two junior counsel, Peter Rawlinson or Sebag Shaw, would have had more appeal to a jury. Just reading the trial accounts, it was clearly a case which any criminal advocate would have longed to get their hands on.

Mr Christmas Humphreys, who must be the only Buddhist to sit on the Bench, opened the case for the Crown on 21 June 1955. Ruth Ellis stood alone in the dock charged with the murder of David Blakely. Humphreys laid emphasis on the fact that Mrs Ellis was conducting simultaneous love affairs with two men: with David Blakely, whom she killed, and with Desmond Cussen. What was never explored was the true nature of her relationship with Cussen, whom she leaned on for emotional support but never considered seriously as a lover: it later transpired that their sexual liaison lasted only a matter of weeks, in June 1954. Mr Humphreys told the jury that Blakely was trying to break off the association and that Ellis was angry about this, even though she had another lover at the time. He described how she took a gun, found David, and shot him dead by emptying the revolver at him, four bullets going into his body, one hitting a bystander in the thumb and the sixth disappearing completely. After the shooting outside a public house in South Hill Park, Hampstead, Ellis was questioned by a police officer who told her that he had seen the body of David Blakely and understood she knew something about it. Her reply was, 'I am guilty, I am rather confused.' She then made a written statement to the police describing how, after putting her child to bed, she had picked up a revolver that had been given to her by a man as security for a loan three years ago, and had put it in her handbag. She had gone out, she said, with the intention of finding Blakely and shooting him.

Christmas Humphreys called only a few witnesses to provide evidence in support of this stark history of the relationship between Ruth Ellis and David Blakely and the events surrounding the killing. After each person completed their testimony, Melford Stevenson rose briefly to his feet to announce that he had no questions. The case for the Crown was over within the morning.

In his opening speech to the jury, Melford Stevenson made great play of the fact that the defence did not challenge any part of the prosecution's version of what had taken place:

It can't happen often in this court that in a case of this importance, fraught with such deep significance for the accused, the whole of the prosecution's story passes without any challenge from those concerned to advance the defence. There is no question here that this woman shot this man. We are not seeking to raise any further doubt in your mind about that. She is charged with murder and one of the ingredients in that offence is what lawyers call malice. The law of England provides that if a woman had been subject to such emotional disturbance as to unseat her judgement, then it is up to you to say that the offence of which she is guilty is not murder but manslaughter.

Melford Stevenson went on to express his opinion of the victim: invidious as he found it to speak ill of the dead, the story could leave no doubt in the minds of the jury that Blakely had been a most unpleasant person:

The fact stands out like a beacon that this young man became an absolute necessity to this young woman. However brutally he behaved and however much he spent of her money on various entertainments of his own and however much he consorted with other people he ultimately came back to her and always she forgave him. She found herself in an emotional prison guarded by this young man from which there seemed to be no escape. It was in these circumstances, driven to a frenzy, which for the time being unseated her understanding, that she committed the crime of which you have heard so many details.

The jury was informed that the defence would call an eminent psychiatrist who would tell them that 'the effect of jealousy upon the feminine mind, upon all feminine minds, can so work as to unseat the reason and can operate to a degree in which in a male mind it is quite incapable of operating'. The two feminine minds on the jury must have loved this description of their frailty.

The defence tactic of keeping clear of the prosecution case may well have been based on the idea that the less said about Ruth Ellis's lifestyle the better, and that what was said should come from her, carefully circumscribed by her own counsel. But juries have a sixth sense when they are not hearing the full story, and their conjectures about what they are not hearing can sometimes be more damaging than the real thing. Sometimes it is better to reveal the defence hand completely. It is as much in those subtle displays of judgement as in fine advocacy that you find great lawyering.

The defence must have realised that Ruth Ellis could appear rather hard-faced because of the way she described the events. Even when there is no challenge to the evidence of prosecution witnesses, they can be the source of crucial material which sheds light on a case and provides corroboration for the defence. Melford Stevenson was unlikely to secure anything very useful from the personal friends of Blakely, who gave evidence for the prosecution. But amongst the witnesses for the Crown was some-one who knew intimately the suffering experienced by Ruth Ellis. Desmond Cussen, her 'alternative lover', was the only real friend Ruth Ellis had, and his love for her was unquestioned. He undoubtedly hoped that in time she would get Blakely out of her system and look upon him with more favour. Cussen knew that Blakely was happy to exploit Ruth Ellis sexually and financially.

Unlike Ruth, a daughter of the lower classes, David Blakely came from a well-to-do family. His father was a doctor of sufficient means to provide his son with a small private income. At 25, Blakely had no steady job but hung around the edges of the motor-racing world, fancying himself as a driver and as the creator of a prototype car. He seems to have been intoxicated with the fast life as well as with hard liquor. When he first met Ruth, who was managing hostess of a run-down nightclub in Belgravia, he was engaged to a 'suitable' young woman from his own background.

No doubt Ruth provided an earthy sexual diversion, but the relationship developed into a compulsive affair in which she was regularly beaten and humiliated. She obviously had hopes that this was the relationship which would provide her with social accept-ability and a real partner, a delusion which was somehow never dispelled even when Blakely had affairs with other women, refused to involve her in certain parts of his life and made it clear to her that she was despised by some of his own circle.

Ruth Ellis gave evidence on her own behalf. Whenever a defendant walks from the dock to the witness box to give their own account there is always a strong sense of anticipation; you can almost feel it, especially in a murder trial. For the defending counsel this is the moment to turn the case round and view it from a different perspective. Taking a defendant through the evidence may seem like a straightforward process to the onlooker, but there is a special skill involved in choreographing a witness's account so that, while coherent, it also gives the jury a sense of the misery and turmoil that can lead to behaviour that would normally never even be contemplated. The counsel's task is to enable the client to communicate their sense of desperation, or whatever other aspects of their emotional state figured in the offence. It should be like watching a *pas de deux*, and the parties must be in step. Defendants themselves often have very little insight into what is needed. They don't say, 'I was suffering from depression,' or, 'I was provoked beyond endurance.' They have to be drawn out so that they describe exactly how they were feeling at the time, the things that were running through their heads, their emotional state in the weeks and days before the crime was committed. Expressing such emotion in a court of law, particularly Court 1 at the Old Bailey, is a daunting prospect and is usually only possible if the person on trial has established a degree of trust and understanding with their counsel.

Any reading of Ruth Ellis's testimony makes it clear that Melford Stevenson had little point of contact with the woman he was representing. At best she was an enigma to him; more likely he saw her as a woman of little virtue. The defence lawyer's theory of the case is inevitably informed by their own attitudes.

She responded to his questions methodically and briefly:

expansion was rarely sought. Even when she was dealing with the violence and rejection which would form the basis of any defence of provocation, weak answers to Stevenson's own questions were left unpursued. She was never asked to explain when she said Blakely 'only hit me with his fists and hands', even though she was clearly subjected to regular beating causing bruising, black eyes and treatment at the Middlesex Hospital, and even though Cussen could have confirmed this. Like many battered women before and since, her reduction of his violence was probably a coping mechanism, and it also displayed the complicated emotions that go with loving someone who treats you like a dog. Her feelings when Blakely finally dumped her, aided and abetted by his circle of friends, were never fully explored, nor was there any probing of the intensity of emotion that she must have experienced during her long vigil outside the building in which she could hear him laughing and socialising. Every sense of herself as an outsider, beyond the pale of his social class, must have been reinforced, and her head must have been buzzing with visions of Blakely with another woman. None of this reached across the courtroom to the jury. Her irrationality was explained as jealousy, the fury of the woman scorned, rather than as the response of someone who had been systematically abused, exploited and humiliated.

Counsel for the prosecution asked only one question in cross-examination: 'When you fired that revolver at close range into the body of David Blakely, what did you intend to do?'

It was not even a leading question. Ruth Ellis replied: 'It is obvious. When I shot him I intended to kill him.'

I can almost hear the silence in the courtroom when she gave that answer, and the gloom it must have invoked in her lawyers. Yet no attempt was made to re-coup in re-examination. No doubt she did intend to kill him at that moment, but the real issue was whether she had been provoked beyond endurance, whether her action was that of someone out of control, a product of desperation in intolerable circumstances. When he came out of the public house, did he see her and ignore her, and did that final act of rejection cause her to snap? It was a case which had to engage the sympathies of the judge and jury in order to surmount the obstacles presented by the law as it then stood.

Where her lawyers had their hardest task was in dealing with Ruth Ellis's decision to take a gun with her when she went to the address in Hampstead where she suspected her lover would be. From such a deliberate action the jury would reasonably assume, in the first instance, that this was a premeditated act of revenge, and that the hours of waiting could have provided a cooling-off time. The immediacy or 'heat of the moment' principle is an important aspect of provocation, and it was bound to fail in this case unless Ruth Ellis had some explanation of how her intentions varied at different times, and how the unexpected sight of him led to a sudden temporary loss of self-control. The questions put to her did not seem designed to elicit such an account, if one existed or had ever been explored with Ruth Ellis in the preparation of her case.

What I read between the lines is a half-hearted attempt to introduce a defence of *crime passionnel* into the English law that was doomed from the start; certainly it gained no credence from the psychiatrist who was called. His proposition was that a woman was more prone to hysterical reaction than a man in the case of infidelity, and that in such circumstances she was likely to lose her critical faculties and try to solve the problem on a more primitive level. Most of the male-dominated court probably agreed with this, but the implications of introducing it into our jurisprudence probably struck terror into the heart of every philandering husband.

The evidence was completed and the rest of the day was spent (in the absence of the jury) presenting the legal arguments to Mr Justice Havers, father of the recent Lord Chancellor. The judge seemed anxious for Melford Stevenson to convince him that he understood the law in relation to provocation, and his questions indicated that he had taken the view that Blakely's behaviour fell short: 'What do you say is the evidence of conduct on the part of this deceased man of a nature which has hitherto been considered by the court to amount to provocation?'

There were then muddled exchanges about the effect of infidelity, jealousy and 'new law'. Finally the judge gave Melford Stevenson the opportunity to clarify the defence position. 'Does your proposition come to this?' he asked. 'If a man associates with a woman and he then leaves her suddenly and does not communicate with her and she is a jealous woman, emotionally disturbed, and goes out and shoots him, that is sufficient ground for the jury to reduce the crime of murder to manslaughter?' No mention whatsoever was made of Blakely's violence, nor of his psychological abuse. Apparently Melford Stevenson was unable to answer Mr Justice Havers's question.

The following morning the trial judge addressed the court before the jury returned. He ruled that there was not sufficient material to support a verdict of manslaughter on the grounds of provocation and that as a matter of law he would so direct the jury. The death sentence was more or less passed at this point. Melford Stevenson made no comment, and indicated that in the circumstances he accepted that he could not make a closing speech to the jury. The judge then summed up, telling the jury that it was not possible to bring in a verdict of manslaughter. The jury retired for 14 minutes before returning with their verdict of guilty. The ritual of the black cap and the grisly formula that she would be taken to a place where she would be hanged by the neck was pronounced. Ruth Ellis was led away.

Despite the uproar at a woman going to the gallows, and many efforts to obtain a reprieve, the execution took place three weeks after the trial, with the traditional crowd gathered outside the prison awaiting the publication of the death notice on the gate.

Given the state of the law of homicide at the time, the same result might well have followed whoever the judge and counsel. What ensued, however, was a public debate over whether a distinction should be made between a killing of this kind and a cold-blooded murder. The important postscripts to the Ellis case are that it lent fuel to the powerful campaign to abolish the death penalty, affected the development of a psychiatric defence to murder which fell short of insanity, and helped to codify the provocation law. That these adjustments to the law can prove inadequate in dealing with the experience of women is powerfully shown by more recent cases.

Self-defence is a complete defence to murder and means a defendant walks free from the court if it succeeds. It is permissible in law for someone to act in self-defence if placed in immediate peril and if some instant reaction is necessary to avert the danger. If the attack is over, or is not imminent, then the employment of force may be seen as revenge, or punishment, or the settling of an old score. The force must also be reasonable. The use of a knife, a heavy weight or a gun is often a crucial handicap for a woman, since the use of a weapon may be regarded as involving excessive force and the act of securing it can allow for the argument that her behaviour was calculated or not in immediate response to an attack. Yet many women are incapable of defending themselves without having a weapon to hand.

When men determined what is acceptable conduct in response to attack and what might constitute self-defence, they were thinking of other men, of similar stature and strength, locked in even combat, where the introduction of a weapon would be bad form, stacking the odds on one side. The law takes insufficient account of the disadvantages women feel in the face of male strength. It is illustrative that the most common murder weapon used by wives is the knife, and the scene of the crime is most often the kitchen, while men kill their wives with their bare hands in the bedroom.

The legal perception of self-defence is the meeting of force with roughly equal force; it is based on what seems fair in the eyes of men. The test is objective, but an element of subjectivity has been introduced to account for the race, sex, or any special characteristics of the person in the dock. This is the narrow opening into which arguments about the history of domestic violence could be crammed, but women are still hamstrung by the spectre of the vengeful wife. It is in the ancient legal authority of Blackstone's *Commentaries* that we find the clear statement that revenge is no defence. The classic pronouncement in modern times, which is used daily to guide us in the courts, comes from Lord Morris of Borth-y-Gest, and in the ordinary case it is a perfect statement of the present law:

'It is both good law and good sense that a man who is attacked may defend himself. It is both good law and common sense that he may do, and may only do, what is reasonably necessary. But everything will depend upon the particular facts and circumstances. Of these a jury can decide. It may in some cases be only sensible and clearly possible to take some simple avoiding action. Some attacks may be serious and dangerous. Others may not be.

If there is some relatively minor attack, it would not be common sense to permit some act of retaliation which was wholly out of proportion to the necessities of the situation. If an attack is so serious that it puts someone in immediate peril, then immediate defensive action may be necessary. If the moment is one of crisis for someone in immediate danger, he may have to avert the danger by some instant reaction. If the attack is over and no sort of peril remains, then the employment of force may be by way of revenge or punishment or by way of paying off an old score or may be pure aggression. There may be no longer any link with a necessity of defence.

The problem with that statement is that battered women feel incapable of leaving, incapable of taking the commonsensical steps which may be possible between equally matched men. They are no match for their husbands, not just pound for pound in the weighing scales but because of their feelings of powerlessness, in the weakness of their low self-esteem. Seeing one event of violence in terms of immediate peril or as a moment of crisis which passes is contextual distortion: when the abuse is constant it is inappropriate to pull out one single fragment of that history. This is a perfect example of the law, which by its letter seems fair but in application is anything but. Treating as equal those who are unequal only creates further inequality. Battered women should not be expected to play by the Marquis of Queensberry rules, and it should be recognised that the peril has not passed for a woman and her children when a wife-beater is merely resting before the next round.

Provocation is a defence to murder and only to murder. In any other case, such as assault, it can only provide mitigation. If a defence of provocation is successful in a murder trial and reduces the charge to one of manslaughter, the court still has to pass an appropriate sentence. Women invoke self-defence or provocation defences infrequently, and the reason is that the legal standards were constructed from a male perspective and with men in mind, and women have a problem fulfilling the criteria. The question for the jury in a case where provocation has been raised is whether a reasonable man might have suffered temporary and sudden loss of self-control so that he was no longer 'master of his own mind' in circumstances similar to those described in the evidence. The issue is one of opinion, not law, but the judge has considerable power in the way in which he presents provocation to the jury.

Little account used to be taken of the cultural differences between men and women and the way that our socialisation affects our responses. Women are much less likely to respond to provocation immediately, for obvious physical and psychological reasons, and therefore self-defence and provocation are less available to them. But the legal standards have been built upon ideas of instant ignition and a hotheaded rush to action. The spark has to be immediate, an assault which requires self-protection or a blow, a curse, an insult that goes to the core of a man's being. Judges have tried to create a parallel analogy, the trigger to violent reaction being terrible insults against a woman's chastity or her way of life, both of which are male ideas of what might make a woman run amok.

Any study of women who kill their husbands (a crime which in former times was indicted as treason) exposes a history of cumulative violence. Most women who kill a spouse or partner have suffered long-term abuse; yet a significant number would fail the test for provocation. Fortunately for most of the women – or unfortunately, from another perspective – the toll of violence usually means they are able to invoke a defence of diminished responsibility, suffering as they almost invariably are from depressive illness or post-traumatic stress disorder as a result of the abuse. By and large this reliance on their psychiatric state takes the sting out of the weakness of the other defences, because the women are then sentenced with appropriate compassion, but there will always be women who slip through that net. There is also the principled concern that women should not so readily be pushed towards a pathological explanation for their behaviour, an argument which seldom troubles women looking at prison bars, who understandably value their liberty and the companionship of their children above all else.

It is well established that retaliation and revenge have no place in our legal code, and if a woman is seen to bide her time and to strike when her attacker's defences are low, she is seen as playing dirty and loses the protection of the law, unless she can invoke mental disturbance. It matters not that she may have been subjected to years of beating and may feel that no other avenue is open to her. If she makes a deliberate decision to kill she is guilty of murder, even if at the time she is no longer mistress of her own mind. Temperature seems to be all important. If the crime is to be reduced to manslaughter the act has to be in the 'heat of the moment' with no time to 'cool off'.

The immediacy principle makes no sense when the provocation takes the form of long-term abuse. When a person lives with persistent violence and alcoholism she often becomes overwhelmed. Her whole life is out of control. She has not been thinking rationally for some time, and her feelings often will not manifest themselves as 'snapping', in the form of the crazed outburst, but may seem more controlled: a snapping in slow motion, the final surrender of frayed elastic.

The case of Sara Thornton came to symbolise all that was wrong with the system and set in train some important shifts in the judicial approach to provocation. Sara Thornton stood trial in February 1990 charged with murdering her husband, Malcolm, having attacked him with a knife as he lay drunk on a couch. The Crown accepted that her husband was deeply alcoholic and violent towards her but maintained that she had attacked him in a calculated way, having deliberately gone into the kitchen and sharpened the knife. Because she had had periods of mental breakdown in the past and because of the delay between her husband's last threat and her strike, Sara's trial lawyers saw this as a case of diminished responsibility, but her plea to that effect was not accepted by the Crown; and she was convicted.

The psychiatric evidence of the defence was that Sara Thornton was in a state technically described as a 'fugue' at the time she killed her husband. This term would seem to describe an interval where the person is not in control. In answer to questions by the prosecutor the psychiatrist agreed that this was not a treatable condition. What Sara Thornton was undoubtedly suffering from was the cumulative effect of domestic violence and the psychological demands of dealing with a chronically alcoholic partner. She had only been married to Malcolm Thornton for ten months, but those months had taken their toll. She was, in the language of provocation, no longer mistress of her own mind at the time of the killing, hence the 'fugue' state, but she was not fulfilling the definition of diminished responsibility: an abnormality of mind. She was functioning in conformance with the classical provocation scenario, except that there was no word or deed triggering her action. It was an accumulation of abuse, evoked as her husband lay on the couch, which drove her to violence.

Unlike English law, which had viewed the elements of suddenness restrictively, Australian law would have had no problem with the delay which preceded Sara's action. Judges there recognise the concept of cumulative provocation, acknowledging that a series of provocative incidents, which may in themselves be trivial, can constitute serious provocation if viewed cumulatively. It is recognised that deliberate preparations for killing may be made while in the heat of passion and that such deliberations are distinguishable from cases of pre-planned killings.

The common law in Australia has developed in a way that is attuned to women's lives, and the judges' decisions have now been consolidated in legislation which specifically stipulates that the provocative conduct of the deceased is relevant, 'whether it occurred immediately before the act or omission causing death or at any previous time'. The statute states unequivocally that provocation is not negated as a matter of law where 'the act or omission causing death was not an act or omission done suddenly'.

However, counsel for the Crown in Sara Thornton's case maintained to the jury that an acquittal would provide Sara Thornton, and I suppose any like-minded women, with 'a licence to kill'.

At her appeal in July 1991, Sara's new counsel, Lord Gifford, argued that 'the slow burning emotion of a woman driven to the end of her tether . . . may be a loss of self-control in just the same way as a sudden rage'. This argument was not accepted in Sara's case; her appeal failed because the court remained influenced by the fact that Sara had equipped herself with a sharpened knife and had in the week before his death threatened to kill Malcolm Thornton. At a later appeal she was released, but on the grounds of diminished responsibility.

Other women have fallen foul of this same problem: their behaviour is seen as premeditated because, evidentially, delay before action is interpreted that way. However, in the context of the abuse, and because of the genuine belief in the omnipotence of the abuser, the killing seems to the woman like a rational and coherent response.

On 9 May 1989 Deepak Ahluwalia had yet again beaten his wife and threatened her with a hot iron. There was a well-documented history of domestic violence. He had beaten her, tried to strangle her, threatened her with knives, pushed her downstairs, sexually abused her and raped her. The attacks often took place in the presence of their children, who cowered in fear of him. His wife, Kiranjit Ahluwalia, had obtained court injunctions against him twice but had failed to get them enforced after threats from his family. He was constantly threatening to kill her and she lived in terror of him. Like so many battered wives, she could sense his mood swings and could read the signals which meant the onset of an attack, but she usually felt powerless. That night she could take no more and, when he fell asleep on the bed, she poured petrol over his feet and set it alight.

Deepak's death led to a charge of murder against his wife, who was not the conventional broken victim but a woman who had accepted long-term violence because of cultural constraints:

> This is the essence of my culture, society and religion, where a woman is a toy, a plaything. She can be stuck together at will, broken at will. Everybody did what they wanted with me, no one ever bothered to find out what kind of life I was leading after I married – one of physical and mental torture.
>
> The culture into which I was born and where I grew up sees the woman as the honour of the house . . . In order to uphold this false 'honour' and glory she is taught to endure many kinds of oppression and pain in silence. Religion also teaches her that her husband is her god and fulfilling his every desire is her religious duty. For ten years I tried wholeheartedly to fulfil the duties endorsed by religion. For ten years I lived a life of beatings and degradation and no one noticed; now the law has decreed that I

should serve a sentence for life. Today I have come out of my husband's jail and entered the jail of the law.

For Kiranjit Ahluwalia, diminished responsibility was not argued as there were varied opinions on the nature of her depression after suffering the effects of years of abuse. She explained her failure to leave or disown her husband in the context of her culture and religion, where community expectations mean enduring domestic violence in silence because of the shame which disclosure will bring upon the family.

The problem for Kiranjit's lawyers was that she had waited for him to fall asleep, and it was this aspect of the evidence that was emphasised by Mr Justice Leonard. Judith did the same before cutting off the head of Holofernes. M. J. Willoughby, an American academic lawyer, expressed the view in her work on battered women who kill their sleeping partners that 'society gains nothing, except perhaps the additional risk that the battered woman will herself be killed, because she must wait until her abusive husband instigates another battering episode before she can justifiably act'.

The requirement that a battered wife must wait until assault is under way before her apprehensions can be validated in law is an acceptance of murder by instalment. If a person being held hostage killed a terrorist captor, the fact that he was sleeping would be of no consequence. The prison of the violent marriage is hard to contemplate for those on the outside, and the question 'Why didn't she leave?' is based on incomprehension.

In 1984, after years of torture, Pauline Wyatt shot her husband as he slept. In her interview with the police she articulated in a way that defeats most women the emotions which ran through her head at the point of killing him:

I was frightened to death of him, but I couldn't get away . . . I couldn't see any way out . . . My mind snapped and I just got the shotgun. I couldn't take any more . . . The end of the gun was very close to him . . . I thought of my kids then fired it . . .
    He drove me to it by the life he was giving me . . . it was living hell.

She was acquitted of murder by a jury and convicted of manslaughter. In his summing-up the judge made very little of the absence of a word or action operating as the immediate trigger for loss of control. Much depends on the attitude of the judge and indeed the prosecutor. In some cases, because of the background, the prosecution and the judge accept a plea to manslaughter even where there has been some premeditation, as in the Maw sisters' case, where their violent father was lying unconscious on the mattress upstairs when agreement was reached that he must be killed (Court of Appeal, December 1980). Similarly, a plea to manslaughter on the grounds of provocation was accepted by the court in *R* v. *Ratcliffe,* May 1980, where the accused borrowed a knife from her neighbour, intending to kill her husband, and did so six days later.

It is wrong to characterise the courts as unsympathetic to the plight of women in violent relationships. In the majority of cases, women who break under the pressure of domestic violence are treated with mercy. However, the vocabulary of the discourse is limited, and the criteria are inflexible, because of a fear that juries will apply provocation too freely.

In the same week that Sara Thornton's appeal failed, a trial judge accepted Joseph McGrail's plea to manslaughter of his wife on the grounds of provocation and passed a suspended sentence. Mr McGrail had lived with Marion Kennedy for more than 20 years. They had two sons, both handicapped and both in care. Ten years previously Marion began to drink and eventually became addicted to sleeping pills. When she had been drinking she used to insult her husband and swear at him. She was a scold, a nag.

One day in February 1991, when Joseph returned from work to find her drunk again, he could stand no more. He kicked her hard enough to cause her to die of internal bleeding. The judge commented that living with Marion 'would have tried the patience of a saint'.

In March 1992 Rajinder Bisla, having strangled his 'nagging' wife in front of his three children, was also given a suspended sentence. No doubt, like Joseph McGrail, he snapped, and we should welcome the humanity which was shown to him. Justice for women does not have to be secured by denying it to men.

However, the willingness to recognise the male experience is a reflection of the male nature of our courts. Nagging is seen as the female equivalent to violence. Yet men married to intolerable women usually have many more alternatives available to them and find it easier to leave.

In July 1992 Kiranjit's case, mentioned above, came before the Court of Appeal. Attempts were made by my colleague in chambers, Geoffrey Robertson QC, to contextualise his client's behaviour against the background of prolonged violence. He tried to press the argument that immediacy has been an evidential development and that no such requirement exists in law. On 31 July the court quashed Kiranjit's conviction. The three judges, headed by the Lord Chief Justice, Lord Taylor, ordered a retrial, on the grounds that new medical evidence, which might have proved a defence of diminished responsibility, had not been brought forward, and should be tested in court. Lord Taylor went to great lengths in his judgment to say that any alteration in the existing legal definition of 'provocation' as 'temporary and sudden loss of control', must be a matter for Parliament, not for the courts, since it involved changing 'a particular principle of law [which] has been confirmed so many times and applied so generally over such a long period'.

However, since the early 1990s the courts have in fact shifted the parameters of provocation in response to the urgings of women seeking justice. Cases like that of Emma Humphreys in 1995, and others, educated the judiciary and the public about the law's shortcomings. As a result the jury is now directed to put themselves in the shoes of the woman on trial and to consider the context of events. There is recognition that the courts must acknowledge cumulative provocation, where after a history of abuse the final act which tips a woman over the edge may not seem very grave but may be the last straw. The question of the time-frame has also widened so that judges make it clear to a jury that 'immediate provocation' should not be interpreted literally. While clearly a woman would not be entitled to go days later to kill her abusive partner, a delay before acting does not preclude the defence. What is not allowed are acts born of revenge rather than anger or despair.

'Of course, we all know there is no such thing as the reasonable woman,' was the law lecturer's joke, but that sort of puerility is well behind us now. That prominent actor in the dramatis personae of the courtroom, 'the reasonable man', seems to be taking his final bow. His long journey on the Clapham omnibus is coming to an end.

The courts became aware that a totally objective test did not operate fairly because once the law, for example, stipulated that words could be sufficient provocation, it was clear that some insults touched a rawer nerve with certain people than others. Insults about race, physical infirmity or some shameful incident in the past may make verbal abuse a more powerful weapon if they are true. A subjective component had to be introduced while at the same time keeping some consensus on what was acceptable in a civilised society. The defence could not be made available to the person with a fragile ego who sees insults in the glance of a passer-by.

'The reasonable man', in the words of Lord Diplock, was 'an ordinary person of either sex, not exceptionally excitable or pugnacious but possessed of such powers of self-control as everyone is entitled to expect that his fellow citizens will exercise in society as it is today'.

However, in the Washington State Supreme Court decision of Wanrow it was held that the traditional instruction to the jury of drawing on the standard of defence acceptable to the 'reasonable man' did not adequately represent a woman's perspective, and consequently threatened to deny a woman equal protection under the law. Mrs Wanrow, whose daughter had in the past been molested by an intruder, shot an unarmed man who tried to enter her home. The court acknowledged that 'in our society women suffer from a conspicuous lack of access to training in and the means of developing those skills necessary to effectively repel a male assailant without resorting to the use of deadly weapons'.

In the United States, the judge's direction from then on has to give special emphasis to the woman's own perceptions of her situation, rather than providing a purely objective assessment of whether the steps she took in self-defence were reasonable.

Our own high-water mark came in the decision of *Regina* v. *Morgan Smith* (2000), where Lord Hoffman said that 'judges should not be required to describe the objective element with reference to a reasonable man. They may instead find it more helpful to explain in simple language the principles of the doctrine of provocation.' It is for the jury to take account of all the evidence relating to the accused and then to ask themselves whether her reaction to the provoking conduct was reasonable. The judges accepted that a line of cases, notably those of Kiranjit Ahluwalia and Emma Humphreys, had firmly established that depressive illness and the mental state of someone provoked into killing should be taken into account when applying the objective test of reasonableness. The judgment accepts that women can lose their self-control out of fear and depression as well as anger.

This shift has created great debate, with some jurists suggesting that the objective test has really been abandoned and complaints that the direction given to the jury in provocation is now so complex that only a judge in the House of Lords would understand it. Juries are in fact perfectly capable of dealing with difficult concepts but it would be helpful if these developments in the defence of provocation could be consolidated into statute form so that no judge is in any doubt as to his or her duty in directing a jury.

Some campaigners feel that it is unjust that a woman is convicted of manslaughter after killing a manifestly brutal partner and have argued for a new 'pre-emptive strike' self-defence. This would provide a woman with a complete defence if she kills her partner when he is asleep or drunk because she has become so convinced that he is going to kill her when he wakens. The very language replicates George Bush's justification for breaking international law and waging war on Iraq. His position was that waiting for Saddam Hussein to take definitive offensive steps towards the West was unnecessary so he was entitled to bomb Baghdad to blazes. But that argument was not persuasive to most of the world. Similarly most people would not be enthusiastic about a perfectly rational woman planning and then blowing out the brains of her sleeping husband, even if she was terrified of him. They may be content to see her culpability reduced to manslaughter but not to see the killing vindicated.

My main concern is always about the unforeseen consequences of such changes. Would we want any tinpot dictator in the world to invade his neighbouring country and claim pre-emptive strike self-defence? Would we want someone to have a full defence to murder if he killed a persistent child burglar, having carefully planned the execution? No government is going to create a gender-specific defence. Would the same campaigners want to see such a defence in the hands of a husband who says his wife threatened to kill him? Legal reform must always be undertaken while looking in your wing-mirrors; otherwise ghastly coaches are driven through your best intentions.

Often in cases where a woman is offered the opportunity of pleading guilty to manslaughter she could be pleading self-defence but feels that she cannot endure a contested trial, and prefers to accept the offer, in the expectation that with the prosecution on her side she will secure a favourable outcome. This happened in the case of Joan Calladine (reported in *Dispatches,* Channel 4, May 1990) who stabbed her former husband. Evidence showed that she had been subjected to 20 years of violence at his hands. She came home one night to find him slumped in a chair asleep. When he woke he started punching her in the face. She went to the kitchen and took hold of a knife. He followed her, continuing the beating, and she stabbed him. Many cases follow these lines, and the women take the course of least resistance in the proceedings which follow.

Over the years it has become clear to me that women in all gradations of case are much more prepared to settle for a plea to a lesser offence than to fight all the way. Who can blame them, when it avoids the horrors of a full trial, with the attendant scrutiny of their life and possibly a less favourable outcome? For similar reasons, women are less inclined to choose trial by jury, in cases where there is a choice, because the delay and terror of a trial is even more intimidating and disruptive of their lives than it is for men. Often they do not have the same will to take on the system.

There are also trials where the defendant is not so compliant and suffers the consequences.

Karen Tyler maintained from the outset to the police that she had killed her father with a kitchen knife in self-defence, and at no time was diminished responsibility countenanced. The Crown charged her with manslaughter, accepting that her violent, abusive father must have provoked her beyond endurance, but said that she was looking for some pretext to injure her father because of the way he had treated her and her mother. In the words of the prosecutor: 'He gave her that pretext by slapping her and causing her minor injuries. It was an unlawful killing.' The Crown made great play of the fact that the teenager was the same height as her father and that, although he was heavier, he was under the influence of alcohol. Karen Tyler was convicted of manslaughter at Chelmsford Crown Court; despite the monstrous record of her father's brutality, and the fact that she had given birth to a baby daughter while awaiting trial, she was sentenced to four years' imprisonment. This was halved on appeal. Karen Tyler was released after eight months after a campaign by her family and neighbours.

Amelia Rossiter ran a mixture of self-defence and accident at her trial. She had killed her husband after a row, and she too was convicted. The jury probably took the view that she had used excessive force because of the number of stab wounds on her husband's body and because of the inconsistent accounts she gave at different times. In evidence, Mrs Rossiter never suggested that she had lost control, despite the injuries having all the signs of a frenzied attack. She also made little of her miserable life with her husband and his abusive and violent behaviour that evening out of a resigned sense of loyalty to him and to their children.

Her conviction was quashed in April 1992 by the Court of Appeal because, in their judgment, the trial judge should have directed the jury on provocation, even when that was not the defence she was placing before the court.

Sometimes women who kill their husband or partner cannot live with the idea that it was anything other than a terrible accident. Jean Harris, the American headmistress who shot her lover, the Scarsdale diet doctor Herman Tarnower, also avoided a middle course, pleading her case on the basis of accident/self-defence, the gun having gone off in a struggle. She too was convicted. Campaigners, rightly concerned with these issues, sometimes fail to recognise the risks involved in criminal trials. Any counsel advising a client who faces a possible term of life imprisonment should be very mindful of her liberty.

Usually a criminal lawyer in a murder trial obtains a psychiatric opinion as to the accused's state of mind at the time of the offence. There are sound reasons for doing this which have nothing to do with sticking a psychiatric label on a woman. Even if psychiatrists do not agree upon diminished responsibility, they can assist the jury in considering provocation. A defence to provocation is only successful if the jury think a reasonable member of the public would also have been provoked. This is to prevent people who fly into a rage at the least slight from invoking the defence. The standard has to be set by the public on an objective basis. However, the courts have come to accept that in doing so the jury should take into account the characteristics of the person on trial. In domestic violence cases the jury is told to consider whether a reasonable woman who has had the experiences of the woman in the dock might have been provoked so that she lost control. The courts now allow psychiatric evidence of the effects of domestic violence on the particular woman, including a heightened sense of fear for her own life as a result of cumulative assaults. If provocation is successful the reports may also be helpful for the purposes of mitigation and sentencing. Psychiatric counselling can eventually be invaluable, because women who kill their husbands, however monstrous they may have been, feel personal guilt and grief, which they have little opportunity of handling in the prelude to their trial.

If the reports support the view that the woman was suffering from a mental disorder, it is then necessary to raise the defence with the Crown to enable them to secure a psychiatric opinion as well. If the experts on both sides agree that the woman was suffering from mental illness at the time of the offence, the Crown almost invariably accepts a plea to manslaughter.

Most often in domestic homicide cases, the woman has available to her a number of different defences, but if one of the avenues affords a manslaughter plea which is acceptable to the Crown, whatever the basis, she is likely to enter that plea rather than fight for a total acquittal and risk conviction.

Pamela Sainsbury was subjected to years of the most extreme violence and degradation imaginable before she killed her husband in 1991. He had treated her like an animal, leashing her with a belt around her neck, forcing her to eat from a dog-bowl, subjecting her to humiliating perversions. She was socially isolated by him and constantly accused of infidelity, so that she never raised her head in the street for fear of his accusations. If she used a word of more than two syllables she was beaten for trying to be smart.

On the night of the killing she had been suspected again of looking at another man, and was beaten savagely. She could take no more and knew that when he woke the violence would start again and this time he could kill her. She could barely walk because of the damage to her leg, and their children were asleep in the house. She could see no escape, and as he lay asleep she tied a rope to the leg of the bed, looped it around his neck and, going to the far corner of the room, out of his reach, pulled the cord with what strength she could muster. The rope garrotted him.

Pamela dragged his body into a wardrobe, where it remained for several days before she dismembered it and disposed of the pieces in a nearby field. She could not face going to the police because she knew it would mean immediate separation from her children, and instead told everyone her husband had left her. Some months later she confided in a friend, who informed the police.

Cases involving the disposal or dismemberment of a body pose additional difficulties for a defendant because of the risk that the jury will transfer the deliberateness of the behaviour after the event and the cover-up to the actual killing. However, the full story of Pamela's life was so terrible that it is unlikely that any jury would have felt anything but overwhelming sympathy for her position.

Pamela Sainsbury's case was prepared on the basis that all the background would go to the jury and they would be invited to consider not just diminished responsibility but self-defence and provocation, despite the inherent difficulties which each presents when the killing is not in the face of the abuse. No contested trial took place, because a plea to manslaughter was acceptable to the Crown and to the court, and she was happy to enter that plea.

The development which went unnoticed in the Sainsbury case was that four psychiatrists, instructed by the Crown and the defence, had all agreed that Pamela was at the time of the killing suffering 'acute stress reaction', which involves no pre-existing mental illness but is a recognised classification of mental disorder, dependent upon the subject experiencing trauma. Not all psychiatrists or courts accept that acute stress reaction falls within the definition of diminished responsibility. Her action was in direct response to her husband's provocative behaviour and there was no suggestion that she required treatment after her trial. Mr Justice Auld commented at the time, 'You killed him in a sudden and impulsive act driven as much by fear and hopelessness as anger.'

Lawyers in the United States have been establishing new precedent by creating a battered woman's defence. In cases involving relentless domestic violence, rather than attempting to secure conviction on the lesser charge of manslaughter by virtue of provocation or diminished responsibility, they are mounting a case of self-defence even where the killing has all the appearances of a deliberate act. The lawyers involved in these American cases feel very strongly the injustice in sending a woman to prison for killing her persecutor, but one of the strongest motivating forces in developing the defence has been the inflexibility of sentencing in the United States. Sentences are generally even longer there than here and, since some form of custodial sentence almost inevitably follows convictions for homicide whatever the degree, they try to go for broke. There have been some extraordinary acquittals, including exoneration for a woman who shot her policeman husband with his own gun while he lay asleep. Before going to bed, he had told his wife that when he woke he expected her to be available for sex and that she had to 'come across' or he'd beat hell out of the kids. Her account of her husband's continuing abuse deeply affected the jury. In another case, a wife hired hitmen to kill her husband, who had terrorised her and would not let her live a life free of him. Again the jury acquitted.

Cases of women who kill are now being handled with increasing comprehension of domestic violence, which is invariably the backdrop to domestic homicide, whether it is husband or wife who is in the dock. Judges and juries can be greatly assisted by hearing from experts like the psychologist Sandra Horley, who as Director of Chiswick Family Rescue has worked for years with battered women, counselling over 2,000. Psychiatrists like Dr Gillian Mezey and Dr Nigel Eastman have extensive experience of dealing with cases of women who kill after a history of domestic violence and regularly testify in court about the dynamic which is set up in abusive relationships.

June Scotland, who killed her husband and buried his body in the garden, was questioned by police about her failure to leave him despite adequate opportunities. The level of her husband's violence was disputed. She had been physically battered, but the real violence was psychological – his abuse of the children, his constant criticism, his despotic rule of their lives so that the whole family was in terror of his moods.

The Crown persisted in a charge of murder against her because of the deliberate steps she took to kill her husband, poisoning his food before hitting him with a rolling pin. However, all the psychiatrists in her case agreed that she was suffering from an acute depressive state by the time she started planning his death and was already mentally ill. In her case, the psychiatric evidence and that of the expert on domestic violence combined to provide the jury with an insight into her powerlessness and fear which they could then apply for themselves as they saw fit. She was acquitted of murder and convicted of manslaughter on the grounds of diminished responsibility. Her sentence was one of probation.

Men who kill their wives are rarely raising their hand for the first time. In appropriate cases the self-defence law will be invoked for women who kill their husbands and, if the courts fail to leave the issue to the jury, legislative change will be necessary. Had the psychiatrists in Pamela Sainsbury's case not spoken with one voice, her case would have begun the process of letting a jury armed with all the facts decide whether she was acting in self-defence. Even though her husband was asleep, the question a jury could have been left to decide was whether, given the history, circumstances and perceptions of the defendant, she could reasonably have believed that she could not preserve herself from being killed by her husband except by killing him first. However, the primary interest must always be that of the individual woman on trial. It is rare that a woman who is offered a plea to the lesser offence and the likelihood of a non-custodial sentence chooses to go on with a fight.

The case histories abound. What Pamela Sainsbury's case taught me was to go in search of evidence relating to the man's previous relationships. Pamela Sainsbury's husband had lived with women before and they provided statements to the police about his violence to them. Sometimes previous partners who have children by the deceased do not want to testify on behalf of the woman who has killed the father of their children; it feels like a betrayal. They may never have acknowledged that they were battered. However, frequently a violent man will have left a trail of victims in his wake and they can be invaluable witnesses.

Carol Peters was convicted in February 1992 of murdering her husband. In November 1990, after years of domestic violence, she fought back for the first time. Her husband died of stab wounds but his body also bore terrible injuries inflicted with a hammer. When Carol was arrested her mouth was so damaged that she could not eat and for many days drank through a straw. The history of domestic violence was minimised in the defence of Carol Peters for fear that its full disclosure would arm the Crown with the powerful weapon of motive. This was a recurring theme in such cases before the courts and legal profession were forced to acknowledge the impact of domestic violence and its effects. Until recently, even psychiatrists knew little of the dynamics that were at work.

Carol Peters's story of the violence she experienced is classic, starting with minor assaults and escalating so that she had to receive hospital treatment on two occasions. Her life was wretched, made bearable only by the presence and love of her children.

The trial concentrated almost entirely on the night of the killing, when her husband's behaviour was especially bizarre and violent, possibly exacerbated by a sleeping drug, temazepan, which was found in his bloodstream. In very large doses temazepan can induce paranoia and disinhibited conduct. When interviewed by the police, Carol's account of the events of that terrible night and her own behaviour varied at different times, but this was explained by a psychiatrist as being consistent with an experience of extreme trauma, after which the memory renders up recollection in piecemeal form. Despite a hard-fought defence, the jury convicted. Carol Peters appealed and a retrial was ordered where her older children testified to their father's violence. She was acquitted of murder, convicted of manslaughter but walked free because she had already served several years in prison.

Carol Peters's case underscores a number of problems which persist.

If the prosecution find that a woman can hold down a job and perform well in that role they maintain that she clearly has the emotional resources to withstand an abusive partner and is capable of taking steps to seek help or leave. The ability to compartmentalise is still not accepted or understood. Carol Peters worked and her employers testified to her capability, which allowed the prosecution to claim that the level of violence was not such as to emotionally undermine her.

Prosecutors also use love letters from women, or e-mails or text messages, to show that the relationship is warm and loving, even passionate, as though that precludes violence. There is an unwillingness to accept that even families which suffer domestic violence can have good times together. Psychiatrists called by the Crown sometimes are encouraged to use their role to debunk battered woman's syndrome as a valid psychiatric condition or to prove that the woman has exaggerated or provoked her partner's abuse by her own behaviour, for example by dressing sexily. In the case of Patricia Lawrence in 2003, the Crown psychiatrist at no time looked at the medical records of Mr Lawrence, which included referrals for psychiatric help for his domestic violence, and his own admissions of abusive behaviour towards his wife. Mrs Lawrence had sent some sexually explicit text messages to her husband and these were used in the court on a questionable claim of relevance when in fact they were meant to prejudice the jury against her.

Prosecutors and police find it hard to understand that a woman may be battered by more than one partner and draw from such a history the conclusion that the woman must make the men batter her. It is her fault. In the case of Patricia Howells in Leeds in 1996, the Crown cross-examined her about earlier abusive relationships to support the contention that she was to blame, that her behaviour must have pushed men to violence. What is so often misunderstood is that men who abuse usually have a radar system, drawing them to women who have underlying vulnerabilities – women who have had rotten lives, who think they deserve no better, who have been sexually abused or traumatised in childhood. It is not always so. Women from a secure and stable background can also be battered or psychologically abused but it is often the case that abusive men seek out women who feel fortunate to be loved at all. Their unerring antennae take them straight to women who are less likely to walk away at the first slap.

The investigation in Patricia Howells's case was based on the premiss that she was responsible for her husband's violence. All the questioning was founded on that assumption. It was revelatory that in the run-up to her trial, the officer who had been in charge of her case and who had conducted her interviews was himself arrested for domestic violence towards his wife.

Samantha Forde was tried in 2004 for murdering the man who abused her mother. She waited until he was lying in a drunken sleep and then attacked him with a hammer, pulverising his skull. All the signs of premeditation were present. She asked her boyfriend who was in the house at the time where on the victim's body was the best place to strike the blows. She looked for the hammer to use as a weapon. She fled the scene and went into hiding after the killing. The case carried all the risks of conviction for murder because Samantha herself was not the victim of the man's violence and in the argument of the Crown she could have sought police help when he lay there in a stupor.

The man she killed was Stephen Cottle, who had battered and beaten her mother Michelle Gyillio to a pulp over a period of months. The jury was asked whether her actions were those of a young woman vengefully punishing a violent man or was she so shocked by the level of his violence towards her mother and in fear for her mother's life that she was provoked and lost control? Was her responsibility diminished because of her mental state at the time?

Samantha's history was tragic. Her mother had been the victim of domestic violence from Samantha's father and other men. Samantha's first memories were of running in terror with her mother from her father's rage and battering. Her mother had become an alcoholic and as a small child Samantha had taken on the role of mother to her siblings, and even to her mother. She had been sexually abused by her grandfather and had grown into an adult feeling self-disgust and worthlessness. She attempted suicide on many occasions and self-harmed. Yet she continued to feel tied to her mother as though the umbilicus had never been severed. She was the carer.

Stephen Cottle's history was also one of emotional deprivation and physical abuse. But in classic conformity to the research on disturbed young men, his low self-esteem led to outward expressions of violence. The trajectory of his violence was plain from police and health records. He terrorised his own mother when an adolescent. His baby sister was put on the at risk register because of fears for her safety. He later beat the young woman who mothered his children; he cut off the ear of a sister's boyfriend. He battered and broke the ribs of another girlfriend and on a later occasion, in a jealous rage, slashed and tore at her body with a knife so viciously that she almost died of the wounds. His violence was so uncontrolled that the police had to use shields to arrest him as he lashed out with a knife. For that attempted murder he was convicted and sent to prison for ten years. On release he was identified in police intelligence reports as a high-risk offender.

It was within weeks of release from prison that he embarked on the relationship with Michelle, Samantha Forde's mother. In the months that followed, he beat and battered Michelle so that her nose was flattened over her face, her teeth were smashed, her body bruised and kicked. He would not let her eat, use the lavatory or move without permission. He held a friend of Michelle at knifepoint to extort money from her, threatened people in pubs, and on buses. This was a one-man terrorist campaign and someone with much more mettle than Samantha Forde would have been just as terrified of him. The lucky person in the whole affair was Michelle, who would very probably have ended up dead. The jury took little time in acquitting Samantha Forde of murder and returned a verdict of manslaughter. However, the judge sentenced her to five years' imprisonment when what she needed was psychiatric help and a community place to help her build a life.

I have no doubt that the judge felt compelled to send her to prison because sitting in court were Stephen Cottle's family who, despite his long history of violence, some of it towards them, still

felt that justice required punishment and sent a letter to the judge
to that effect. The woman whom he had nearly murdered six years
before might not have felt so benevolent towards him.

In 2001, Mikaela Wrenn stood trial for murder of a young man
called Jason Chant. The allegation was that she, along with her
older partner, Stephen Sullivan, and a young man called Lee Smith,
had held Jason Chant captive and starved him to death. The facts
were horrifying, describing a cruelty beyond measure. What Jason
Chant experienced would have constituted torture in any
international tribunal – food deprivation, no drinking water,
deafening sound, a freezing cold shower, confinement in a space
where the tiniest movement was impossible, no sanitation so that
he had to wallow in his own excrement. He was held in a state of
uncertainty as to what might happen next. Kept in the dark, he was
then brought cowering into the light to be subjected to verbal
abuse, intimidation and aggression. The level of fear engendered
was so great that Jason Chant did not ever cry out for help, not a
sound. These activities which compared to the behaviour of Latin
American death squads and torturers were taking place in a council
flat in Essex.

The orchestrator of this prolonged punishment was Stephen
Sullivan, a small-time crook and drug dealer, who reigned like a
tyrant over his tight coterie of confederates. All the people he drew
around him were vulnerable; boys like Jason Chant who had been
in care, like Lee Smith who was physically disabled and lonely, or
his girlfriend Mikaela Wrenn who had been abused by her
stepfather and run away from home when she was only 16 to be
with Sullivan, a man twice her age. Stephen Sullivan's persecution
of Jason, who was already treated like a slave, was for some trifling
misdemeanour. The prosecution case was that Sullivan was indeed
the central killer, a malevolent dangerous man, but their argument
was that Mikaela Wrenn and Lee Smith had willingly participated
in the torture and death by doing nothing to secure help or to
alleviate the suffering of their victim.

As the Crown prepared their case, an extraordinary picture of
Sullivan came to light. More and more women gave statements
telling of their suffering at his hands. His own mother had been

battered by him when he was still a boy. His sisters lived in terror of him. One after another ten women gave accounts of the most horrifying abuse against them and their children. The judge ruled that the Crown could not use the material as part of their case as it was so prejudicial to the accused but for Mikaela Wrenn and Lee Smith the evidence was vital as it explained their terror and manipulation by Sullivan. After lengthy legal argument during the trial, the judge conceded that the evidence was admissible to support the defence of Mikaela Wrenn that she was a battered woman who was so paralysed by fear for her own life that she could do nothing to help Jason. The fear Stephen Sullivan generated, even after many years without contact, meant that witness summonses had to be issued; the women with whom he had had relationships were so afraid to come to court, so afraid to face him, even when he was in the dock between two prison officers and behind a security screen, that the court had to order their attendance.

Once there, the women recounted violence and cruelty of such magnitude that it was hard to listen. Some of it was indescribable. He had shoved his hand into one woman's mouth and forced it open with such ferocity that her mouth tore, leaving a scar which extended up the side of her face. He had beaten, kicked and humiliated these women when they were expecting his children. He had broken into their homes when they dared to change locks. When they tried to escape, he found them. The women had no connection with each other but patterns emerged, creating a vivid picture of a controlling, dominating bully who surrounded himself with pliant vulnerable people many years his junior, who became enslaved to him out of terror. The evidence showed a man who never reached maturation, who was car obsessed, driving around in flashy vehicles, spending hours cleaning them or getting others to do so; touring the streets with loud 'look at me' music blaring from his woofer; it documented his obsessional concern about clothing, insisting that seams were pressed in his T-shirts, that his socks were ironed, that the undersoles of his trainers were cleaned; his bragging connections with criminals; his demands for constant attention that meant he was even jealous of a woman's child; his extraordinary control of women by impregnation. This was a man who had fathered 18 children, as if tattooing himself on these women so that they could never be beyond his control.

A number of the women described attempting suicide because of their despair. Some of the hardest pieces of evidence for the jury related to children: the smashing of a child's face for crackling a crisp packet; a small boy, little more than a baby, hiding wet pyjama bottoms for fear of the punishment that would be exacted – being locked in a dark cupboard; a hungry baby being left to scream while its mother wept because Sullivan decided when babies were fed; the pouring of a child's antibiotics down the sink. Another mother described the day her daughter did not return home. She watched the clock and knew with each passing minute that she had run away, that her daughter was free. Although she had lost her child, she was happy for her because 'at least she had got away'.

Mikaela Wrenn remained under Sullivan's spell until shortly before her trial: even from prison he was able to exert control over her. It was with the support of decent, kind people that she began to recover her self-worth and to see that she could be free of him. Her greatest act of courage was going into the witness box and testifying against him.

The question for the jury was whether Mikaela Wrenn, as a free agent, was a party to the murder of Jason Chant. The jury had no difficulty acquitting her and also Lee Smith. They knew that she was no more able to stop Sullivan's cruelty towards Jason Chant than she was able to stop his cruelty towards her. Stephen Sullivan was sentenced to 23 years' imprisonment. Most of the women he had abused came to see him sentenced, to be sure that he was really going to jail.

This was a case at the extreme end of the scale but only because one woman after the other told her tale. Had any one of those women appeared in court as a solitary complainant of abuse, they would have faced the same old claims of exaggeration and invention and they would have been asked sceptically, 'If it was so bad, why didn't you leave?'

There has been a quantum leap in the court's understanding of domestic violence and the forces which drive women to kill but there remain myths and misperceptions, which must be addressed.

Justice is likely to remain a lottery while so much depends on the woman's fulfilment of society's expectations. One of the factors which undoubtedly affects the outcome of murder trials is, as always, the persona of the woman in the dock. It is my view that this is what really determines the outcome. Women who conform to the conventional image of the cowed victim fare better than those who come to trial angry that they are being blamed for what ultimately took place.

As in rape trials, women on any kind of charge frequently experience irrelevant questioning which discredits them as women in the eyes of the jury. In Sara Thornton's case, efforts were made to find a motive for the killing aside from vengeance. It was suggested that she stood to gain financially, had had an affair, and lived an unorthodox life, all of which apparently justified the Crown's asking her why she wore no knickers and whether she occasionally smoked cannabis. Ordinarily assertive and lively, Sara became totally demoralised in her marriage to a drunken, violent man. However, by the time she came up for trial her confidence was returning. She cavilled with prosecuting counsel, drew distinctions when she answered questions, and had all the disadvantages of a now rational person attempting to speak about a period of irrationality. To a jury she probably seemed too feisty and in control to be a victim. She also articulates a complaint that is made with growing frequency by women: that they are infantilised by lawyers, who fail to recognise their intelligence and do not listen to their views about the conduct of their cases.

Approximately ten years later, in 2003, Patricia Lawrence faced the same set of assumptions. Feisty, glamorous and flirtatious, she had the uphill task of confronting the stereotype that a victim must be mouselike, submissive and totally crushed. She herself challenged the equally damaging stereotype that abusive men have to be like Stephen Cottle. She explained that she loved her husband but, as was shown by his family and psychiatric history, he himself had been sexually abused as a child. When he felt bad about himself or his self-confidence was low, he would take drugs or drink, become violent and she would be at the receiving end of all his pent-up rage. On the night of his death he felt she had embarrassed him in front of the caretakers of their accommodation and caught her by the throat. Passing out from the pressure on her neck, she felt for a knife in the cutlery drawer and stabbed him. Patricia Lawrence was acquitted on the grounds of self-defence and walked free from the court, but she had lost her man when all she wanted was for him to get help.

What is needed is a root and branch review of the homicide laws. Judges complain that current rules force them to treat all people convicted of murder in the same way. The mandatory life sentence should be abolished. It fails to reflect the wide variations in crimes now classified as murder – at one extreme, the sadistic killing of a child and at the other, the injection by a doctor of a patient who is dying and begs for the pain to be ended. Life should be made the maximum sentence, rather than mandatory, and it should be left to the judge to sentence according to the circumstances. However, the government is committed to the mandatory life sentence and although a review of homicide law will take place that aspect is non-negotiable. The law and order lobby holds too much sway and the mandatory life sentence was the price for abolishing capital punishment.

A new and simpler statement of the law of provocation is needed, with a formulation which makes it clear that cumulative provocation can lead to despair and a loss of control and specifying clearly that the test must not involve strict immediacy when there has been cumulative abuse. The standards of the community or objective test should still exist for provocation but it should take into account the toll taken by domestic violence or other abuse and this should be spelt out in any new legislation. The language in the tests for diminished responsibility should also be simplified and made to correspond to the developments in psychiatric understanding which have taken place in the last 50 years.

Given the intransigence on the mandatory life sentence for murder, there should also be a new partial defence created of 'killing *in extremis*', which would cover a carer who kills purely to end the suffering of someone who is terminally ill, or a person who kills in circumstances where there is extraordinary mitigation, for example after rape or the killing of one's child. Such mitigatory circumstances should reduce murder to manslaughter. The latter suggestion is likely to be highly controversial but I make it knowing that the alternative of ending the mandatory life sentence altogether is off the agenda. This new mitigatory defence could cover situations where a woman deliberately killed her partner after terrible abuse or provide a defence for someone involved in a mercy killing in appropriate circumstances.

9

Justice Miscarried

Although women commit very little serious crime, they have been a real presence in the infamous miscarriages of justice; Carole Richardson, Annie Maguire, Judith Ward, Jacqueline Fletcher, the Taylor sisters, the battered women who have killed their partners, the women more recently accused of killing their children: Sally Clark, Angela Cannings and Trupti Patel. Their numbers are out of all proportion to the numbers of women who kill or conspire to kill. The question which haunts these cases is whether gender plays any part in the failure of the criminal justice system.

Miscarriages of justice result from a multiplicity of causes, and individuals have often been subjected to more than one form of abuse by authority. There are common threads which run through most miscarriages: wrongful identification, false confessions, perjury by witnesses, police misconduct and bad trial tactics by defence lawyers. Police are in a powerful position to manipulate evidence, for example by verballing the accused – inventing damning admissions or comments – as well as encouraging witnesses to lie or planting evidence. As well as those gross intentional violations, fabrication can come through a more subtle process of police and prosecutorial overzealousness, which can lead to a willingness to use improper and unethical means to obtain a conviction against someone because he or she is believed to be guilty. Women suffer a double disadvantage when the justice processes underscore a woman's vulnerabilities and sexism can be an unacknowledged germinator of hunches which have no basis in evidence.

Identification testimony is notoriously unreliable although witnesses will swear blind that they are right. The value of expert evidence has also been overestimated as we saw in the cases of sudden infant death like Sally Clark but also in the famous Irish cases in relation to forensic science – the Birmingham Six and the case of the Maguire family. The non-disclosure of relevant evidence by the police or prosecution or by experts to the defence may be another issue.

The BBC's *Rough Justice* series, sadly abandoned in the search for cheaper television, looked at cases where there may have been a miscarriage of justice. A number of their most poignant investigations involved women. I dealt with *Rough Justice*'s last successful appeal before the courts in 2000, the case of Mary Druhan, where the meticulous and committed research of David Jessell's team effected the release of a sad, elderly woman wrongly accused. One of the great handicaps for women who are convicted unfairly of crime is that they often have no large support system to mount a campaign on their behalf. Women like Sally Clark, Angela Cannings and Trupti Patel had supportive husbands and families who stoically persisted in their efforts to secure justice but many women who are convicted feel alone and powerless. Few husbands or lovers stay the course when women receive prison sentences.

Mary Druhan had been happily married. When she found her husband dead in bed beside her after a sudden heart attack, her world fell apart. She started drinking so heavily that she lost her job and fell into debt. Then she lost her home. Her daughters, now young women, were unable to help her. She ended up sitting on park benches with vagrants, sleeping rough and drowning her wretchedness in alcohol. A bag lady.

One night a house where indigent people used to huddle for warmth went up in flames and two men were burned to death. Mary Druhan was blamed. She had been seen to argue with one of the men in a pub earlier that day and in the drunken exchanges it was claimed that she shouted 'I'll kill you.' Highly questionable identification evidence was given of a woman seen in the vicinity shortly before the fire. It was also maintained that, when told of the deaths, she had made some strange ambiguous comment which may have suggested knowledge on her part. The whole trial was a fiasco, with insufficient attention paid to whether the fire just might have been an accident caused by the careless abandonment of a cigarette end. The drink-addled Mary Druhan became an easy scapegoat, particularly as she did not cut a prepossessing figure in court and was confused about distinguishing one day from the next.

Rough Justice found new evidence about events at the pub and secured expert testimony showing that the fire was most likely caused without intention, since the premises had been used to store paint and paint thinners and would go up like a light. In 1998 Mary Druhan came blinking into the light, freed by the Court of Appeal after seven years in prison. In that period one of her daughters had committed suicide and Mary had become, like so many long-term prisoners, institutionalised.

Almost 20 years earlier *Rough Justice* had gone to work on another woman's case. Margaret Livesey had always maintained her innocence of the murder of her son, Alan, and the BBC team tried to reopen her case. She was convicted in July 1979 after a second trial, the first having been abandoned at a very late stage when the relative of a juror became seriously ill. The problem with abandoned trials is that witnesses have time to consider answers to the questions they were asked the first time round, and the prosecution's case has usually been well rehearsed in the papers. There is a risk that people are already establishing their views before they are even empanelled as jurors. Press interest was particularly great in a trial where a mother had allegedly killed her 14-year-old son, especially when it emerged that Margaret Livesey's alibi for the time of the murder was a man with whom she was conducting a secret affair while her husband was on night shift at British Leyland.

According to the Crown, Mrs Livesey arrived home late, having been out with her man-friend, and embarked on a terrible row with her son. During this row, it was claimed, she lost control and stabbed him repeatedly with a kitchen knife that she had used earlier for peeling potatoes. The prosecution then maintained that the defendant attempted to cover her tracks by tying the boy up, cleaning the murder weapon and leaving the house so as to ensure that the discovery of the body was made by someone else.

The allegations were deeply flawed. When the murder came to light, Margaret Livesey was by all accounts in deep distress, but after five days' interrogation eventually said to the police, 'Well, if you say I've done it, then I must have, but I can't remember.' She then began a lengthy confession based largely on knowledge which by this time was shared by most of those investigating and by most of those who had been around after the discovery of Alan's body. She retracted her confession two days later.

Margaret Livesey told the police that she had been having problems with her adolescent son in recent months. Concerned that he was getting into trouble, she had been trying to exercise some parental control; this had placed a strain on their relationship. According to her confession, on this particular night the argument got so heated that it ended in a physical struggle. She went into a complete frenzy and stabbed the boy time after time. Yet much of what she said was totally inconsistent with the forensic evidence. For a start, the position of the body was not as she described it. Then she maintained that she had put socks over the boy's wounds after the stabbings because she could not bear to see them, but the evidence showed that the stabbing had in fact been done through the socks. Nor was the nature of the stabbings and the absence of blood-spurt staining consistent with a frenzied attack; indeed, the socks accounted for the absence of bloodstains.

One of the most bizarre aspects of the forensic evidence was that four of the incisions were pricks with the point of a knife, including a prick to the eyelid, more in keeping with carefully inflicted injuries than with a struggle. And the boy bore no sign of defensive injuries. Wherever someone has attacked another with a knife, the first things to look for in courtrooms as well as in mortuaries are wounds on the forearms or the palms of hands, where the unarmed victim has tried to fend off the weapon or protect their own face. None of those signs of struggle existed, and the knife which was supposed to have inflicted the injuries had no trace of blood on it, although it had a handle of unvarnished wood which would have been particularly receptive to staining.

Crucial to the whole case was the timing of the death. At the trial, the prosecution claimed that it would have been around 11 p.m. This was deduced from the temperature of the room, which was taken by the scene-of-crime officer; what was forgotten was that the windows had been thrown open because the gas taps had been turned on. Reappraisal of this as well as examination of the stomach contents provided evidence on appeal that the death could have taken place an hour earlier than was believed at the time.

Margaret Livesey's lover gave evidence that he was with her until after eleven o'clock, and she was at her neighbours' house by 11.10. It is hard to believe that she could have committed the murder and trussed the boy up in a complicated series of knots in such a short space of time. The neighbours described her as completely unruffled and unstained with blood.

However, neither Margaret Livesey nor her lover were believed. There was even evidence at her trial that she had been reported to the NSPCC for abuse of her son prior to his death, although there was no evidence to support the complaint. It came to nothing, but 'no smoke without fire' hints were being made. Clearly this was a defendant who had failed both the mother and the wife tests.

If Margaret Livesey did not kill her son, then who did? At the trial the evidence of a mentally handicapped boy, who said he saw an intruder leave the Livesey house by the back door around 10 p.m., was discounted: the prosecution claimed the boy was unreliable. Furthermore, in the house there was an unaccounted-for cigarette packet and some cigarette ends. A forensic pathologist who was called in years later believed that the murder had the hallmarks of a sadistic and ritualistic homosexual murder, which would explain the elaborate knots, the teasing pricks with a knife and many other features. The police had been so convinced that this aberrant mother was guilty that no forensic tests of the cigarette packet or ends were ever conducted.

Margaret Livesey confessed, and for most people in the court, whatever the quibbles over the evidence, that was good enough – after all, who in their right mind confesses to something they did not do? What was not sufficiently taken into account was that this was the confession of a woman who was experiencing a profound reaction to the monstrous death of her child. Not only was she filled with guilt over her contentious relationship with him and her feelings of failure as a mother, but his death had also exposed her affair and the turmoil of emotions around that aspect of her life.

*

It is only recently that we have come to understand that certain people in certain situations are more likely to confess to crimes they did not in fact commit. Sexual discrimination can actually take its toll in the investigation process. When any person comes to the attention of the police, they are confronted with an authority figure who from childhood has been held up as frightening and all-powerful. For women, this can be especially potent, and their response may be to act submissively and co-operatively. If they feel guilty, for any reason, they may be manipulated into confessing to intentional killing, whatever the reality. They may acquiesce to propositions put to them in a leading manner which distort the truth of what happened. Policemen, trained in a culture which is not attuned to women's lives, are likely to ask questions from a perspective quite alien to the experience of women, imposing their own conditioning on the woman's perceptions.

The record of interview is a crucial part of the evidence. The jury are given a transcript of the taped interviews and they take it with them into the jury room. Great weight is attached to the account a defendant first gives to the police, because it usually takes place so soon after the event, sometimes within hours of the incident or, in a murder case, of the realisation that someone with whom they have been intimately involved is dead. Rarely is this going to be their best and most complete account, because of the state they are likely to be in. Yet their answers will be scrutinised, and any slight discrepancy between them and their evidence to the jury will be leapt upon. Inevitably interviews are interrogator-led, and one frequently finds that the defendant's story is told inadequately because the answers reflect the limitations of the questions. If, for example, a woman is never asked whether her husband beat her, she may not mention it at that stage, especially if she is finding the atmosphere unsympathetic. If she is being required to re-create in answer to questions, blow for blow, a nightmare of violence, she may disturb the sequence or leave out matters which later seem central.

Professor James MacKeith of London University and his psychologist colleague Dr Gisli Gudjonsson have been conducting research into false confessions and how they come to be made. Their work has moved beyond those confessions made under pressure or in response to inducements, to those where the defendant has experienced a short-term mental state triggered by great distress or bereavement, or where their intelligence quotient or psychological make-up put them at risk. Both sexes can be vulnerable. The Blakelock appeal in March 1992 exposed how Engin Raghip, a man with low intelligence, had confessed to a crime he did not commit. In 1977 Stefan Kiszco also confessed to a terrible crime. He was said to have admitted the rape and killing of a little girl, although he had an alibi for the time of her death. A comparison of his seminal fluid with that found at the scene showed he could not have been the killer, but the shame of his conviction was not exposed until he had spent 15 years of his life in prison.

The cautionary tales emanating from the research should be included in the training of all criminal lawyers. There is a lesson too about the rigour lawyers should bring to the cases they handle.

One of the factors MacKeith and Gudjonsson have considered is the susceptible personality, the person who adopts the perspective of the interrogator and desires to please. *In extremis*, and under constant questioning, such people do not measure the consequence of their statements but simply say whatever they think will satisfy the person asking the questions. This was the core of the evidence which Professor MacKeith would have given at the appeal of Carole Richardson, one of the Guildford Four, had that event not been overtaken by the Crown's own disclosure that police interviews had been improperly conducted.

Carole Richardson's case was the key to that particular miscarriage of justice and, because her alibi was so strong, galvanised much of the support. A friend repeatedly testified that she had been in his company elsewhere when the bombings took place. Once those who took up her case accepted that she had been wrongly convicted, the whole edifice had to crumble, because no individual case could be separated out from the others. But the question always remained, why did she confess? The account she gave after long periods of interrogation was inconsistent in itself and at odds with much of the other evidence, even though she 'admitted' her involvement. She was, in the view of Professor MacKeith and Dr Gudjonsson, a classic case of the 'susceptible personality'.

One miscarriage of justice concerned a young woman, Jacqueline Fletcher, who was convicted of murdering her baby son. The most damning evidence against her was her confession to the police, made during a six-hour interrogation. She was tested in prison at the request of the *Rough Justice* programme and found to have an IQ of 70, at the edge of mental handicap and equivalent to that of a ten-year-old. Evidence of her low intelligence was not placed before the trial court. Half an hour into the questioning, Jackie had had a private conversation with a policewoman, after which her language noticeably changed and her vocabulary included professional terminology and references to postnatal depression. She also gave a description of drowning the baby in a manner which proved impossible when a reconstruction was undertaken. However, a pathologist who examined slides of the baby's lung tissue had described them in court as waterlogged, an unfortunate expression; what he saw was the body fluid frequently found in the lungs of cot-death babies.

Jackie Fletcher had a tragic history with her children. She had become pregnant in her early teens and had been deemed unable to look after the child, who was taken into care and subsequently adopted. She had another child by the same father, and it was this baby who was found one morning dead in his cot. An autopsy was conducted and nothing at all suspicious was found. The verdict was cot death. It was when her third child was small that she was overheard by a landlady to tell the crying child to shut up 'or I'll do the same what I done to the other!'

It was the view of David Southall, consultant paediatrician at the Royal Brompton Hospital, that Jackie, of limited intelligence and with one baby already taken from her, shared the guilt felt by all mothers who have lost babies through cot death. The grief and sense of responsibility can go on for years.

Jackie Fletcher's conviction was quashed by the Court of Appeal in February 1991. A case which had a less happy conclusion was that of Beverley Weightman, who was convicted of murdering her only child, a two-year-old girl. The child had inhaled a plastic bag and suffocated. Mother and child had returned home from a neighbour's house where all had been well. Within 45 minutes Mrs Weightman returned to the neighbour's with the child dead in her arms. She was hysterical there, and equally distraught later at the hospital.

In a statement to the Coroner's officer, Beverley Weightman described going to the bathroom to wash her own hair:

> I went into her room and found her on her back on the bed with a plastic shopping bag plastered over her face. Her head was not inside the bag. I rushed to her and peeled the bag off, she was not breathing . . . Ruth kept her toys in a plastic shopping bag but she may have taken another bag upstairs when she was pretending to go shopping. She was fond of playing shopping.

The bag made a 'whooshing' sound when it was removed.

The post-mortem report concluded that the cause of death was accidental asphyxiation. Three months later, in the course of an argument, Beverley Weightman's husband accused her of killing their little daughter, and she agreed. The following day she went to her probation officer and made the same claim, saying voices had told her to do it. In the presence of a senior probation officer she repeated what she was saying and wrote a note to her husband, asking his forgiveness. In turn, she confessed to the police, having declined a solicitor, and, two days later, repeated her confession with a lawyer and psychiatrist present, saying that she had confessed because 'there had been four deaths in the church' which she attended and death was preying on her mind. The fact that she was directly responsible for this other one, she claimed, became too much for her. She also explained that she was in regular contact with young children and was frightened of the responsibility. She denied to the police that she was confessing to focus attention on herself or to seek assistance by roundabout means.

At her trial Beverley Weightman denied murdering her child with the plastic bag. She could not explain why her story changed, nor provide an adequate reason for confessing. The defence sought to call the psychiatrist, Dr Earp, who had been present at the second stage of police interviews, to testify that in his view Beverley Weightman suffered from a histrionic personality disorder, characterised by emotional superficiality and impulsive behaviour when under stress. He called the condition 'La Belle Indifférence', a recognised syndrome. Two psychiatrists instructed by the Crown also took the view that she had a histrionic personality. The woman's own probation officer had agreed in cross-examination that she was theatrical by nature and could say things to draw attention to herself. Of the two, the view of a professional psychiatrist would have carried greater authority with the jury, yet it was for this very reason that the evidence was excluded by the trial judge, who said he was 'very concerned lest the jury see it as a suggestion that their function should be usurped by an expert witness . . . Jurors do not need psychiatrists to tell them how ordinary folk who are not suffering from any mental illness are likely to react to the stresses and strains of life.'

While Beverley Weightman is not someone of abnormally low intelligence, and her condition could not be characterised as mental illness, it is hard to imagine that she would be included in the run of 'ordinary folk'. Few jurors would have come across a personality of such an hysterical type as to confess to a crime of which they were innocent; the possible vulnerability of certain types of people is not within their normal purview. Mrs Weightman was convicted and, although she appealed, her conviction was upheld on 18 October 1990 on the grounds that the judge was right not to permit the calling of a psychiatrist's evidence where the defendant was not suffering from a mental disorder. She is serving life imprisonment.

The phenomenon of wrongly confessing to crime is not new. On 24 March 1935 Francis Rattenbury was bludgeoned to death with a carpenter's mallet as he sat sleeping in an armchair in his drawing-room. Alma Rattenbury claimed that she found him there already unconscious. By the time a doctor and then the police arrived, Alma was extremely drunk, and was making statements to the effect that she had killed her husband. An account of the case appears in a series of books called *Notable British Trials,* and a revealing passage describes her as a 'highly sexed woman . . . and six years of being deprived of sexual satisfaction had combined with the tuberculosis from which she suffered to bring her to the verge of nymphomania'. We should be grateful for penicillin.

Mr Justice Humphreys's summing up was no more generous: 'Members of the jury, having heard her learned counsel, having regard to the facts of this case, it may be that you will say that you cannot possibly feel any sympathy for that woman; you cannot have any feeling except disgust for her.'

In fact, Alma Rattenbury was a rather dizzy, good-hearted woman married to a man many years her senior with whom she no longer had any sexual life. She had embarked upon a crazy love affair with their 18-year-old chauffeur cum handyman when she was still only 31. Because of their age difference, Alma was assumed to be the dominant partner – which, given her temperament, was probably not the case. It became apparent during the trial that she cared greatly for her husband and that he probably knew of the affair but chose to ignore it because of his own attachment to her. When she found him dead she drunkenly accepted responsibility because she felt guilty and knew what the consequences would be for the chauffeur, George Stoner.

Although Alma was acquitted, she was destroyed in the process, hounded by the press, socially despised, and tortured with guilt about the imprisonment of her former lover and the shame she had visited upon her children. She stabbed herself to death soon after the trial.

Irish trials import particular problems into the courtroom. As with sex and race cases, another agenda operates in addition to that prescribed in every criminal trial. People have strong views which can influence the proceedings and the risk of miscarriage of justice is real. The campaigns arising out of the convictions of the Birmingham Six, the Maguires and the Guildford Four have drawn attention to the powerful feelings which can deny a fair investigation and trial. Throughout their long sentences, the convicted prisoners in these cases at least had the support and sustenance of families and close friends, who refused to give up the fight on their behalf. Even less fortunate are those prisoners who do not have people on the outside to hammer on doors and write letters to influential public figures. Many women on the inside lose family and friends in the face of convictions, and the shame of imprisonment silences protest even in those cases where there is serious doubt about the outcome.

*

Judith Ward was convicted of the M62 motorway coach bombing, a horrible explosion which killed Corporal Clifford Houghton, his wife and two young children, as well as eight other British soldiers. In 1974 she received 12 sentences of life imprisonment, plus 30 years for the M62 and two other bombings. Her father disowned her after her trial. Until her release by the Court of Appeal at the end of April 1992, she was the longest-serving woman prisoner in Britain or Ireland for offences connected with the Irish conflict. Like the Guildford Four, the Maguire family and the Birmingham Six, she had never been acknowledged by the IRA as one of its adherents. For years people hardly knew her name, and she received little media attention or campaigning interest during her 18 years of incarceration. Judith Ward did not campaign or write letters over the years but quietly maintained her innocence. Prison officers and probation officers involved with her had deep misgivings about her conviction, but felt that she became resigned to biding her time in hope of eventual release on parole. She had to settle for a fate she felt she had brought on her own head.

The evidence against Judith Ward was paralleled by that in the Birmingham case. She made confessions which were deeply flawed and in significant respects unreliable and fantastical. At trial her defence lawyers described her as a 'Walter Mitty' character who made claims which were manifestly untrue. Forensic evidence was supposed to show that she had been in contact with explosives. However, the expert was Dr Frank Skuse, also of the Birmingham case, who was forced to resign in 1985 because of his 'limited efficiency'. He used the infamous Griess test for detecting the presence of the explosive nitroglycerine on swabs taken from Judith Ward's hands. This simple presumptive test was called into serious doubt in the Birmingham case because positive reactions can also be obtained from innocent material such as soap, Formica and the coating on cigarette packets. It is usually followed by a more sensitive procedure called thin-layer chromatography. When the more sophisticated process was applied to Judith Ward's swabs, the results were negative.

While the mental state of women is usually seized on to explain their aberrations, at her trial the emotional vulnerability of Judith

Ward was never allowed to explain her behaviour. This was terrorism, where different rules seem to apply. She was questioned extensively by police over many days without a solicitor or outside contact. Sixty-three interviews took place, an unbelievable number, and beyond the experience of any lawyer I know. Thirty-four of those interviews were not disclosed to those who defended her at her trial, and the jury heard nothing about them. The failure of the Crown to disclose this evidence was quite extraordinary. It meant that the full extent of the contradictions in her interviews was never fully before the court. The reason why such a volume of questioning took place was because the versions of events were so ludicrous and did not quite fit the evidence. Judith Ward has described in letters and statements her exhaustion and her desire for the interviews to end. The confessions she made contained statements which were shown not to be true and names which she could have readily known. There was also invention, which people from her past claimed was typical of the kind of lies she used to tell to glamorise herself.

Judith Ward was born in Stockport, but claimed to people that she was Irish and that her father was Irish, which was not true. Her childhood had been disrupted by her parents' divorce and a period in care had left her lonely and rootless. She went to live in Ireland for a while, and those who knew her there described her as insecure and desperate for attention. She became 'a Republican groupie', romancing that she had had a relationship with an Irish folk hero, Michael McVerry, who had been killed. There is no evidence that she ever even knew him, although she claimed they had a cathedral wedding on a day when he was somewhere else. The Crown knew this story was a fabrication but, according to Michael Mansfield QC at her appeal, the trial was conducted as though she were an IRA widow. She also told stories of having a baby by another IRA man, but was never seen pregnant. She had taken to wearing a rather conspicuous Provo-style uniform of military jacket and beret when selling Republican newspapers and hanging around Irish bars. She tried to get a job working for Sinn Fein, but they would not accept her, taking the view that she was unbalanced. On a number of occasions before her eventual arrest she had been taken into police stations by police and while in custody had confessed to being complicit in IRA offences; her stories were so obviously absurd that she had been released. When a bomb went off at Euston station, she and another woman who were living rough went to the station and shouted IRA slogans at the police. She was arrested then too, but no one believed for a minute that she was anything other than a sadly disturbed young woman.

Dr James MacKeith testified at Judith Ward's appeal that she was at the time of her confessions suffering from a personality disorder which had developed into mental illness by the time she was charged. The disorder manifested itself in attention-seeking, memory problems, mood swings and depression – a condition of 'hysteria' making her removed from reality. His assessment was based on interviews with her, her family, and people who knew her, but also on police and prison records and all the documentation which has subsequently come to light.

After each account given to the police of her involvement in the bombing, the story would be checked, only to find that her alleged supplier of explosives was out of the country at the time and that her movements did not fit. They would return to question her further, and, anxious to accommodate them, she would produce a new and equally untenable yarn. Interview after interview was filled with palpably false information.

After she was charged, Detective Chief Superintendent George Oldfield conducted yet another interview with her in which she spoke of participating in helicopter manoeuvres with an IRA flying corps over the Yorkshire moors, a fantasy so absurd that the officer stated in a report at the time that he had reservations about her veracity. He had written that he would be 'extremely reluctant to rely on her . . . Her mood changes from day to day, hour to hour and minute to minute.'

The medical officer at Risley Prison, where she was held on remand, prepared a pre-trial report (which juries do not see). It said: 'Ward cannot be described as a very truthful person in that she has changed her story to me several times . . . She is a most difficult person to evaluate. At times she is feminine and well-mannered. At other times she is rough, foul-mouthed and coarse.' In the months just before trial Judith Ward was so mentally ill she attempted suicide twice; the defence lawyers were never informed.

Someone who is unstable could, of course, be responsible for terrible crimes, and it could be argued that they are particularly eligible candidates for suspicion. However, it was the view of a detective sergeant in the Royal Ulster Constabulary who knew her that it was 'total nonsense that the IRA would have trusted a person with the mentality of Judith Ward. She was not a stable person.' A wealth of material pointing to her instability was available to the prosecution but never put in the hands of the defence. The inexplicability of this situation is still a source of bewilderment to the legal profession, and was described by her lawyer at the appeal as a dereliction of duty.

Dr Gisli Gudjonsson, the clinical psychologist, also gave evidence in the appeal. His tests on Ms Ward showed she was abnormally suggestive and prone to confabulation, filling in gaps in her memory with fictional material.

When giving evidence at the appeal, Dr MacKeith said that it would not have been reasonable to expect the jurors in her trial to be conscious of Ms Ward's mental state. The full body of interviews showed clearly how disturbed she was, but the jury and defence were never provided with that information, having heard less than half the possible evidence. The lawyers were putting together a jigsaw with most of the pieces missing. It is a scandalous indictment of the prosecution that such non-disclosure could ever have taken place, especially when a sense of concern about the woman's reliability was already in the minds of some police and expressed in their reports.

Michael Farrell, a staff journalist on the *Irish Press* and a respected writer, interviewed a woman who claimed that she had planted the M62 bomb; the detail of her account led him to believe that it was decidedly more credible than any of the multiple stories proffered by Judith Ward.

Judith Ward was not a woman likely to evoke much empathy when she came to trial. From her own mouth she was a Republican supporter and her behaviour, unless explained psychiatrically, marked her to many as an enemy of the state. The obvious and heavy-handed security arrangements accompanying trips to court and her quarantined appearance in the dock inevitably conveyed an impression of guilt and menace. During the course of her case the bomb at Guildford exploded, a factor which it would be hard for a jury to ignore. The temptation to say 'better safe than sorry' and to convict in that spirit is especially strong in cases where public safety is an issue.

Her case added to the catalogue of shameful conduct in Irish cases, but it also raised important concerns about vulnerable suspects. Even if interrogators do not use threats or physical violence, hostile and aggressive questioning by men can be oppressive to women, especially if they are psychologically fragile. This is not pleading kid gloves for the weaker sex. The research of psychiatrists working in this field indicates that the personalities most likely to admit offences they did not commit tend to be passive in the face of authority and anxious to avoid confrontation. The way most women are socialised inevitably means that they are especially susceptible, the more so if they have lived with an authoritarian man.

On 4 June 1992 Judith Ward's convictions were quashed by the Court of Appeal as unsafe and unsatisfactory; the judges, in an excoriating judgment, made clear their disgust at the non-disclosure of important evidence by the Crown, a doctor in the prison service and the scientists in the case.

The labelling of cases as 'terrorist' carries the clear risk that everyone from police through to the jury will apply a different standard because of the culture of fear which surrounds these cases. The people who could next be at risk are those of Muslim faith who stand trial for connections with Al-Qaida or other terror organisations. All of us have a responsibility to ensure that the principles which have been established from raw experience are applied to ensure just outcomes.

Because so few women are involved, the investigation and trial of serious crime is not designed with them in mind, and little consideration is given to the impact of conventional policing methods and trial procedures on women. There should be greater use of women police officers in primary roles where women are accused of crime; and officers should be better trained in good interrogation practices, creating awareness of the inherent risks. In her book *Women in Charge: Policing, Gender and Leadership* (2003), M. Silvestri argues that the structure and the culture of the police service remain deeply gendered and unsympathetic to women. She points out that while policing is supposed to be about care and control, the control element is the one that is valued.

One of the great advances in protecting the rights of those accused of crime has been the unpacking of what 'the right to due process' under human rights legislation actually means. The presence of solicitors at police stations is now almost a matter of course; statements made in their absence are normally inadmissible. The police do still try to cheat and claim that incriminating statements were made in the back of the police car on the way to the station when the solicitor was not around, but the courts are less accepting of those shortcuts. The non-disclosure of evidence to the defence is still an issue. As we saw in Sally Clark's case, the results of certain tests on one of her babies were never disclosed to her lawyers and they would have shown that the child had an infection. The code of professional conduct for experts and prosecutors must make it clear that the defence have a right to see all the material in a case. If evidence is being withheld because the security of the state would be put at risk by disclosure, the defence should be told the nature and ambit of the evidence so that a challenge can be made in court to that decision.

In examining the ways in which women experience injustice it is vital to recognise the role played by the media. The powerful sway of the tabloid press was a key element in producing a wrongful conviction for the Taylor sisters. During their trial, the press went beyond presenting a set of facts and actually constructed a set of facts, using manipulated photographs from a video-recording in order to present a story other than the truth. Michelle and Lisa Taylor were charged in 1992 with the murder of Alison Shaughnessy but were acquitted in 1994 in light of the suppression of evidence – an inconsistent statement was never revealed to the defence – and, in the words of the judgment, because of the likely impact on the trial of 'unremitting, extensive, sensational, inaccurate and misleading media coverage'.

The Crown's case was that Michelle, a jealous mistress, had murdered her lover's wife. Her sister Lisa was accused of being an accessory to the killing. Photographs and a video had been taken at Alison's wedding, which Michelle had attended. What was in reality a civil greeting between the bridegroom and a wedding guest became in the hands of the tabloids an impassioned embrace between a killer and her lover. This was achieved by splicing the video to close any distance between the parties, thereby turning a peck into a clinch. The headlines read: JUDAS KISS, CHEAT'S KILL and the *Sun*'s page ran THE 'KILLER' MISTRESS WHO WAS AT LOVER'S WEDDING with an arrow running from the word 'killer' to the face of Michelle. Even the perspective of the broadsheets was one of assumed guilt. The judges agreed that it was quite impossible to say that the jury had not been influenced in their decision by what they read in the press. Had the media succeeded in their campaign of unsubstantiated accusation, the two women would have been wrongly imprisoned for approximately 20 years.

Women are doubly at risk of miscarriage of justice: in addition to all the usual faults in the system, they face the prejudices which are particular to women. Susan May, who was convicted in 1993 of the murder of her much-loved elderly aunt, Hilda Marchbank, is still protesting her innocence in prison. She was her aunt's carer and testified that she discovered the brutal killing when she visited the house to bring food. A large support campaign has now developed despite two unsuccessful appeals and new analysis of a bloodstain on the wall of Mrs Marchbank's bedroom suggests it is neither hers nor that of Susan May but belongs to someone as yet unidentified. Susan May has been told by the prison authorities that unless she changes her attitude and admits her guilt her release on parole will be delayed indefinitely but, even after 11 years in jail, she is adamant that she will not perjure herself even to gain her freedom. The starting point of the Home Office is that a prisoner's refusal to come to terms with their conviction means that he or she will be a danger to the public if released.

It would be wrong to pretend that nothing has changed since the great scandals of the early 1990s. However, progress has been painfully slow. The consolation is that the criminal justice system has at least become more open in recent times. So the hope for the future is not that miscarriages will never occur – that would be crying for the moon – but that their occurrence will become more evident, more quickly than in the past.

10

She-devils and Amazons

In almost every culture and every period of history, a she-devil emerges as an example of all that is rotten in the female sex. This Medusa draws together the many forms of female perversion: a woman whose sexuality is debauched and foul, pornographic and bisexual; a woman who knows none of the fine and noble instincts when it comes to men and children; a woman who lies and deceives, manipulates and corrupts. A woman who is clever and powerful. This is a woman who is far deadlier than any male, in fact not a woman at all.

Other courtroom allusions are often classical. Such women are gorgons, sirens, harpies; Medusa is invoked, and Circe the seductress. Literature is rich with comparisons: Lady Macbeth, Lucretia Borgia, Messalina. Witches and Salem and all the hellish ghosts of the past rise to haunt the trials, conspiring to make woman central to the human fall from grace.

The perversion of the human spirit that underlies crimes of desperate cruelty invokes an atavistic desire to punish those who inflict such pain, not just on the victims, but on the scarred families who are left to mourn. It is all too easy to characterise women criminals as victims, because so many of those who go through the system have themselves been at the receiving end of criminal behaviour. However, the inhumanity of women can be as terrible as that of men, who enter the pantheon of monsters more often: one thinks of John Christie, Peter Sutcliffe, Dennis Nilsen. But those convicted of killing who do not belong to the dominant culture are more likely to be mythologised. Until his successful appeal, Winston Silcott, who was convicted of murdering PC Blakelock, was subjected to wilful demonising by the media, much of which was blatantly racist: the Black Beast of Broadwater Farm, the Evil Warlord, the Dark Demon. There were unsupported suggestions that he was a pimp, a drug dealer, a black Fagin who operated gangs of young criminals around London. And the imprisonment of Myra Hindley came to stand for more than simple punishment for an abhorrent crime: her continued incarceration symbolised our fear of returning to a more primitive past. In an increasingly secular world, a woman like Myra Hindley is the vessel into which society pours its dark secrets: like a war criminal, such a 'she-devil' is a reminder of what is horribly possible.

Myra Hindley is still the embodiment of all that is unnatural in women. Yet if you ask people under 40 what she actually did, they are uncertain, apart from a hazy appreciation that children were killed and that the case had sadistic sexual overtones.

It is impossible to fathom what corruption or disturbance of the human spirit can account for the horrible crimes Ian Brady and Myra Hindley committed, and no lawyer is going to be able to provide the answers.

The investigation began in October 1965 when David Smith, the brother-in-law of Myra Hindley, informed the Manchester police that he had been witness to the savage murder by Ian Brady of a 17-year-old youth. On the information he provided, the police went immediately to the address of Ian Brady and Myra Hindley and found the boy's dead body cleaved by an axe. Brady maintained at his trial that the boy was homosexual, that he had picked him up with Smith to 'queer roll' him for money, and that the death resulted accidentally when the boy struggled.

In a notebook discovered in the house was a list of names, including that of John Kilbride, a 12-year-old boy who had gone missing two years before. The police sensed that they might be dealing with a complex investigation and scoured the couple's property for information on John Kilbride's whereabouts. They found a quantity of photographs taken on the nearby moors, and with the assistance of a neighbour's child the locations in a number of other photographs were identified. A search of Saddleworth moor unearthed the body of another missing child, Lesley Ann Downey, who had disappeared the previous year.

The case began to come together when David Smith also recollected that he had seen Ian Brady remove two suitcases from the house. When they were discovered in the left-luggage office at the city's central station, they contained crucial evidence linking the pair to the body of the little girl. Days later, the body of John Kilbride was also found on the moors.

The contents of the cases included books on sexual perversion, coshes, photographs of Lesley Ann naked, and a tape-recording of her screams as she pleaded not to be subjected to whatever was happening. The voices of Ian Brady and Myra Hindley are clearly audible, remonstrating with the little girl, telling her to shut up and to co-operate. The child is threatened and told to put something in her mouth. The playing of that tape in the court did more than any other piece of evidence to secure the convictions.

At their trial in 1965 at Chester, Myra Hindley was presented by both Brady himself and the prosecution as his faithful lieutenant. In the popular press she was described as his sex slave, and there was little doubt at the time that, while her role was criminal and appalling, she was not the prime mover in the murders. The trial judge, Mr Justice Fenton Atkinson, suggested she might be capable of reform. He said: 'Though I believe that Brady is wicked beyond belief without hope of redemption, I cannot feel the same is necessarily true of Hindley once she is removed from his influence.' Yet as the years passed she moved to centre stage. Brady's psychosis is long since established, and he is now serving his sentence in a penal institution for the mentally insane. The mad dog is safely caged; whatever power he once wielded, he is now, we are told, a pathetic, demented specimen.

Not so Myra Hindley, whose survival and persistence in seeking parole right up to her death in November 2002 was seen as a testament against her. Her academic success and her support from prominent campaigners like Lord Longford and Lord Astor served only to compound public perceptions and to put paid to any suggestion that we were here dealing with a psychiatric case.

In 1994 she published a letter, begging: 'After 30 years in prison, I think I have paid my debt to society and atoned for my crimes. I ask people to judge me as I am now, and not as I was then.' She claimed in 1998 that she had been abused by Brady, who had threatened to kill her mother and grandmother and sister if she did not participate in the killings. But successive Home Secretaries refused to relent, knowing that the public would be enraged.

Dreadful crimes challenge belief in fundamental goodness, and if there is no understandable motive, such as jealousy or greed or a response to some form of provocation, we cannot comprehend them. We are disturbed at our failure to categorise the conduct, beyond accepting that it falls well beyond the bounds of moral acceptability. We are happier to catalogue the deed as a result of madness, because we do not then have to deal with the troubling concept of wickedness. Madness, for all its elusiveness, is a label which gives us comfort in the face of inexplicable behaviour. Yet there is ambivalence about how it is used. The public want murderers convicted as 'murderers' rather than madmen if they have killed in cruel and vicious ways; they want lunacy to be diagnosed after the magnitude of the crimes is recognised, not before. The catharsis of public condemnation has to be ritually experienced.

In the case of Peter Sutcliffe, the Yorkshire Ripper, the judge felt that the issue of the accused's sanity should be tried by a jury. It would have been wrong for a decision about the state of Sutcliffe's mind to have been resolved by a cabal of lawyers and medical men, even if their opinions were completely sound. Public involvement in such decisions is crucial, because it maintains a balance between the *vox populi* and the law. If it had been decided that Peter Sutcliffe was not guilty by reason of insanity and he had been sent to Broadmoor, a secure hospital, under section 60 of the Mental Health Act, the public would have felt aggrieved. That a serial killer who had stalked women, attacked them, sexually assaulted, mutilated and killed them, and also put all women in fear of their lives, should not carry the label murderer would have seemed like an affront. In fact, the jury decided that he was not criminally insane, but since his initial incarceration he has been transferred to Broadmoor in recognition of his deep psychopathy.

Many lawyers in the Temple felt that the trial was a show put on for public consumption; they thought it was an abuse of the process, as Sutcliffe's psychiatric state should have been recognised. Psychiatrists of considerable reputation were publicly undermined, but it was subsequently shown, by his move to a mental institution, that what they were saying was true. It is all too easy to make fun of a defendant's descriptions of hallucinations or divine injunctions to commit crime, but psychiatrists with a wealth of experience do know when they are dealing with a psychopath. Although the jury had no hesitation in deciding that in their view Sutcliffe was not criminally insane, that does not necessarily mean they doubted his madness. They wanted an acknowledgement of his wickedness and were unable to contemplate returning verdicts of not guilty. I have no doubt, however, that the jurors who listened to the roll-call of Sutcliffe's violence ultimately found it reassuring that his crimes could be attributed to some deep-seated mental abnormality which did not defy diagnosis.

There is a conflict between seeking an explanation for the inexplicable in madness and an unwillingness to allow madness to become an excuse. When we ask ourselves, how could anyone do that to another human being, to an innocent child? we want someone to make the behaviour intelligible to us. We hoped that psychiatry might have all the answers and that evil might be rendered obsolete, but the medical profession is not as magical or all-powerful as we like to believe. Explanations for deliberate acts of criminality are sometimes not available; although these occasions are comparatively rare, there are motiveless crimes with no suggestion of diagnosed disease of the mind. And, of course, if they are denied by those charged with their commission, no insight comes from the offender.

Evil as a concept is resisted by some people, but the majority do accept the idea of evil and want punishment for its perpetrators. Sexual depravity as a component in killing heightens our revulsion, and our inability to understand becomes the more pressing if children are involved. However, countless men have been convicted of revolting crimes, beyond the imagination of most people – raping and mutilating, torturing and killing, severing and dismembering – in a nightmare of atrocities that make one long for the simple bullet in the head or the knife wound. These men fill the pages of true crime compilations and chambers of horrors, but few of them are remembered by name.

We feel differently about a woman doing something consciously cruel because of our expectations of the 'gentle', nurturing sex. It defies explanation that someone like Myra Hindley, a woman, can stand by and allow torture to take place. Similarly, Mary Bell, the 10-year-old girl who said she strangled two small children 'for fun', perplexed and terrified the British public because her behaviour contradicted the sugar and spice make-up that little girls are expected to have. Yet in every child's fairy story the delicate heroine is contrasted with a wicked woman who is there to put fear into the hearts of little boys (and girls), a reminder of corrupted womanhood. Wicked witches, old crones, evil stepmothers and ugly sisters leap from the pages in greater numbers even than the giants and ogres. Terror is a man, but wickedness is a woman. These women, who either have a cruel beauty like the stepmother of Snow White or are as ugly as sin, insinuate themselves into positions of power over children and grown men, luring them to danger, plumping them up for a final devouring, cutting them to pieces.

Most police mug-shots are less than flattering, but the photograph of Myra Hindley which is forever used in the press is in a class of its own, and bears little resemblance to the woman. The female who looks out with steely eyes has badly dyed, dishevelled hair and a heavy face. Her mouth is tight and mean. This is a woman to hate. When an artist displayed a portrait of Myra Hindley based on that infamous photograph, in a Royal Academy exhibition called Sensation in 1997, it was vandalised despite the passage of time.

A female client spoke to me back in 1985 about a woman incarcerated with her called Carol Hanson, who she said was serving 20 years for child murders. The story amongst the prisoners was that she had been employed as a foster mother and had killed the babies in her care. She was supposed to have cut them up and sent the pieces of their bodies through the post to their natural mothers. To the other convicted prisoners, many of whom had had their own children taken from them, she was a pariah. She had to keep away from them for her own safety and had hung a notice on her cell door saying she killed only one child.

I was interested in this woman. If she had committed crimes against children, why was her name unknown to us? What made Myra Hindley so different? I had great difficulty in tracing reports of the crime and eventually found out that she had been convicted of murder in circumstances very similar to those of Myra Hindley, but bearing no relation to the prison mythology of cutting up babies.

Carol Hanson and her husband Michael were convicted in 1970 of murdering Christine Beck, who was 10 years old. Michael Hanson, a soldier, was also convicted of unlawful sexual intercourse with the child. The court had heard evidence of 'sex games' played regularly by Mrs Hanson and numerous children aged between 11 and 15. At least five of them had been sexually assaulted. The Crown's case in relation to the death was that, as part of 'some form of perverted sexual pleasure, Christine was sexually assaulted, partially strangled and then stabbed twice through the heart with a flick-knife'. The defendants blamed each other, Carol saying that the killing happened when she was downstairs, unaware of what was going on.

My client described Carol Hanson as someone who had become 'noncified', an elaboration of the prison term 'nonce' which is used for sex offenders. She explained that the woman was now a broken creature, despised by all the other inmates. This was not true of Myra Hindley, who had her share of physical attacks and rejection but survived intact. If punishment had not bowed her, the public expect guilt and remorse to achieve the same effect. That is what separated Myra Hindley from other women offenders, and gave her the status of high priestess of wickedness.

In 1986 the Moors Murders case was reopened when Ian Brady was said in the press to have confessed to reporters that he had also killed two other young people, Keith Bennett and Pauline Reade. In the prison interviews with the police which followed this disclosure, Ian Brady refused to help, but Myra Hindley admitted that they had also been murdered. She described the unbearable pain of confessing to crimes of such enormity, but wanted the whole thing to be laid to rest for herself and for the families. Her years of imprisonment had provided ample opportunity for self-analysis and introspection, and she was able to describe the fierceness of her passion for Ian Brady, who had such a powerful hold upon her at the time, but her attempts at explanation only fuelled the cynicism of police and public. The lucid explanation that Myra Hindley herself put forward to explain (but not excuse) her involvement in the killings – that she was then a naïve young girl totally in thrall to a complex, experienced man – missed its mark because of the very coherence with which it was expressed. From the knowledge of her as she had become, the public found it hard to extract a sense of the woman that she was then.

An obsessional quality, which she continued to possess, was clearly revealed in the personal diary that Myra Hindley kept when she first met Ian Brady at their place of work. The entries are a catalogue of childish desperation for him to show some interest in her, and since they were not written for public consumption and were penned before the spiral of degradation was under way, they support her contention that she was deeply immature. But it is hard to see beyond the strength of character and force of will which she came to exude in middle age. Her all too late confessions of guilt in relation to the original charges and the further admission of two additional murders were hard to interpret as genuine repentance, and appeared rather as part of calculated machinations to get herself released. Press revelations of her lesbian relationships in prison had further stoked the fires of abhorrence.

There are very few female serial killers who stalk and kill strangers. The nearest in recent memory was the American, Aileen Whornos whose pathetic life was immortalised in the film *Monster* in 2003.

No case has emerged, however, where the killer is a lone female operator, who stalks successive, unfamiliar prey. Despite efforts by Hollywood to create movies on those lines, there seems to be no female Boston Strangler or Yorkshire Ripper. The nearest women have come to this systematic taking of life are when women carers, such as nurses or keepers of old people's homes, kill their charges, or bizarre instances like Mary Beth Tinning, an American, who gave birth to nine babies in 14 years and killed them all, year after year. When the nurse, Beverly Allitt, stood trial in 1993 for the killing of babies and young children the public were horrified. She was diagnosed as suffering from Munchausen's Syndrome by

Proxy in which women use the ostensibly caring role of mother, nurse or nanny to inflict harm on children. While she was clearly shown to be highly disturbed and dangerous, the degree to which her offences were treated with disbelief and then moral panic reflected the extent to which she, as a nurse caring for children, had shattered the image of womanhood held most sacred by the general public.

Men who commit multiple crimes are usually involved in a misogynistic power-play deriving from a deep-rooted anger against women, and often direct their perverse rage at women they perceive as bad. The blame for the criminality of the serial killer is frequently put on his maternal relationship or lack of one. Interestingly, the experience does not seem to operate in reverse, with powerless women seeking indiscriminate vengeance against men. The physical imbalance between men and women might again be a factor here, but why do we not see women with access to guns mowing down their oppressors at random?

On the few occasions when women have played a role in serial killings, as in the Moors and Manson murders, they have functioned as handmaidens to a master. This is not the same dynamic as that of the battered wife who submits or colludes because of her own passivity in the face of violence. These are women in the power of strong-willed men who kill to express their scorn for humanity, men who see themselves as superior and are empowered by exacting the ultimate price from their victims. Some women feel strangely flattered at being chosen by such men, as though they had been singled out from the ordinary run of womankind.

There are people whose sexual make-up seems to require a relinquishing of personal will; it implies never having to face moral responsibility for sexual indiscretion or having to accept guilt if your deviance becomes criminal. It may be that at that time in her life Myra Hindley needed Brady's sexual control just as much as he needed a witness to his atrocities, and that they became welded together by their mutual knowledge.

No one should be surprised at Myra Hindley's reconstruction of the past. We all do it, and the enormity of her shame must require some delusion. But every attempt she made to explain her acts only fed the view of her as a devious, manipulative woman. Her own gender is especially repulsed by her crimes.

Rosemary West has now replaced Myra Hindley as the female monster within our jails. She is still an enigma because she failed to testify at her trial and has withdrawn into silence, having said she wishes to remain in prison for the rest of her life. Frederick and Rosemary West were arrested in February 1994 after their garden was dug up during a search for their daughter, Heather, who had gone missing seven years previously. The police unearthed more than one body. In interview, Fred West admitted having killed his daughter and two other young women but insisted that Rose knew nothing at all. However, in the excavations of the house which followed, six other bodies were found. Fred was not a novice at murder when he met Rose. He admitted murdering his first wife and a previous lover and hinted that other bodies were buried in shallow graves, but it was in his relationship with Rose that a desperate campaign of sexual depravity reached its apotheosis. Together they would lure hitchhikers into their car – young women reassured by the presence of a woman. They would abduct their victims, violate them sexually and then kill them. The vile torture to which the women were subjected was so terrible that the press felt inhibited about printing all the details. Rosemary West may have been drawn into killing because of her infatuation with Fred but she could not claim immaturity as Myra Hindley did. Rose took part in serial killing over many years. There was direct evidence that she herself was a sexual abuser and not just an aider and abetter. On New Year's Day 1995 Fred West committed suicide in prison, leaving Rose to stand trial alone in October 1995. She was convicted on ten counts of murder and sentenced to life imprisonment.

The idea of contemporary witches may seem laughable, but women who murder summon up a special revulsion. The Lindy Chamberlain case in 1980 in Australia became a *cause célèbre* for a mixture of reasons, one of which was undoubtedly that the person at the centre of the allegations was a woman and a mother. The Chamberlain family had gone on a camping holiday to Ayers Rock, which is to Australians what Stonehenge is to the English. The parents had with them their two young sons as well as a newborn daughter, Azaria. Lindy Chamberlain put the baby to sleep in its bassinet and had only just rejoined a group of campers when a cry was heard and she flew back to the tent. Her story remained consistent from the outset: seeing a dingo (wild dog) emerge from the tent, she ran in to the baby, but it had disappeared, snatched, as she assumed, by the animal. There was blood spotted about in the tent and a search by campers and subsequently by the police discovered no infant, nor any remains. The couple were interviewed repeatedly by the media, and after their initial grief displayed a calmness in the face of questioning which they attributed to their religious faith as Seventh Day Adventists. They explained that they had accepted the baby's death as part of God's great design and had resigned themselves to their loss.

Some time after the death, the baby's stretch-towelling suit and her vest were found, allegedly in a neat pile. Zoologists testified that, though they had not known a dingo to kill a human baby before, they did think it was capable of peeling and shaking a baby out of its clothes. They also believed that a dingo would devour every last fragment of an infant, leaving no debris behind.

Speculation and gossip mounted, and even by the time of the coroner's inquest the couple were being accused behind hands of killing the baby. The problem was absence of motive. The mother showed no signs of postnatal depression, and the baby had seemed to be particularly welcomed because she was a little girl in a family of boys. She was to all appearances well cared for and loved. Why would they do it? There were rumours about human sacrifice in biblical fashion, as though anyone who belonged to a peculiar religious sect might be tempted to surrender unto the Father what was really His. It was even suggested that there were links with the Jonestown mass suicide a couple of years before, when whole families had surrendered themselves to the higher good. The hiss of 'burn the bitch' followed Lindy Chamberlain wherever she went. There were stories that she had dressed her baby in black and behaved strangely, all part of the hatred that the Australian public was developing for her. The family received calls from people who found her composure 'affronting' and accused her of treating the baby's death as 'a big joke'. She was not behaving in the manner expected of a grieving mother.

By the time Lindy Chamberlain stood trial for murder, she was expecting another baby and her pregnancy was obvious to the world. This was seen as an attempt to manipulate the sympathies of the court, although the trial had originally been set down for many months before, when no one would have been aware of her condition. She appeared in the dock with her husband, who was charged with aiding and abetting her after the event. The prosecution case turned on the forensic evidence of a bloodstain on the baby-suit, which a British expert said was in his view the imprint of a small, bloodied hand, a contention which did not withstand cross-examination. Splatters of blood were allegedly found in the well of the Chamberlains' car, but there was evidence to suggest that other substances might have created the same response to the haematology tests. As against the forensic case of the prosecution, an independent witness for the defence said she heard the baby cry out when Lindy Chamberlain was standing in front of her. It was as a result of that cry that the mother ran to the tent, and therefore the baby could not have already been dead as the state was maintaining.

In the theatre of the criminal court, Lindy Chamberlain was a bad witness. She did not disclose the emotional torment which the situation (and public) seemed to demand. She was disgusted and angry with the way the media had treated her, and made no attempt to conceal her feelings. Her anger at the prosecution meant that she came across as a cold, hard-faced woman. She was damned if she was going to give them the show they wanted to prove her innocence, and damned she was as a result.

In this country, the professional rule against speaking to your client when he or she is in the middle of giving evidence is religiously observed, but in Australia there is a slight relaxation, in that whilst counsel cannot talk to the defendant about the content of their evidence, they can discuss extraneous matters such as the client's demeanour in the witness box. John Bryson, who wrote the definitive account of the trial, recorded a conversation relayed to him by someone who was present. Andrew Kirkham, Lindy Chamberlain's counsel, was worried about the impression she was making and warned her against sounding 'like a fish-wife' as she answered the prosecutor's questions. He advised her to hold her temper, not to sound too harsh or angry. He suggested she should try to be more 'demure'. This was a lawyer who knows his trade attempting to squeeze his client into a more acceptable manner; there is no criminal lawyer who has not done the same in his or her time. Lindy Chamberlain's reported response was, 'I am the way I am. The jury will just have to get used to it.' The jury did not, and she was found guilty, although no reason could be found to explain why she might have killed her baby. Benjamin Cardozo, the American Supreme Court judge, recognised this type of problem when he wrote, 'Deep below consciousness are other forces, the likes and dislikes, the predilections and the prejudices, the complex of instincts and emotions and habits and convictions, which make the man, whether he be litigant or judge.'

We should add jurors to the list.

After the failure of successive appeals, Lindy Chamberlain and her husband were eventually cleared because the forensic evidence was discredited. But the gender factor was the one that really counted.

Lindy Chamberlain did not cry. Ruth Ellis did not cry. Myra Hindley did not cry. Real women cry. Yet even when they do, it can be met with scepticism. When Ian Huntley stood trial in 2003 for the murder of Holly Wells and Jessica Chapman, two 10-year-old girls, his girlfriend Maxine Carr was also in the dock, charged with providing him with a false alibi. Carr's account to the police was that she was upstairs in the bath when the girls came to the house asking for her. She claimed that she heard Ian speak to them outside but that they then left without anything untoward happening. She was in fact 100 miles away in Grimsby. In the week before being arrested she helped Ian Huntley clean the whole house from top to bottom, which meant that possible forensic evidence was unavailable.

At her trial Maxine Carr admitted lying but described her relationship with Ian as one in which he was controlling, jealous and at times violent. She said that she had covered up for Ian Huntley at his insistence because he had been falsely accused of rape in the past and said he might face the finger of unjust blame again because of that history. She said she could not let herself believe that he had killed the girls. However, Detective Chief Inspector Hebb, number two in the inquiry team, was unimpressed by Carr's tearful performance in the witness box, still convinced that she must have had her suspicions about what Huntley had done. 'Rather cynically is how I view it,' he told the *Observer* in December 2003. His view, so publicly expressed, fed into the general vilification of Maxine Carr in the press. Public vitriol was such that she had to be given a fresh identity and placed in a safe house on her release from prison.

In her authoritative book, *Women Who Kill* (1991), Ann Jones suggests that moral panics about women and crime coincide with the periods when women make strides towards equality, and that such panics may be a crude and perhaps even unconscious attempt at controlling these advances. She cites the cases of two twentieth-century American examples of the female criminal, Ruth Snyder and Alice Crimmins, in support of this view, placing both historically in times of dynamic change for women. Ruth was tried with her lover Judd Gray in 1927 for the killing of her husband, who had been bludgeoned to death with a sash-weight. The couple had been conducting a clandestine affair and the murder had been made to look like a robbery, with Ruth left tied up and some jewellery missing. The sophistication of this plot was somewhat undermined by the discovery that the seductress had simply hidden the supposed proceeds of this robbery under her mattress. When asked about the name of Judd in her address book, she immediately asked if he had confessed.

The attorney who represented Judd Gray went to great lengths to describe the wiliness of Ruth Snyder's character:

That woman like a poisonous snake drew Judd Gray into her glistening coils, and there was no escape. It was a peculiarly alluring seduction. Just as a piece of steel jumps and clings to the powerful magnet, so Judd Gray came within the powerful, compelling, attractive force of that woman. She held him fast. This woman, this peculiar venomous species of humanity, was abnormal, possessed of an all-consuming, all-absorbing passion, an animal lust, which seemingly was never satiated.

Every detail of the adulterous affair was pored over in court, and in the press. There Ruth Snyder was described as having no heart, being a bad woman, a bad wife, a bad mother, who did not even look like a woman. Comment was made on her dyed blonde hair, her 'masculine' jaw and her mouth, which was 'as cold, hard and unsympathetic as a crack in a dried lemon'. Ruth Snyder and Judd Gray went to the electric chair.

In 1967, with the rise of women's liberation, came Alice Crimmins, who was tried for the murder of her two children. Again, Alice did not look like a decent woman, let alone a proper mother: she was a sexy blonde who wore tight trousers and had affairs and, like Ruth Ellis, had been a nightclub hostess. The police officer in the case took one look at her and decided he had his murderess. He took her to the scene where her little girl's body had been found and showed her the corpse. She failed the test by failing to cry, although she did faint. It took him two years to put together a case against her, and it later came to light that this had involved bribing and suborning witnesses.

Alice Crimmins suffered the same fate as Lindy Chamberlain. A campaign of attrition was mounted against her by the press and by the time she came to trial she was angry and defiant. She too was hurt that her grief was not recognised because her manifestation of it did not conform to expectations. Apparently she too was coaxed and cajoled into dressing more appropriately, wearing her hair differently and generally presenting herself in a more acceptable form. However, she was certainly not going to break down in court just for the spectators, which meant that she was seen, as usual, as unnatural and hard. This being the 1960s, she was described by the press as a 'sexy swinger': an example of what freedom for women brought. Alice was convicted on the doubtful evidence of having been seen in a car with a bundle, supposedly a body, and an unknown man. A former lover of little credibility claimed she had confessed to the killing to him, but little credibility is more than none, which was the status attached to Alice's own account. After a successful appeal she was retried and again convicted; another appeal led eventually to her having the conviction reduced to manslaughter.

It is difficult to assess accurately whether Ann Jones's theory about moral backlashes against female advances holds true in Britain. Serious crime by women here is still sufficiently rare to invoke horror whenever it happens, and it is hard to link the outrage to specific periods in history, but a number of notorious cases are remarkably similar in their facts and in the response they evoked to the ones cited by Ann Jones.

Edith Thompson was hanged at Holloway Prison in January 1923 at precisely the time when women were being admitted to the professions, having successfully secured the vote. She had been convicted of murdering her husband.

The Crown alleged that the Thompsons were walking home in a dark road in Ilford, Essex, in October 1922, when a figure emerged from the shadows and stabbed Mr Thompson to death. The assailant was later proved to be Frederick Bywaters, a young ship's purser and Edith's lover, once a lodger at her house. From the moment of her arrest, Edith denied complicity in the killing and insisted that she had no idea that Bywaters was anywhere in the vicinity or had any intention of harming her husband. Bywaters himself confirmed this. However, the core of the evidence against her at her trial at the Old Bailey was her correspondence with the man she loved whilst he was at sea. Her love letters seemed to indicate that she was learning about poisons and wanted him to send her something to do away with her husband. The defence were able to show that much of the contents were fanciful, that she was merely using the letters as a means of indulging her fantasies of being free to share a life with Freddy. The autopsy report from a celebrated pathologist, Sir Bernard Spilsbury, proved that her claim to be adding broken glass to her husband's food was nonsense, wholly unsupported by the findings at the post-mortem.

The picture that comes across clearly today is of a woman trapped in a loveless marriage to a less than admirable man who physically abused her, but she received little understanding from the trial judge, Mr Justice Shearman, and his bias against her repeatedly filtered into his summing up. The same old judicial formula was used whereby judges absolve themselves from any responsibility for prejudicing a jury when they indicate their own interpretation of the evidence. Mr Justice Shearman invoked this when he chose to assert his view, and followed it with the rider that the final decision was, of course, in the hands of the jury: 'That is for you and not for me.' He was clearly convinced that Edith had incited Frederick Bywaters to murder. Even if she was not privy to the fine detail of the ultimate plan or its execution, it was she, as an older woman, who had to be held responsible. His moral outrage on behalf of husbands was obvious, and he was particularly offended by the descriptions of the defendants' great love.

At the end of one of Edith's letters to Freddy, she referred to her husband as having 'the right by law to all that you have the right to by nature and love'. Mr Justice Shearman vented his spleen:

Gentlemen, if that nonsense means anything it means that the love of a husband for his wife is something improper because marriage is acknowledged by the law, and that the love of a woman for her lover, illicit and clandestine, is something great and noble. I am certain that you like any other right-minded persons will be filled with disgust at such a notion.

His Lordship also suggested that some strange chivalry, rather than an expression of the truth, might account for Freddy's exculpating Edith.

In the press, Edith was portrayed in a covert way as the New Woman: she earned her own living as a supervisor in a clothing manufacturer's, taking home more than her husband, who was a city clerk. She was portrayed as a flapper, who liked to go to a show in the West End and have a port and lemon with her girlfriends. She showed little interest in having children. Was this the kind of woman society wanted?

Poor Edith went to the scaffold amidst some public concern about her conviction. Horrible stories were told in the press alleging that she disintegrated emotionally at the point of hanging, that she fought, kicked, screamed and protested her innocence to the last, and that five warders had to hold her down as she was carried to the gallows. It was even suggested that 'her insides fell out'. As late as 1956, during the death penalty debate, the then Home Secretary denied these accounts, but accepted that she had to be given sedatives before the hanging. Recent investigations into the case suggest she may have been pregnant at the time of the hanging, but her Home Office file has been withdrawn without reason and is no longer available to the public.

The trial of Ruth Ellis took place in 1955 at a time when women, having been shooed back into domesticity after the war, were being portrayed in advertisements and on the radio as the core of the modern nuclear family. There had been a general outcry against the collapse of morals due to the pressures of war, and calls had gone up for the re-establishment of 'traditional values' – always bad news for women. Ruth Ellis served as a perfect example of the consequences of female venality, and the double standard relating to sexual behaviour was never questioned. It was one thing for David Blakely to hang around nightclubs picking up hostesses, but quite another to be that hostess. And while it wasn't altogether decent for Blakely to slap Ruth Ellis about, had she not an illegitimate child and a daughter by a failed marriage whom she did not even look after? She failed society's expectations on all fronts. The only criticism made of David Blakely was that he gave her false encouragement, letting her believe that they might have a future together. Leslie Boyd, who was the chief clerk at the Old Bailey at the time, described Ruth Ellis in his reminiscences as cold and calculating, an example of evil womanhood.

One of Britain's 'swinging sixties' cases took place at the High Court in Aberdeen. On 2 December 1968 Sheila Garvie, who was 34, and her lover Brian Tevendale, who was 22, were sentenced to life imprisonment for the murder of her wealthy farmer husband, who had disappeared in mysterious circumstances the previous April. Not until August was the decomposed body of Maxwell Garvie found by the police in an underground tunnel some miles from his farm. During the trial it was said that Mrs Garvie had wined, dined and slept with Tevendale in the knowledge that he had bludgeoned and then shot her husband to death in their own home while her three young children slept. She was described variously by counsel as Lady Chatterley, Lady Bountiful and Lady Macbeth.

As with Edith Thompson, it was suggested by the Solicitor-General, who was prosecuting, that because of her age Sheila was ultimately responsible for the crime. Particular exception is taken to women having young lovers. 'Is Mrs Garvie the real brains behind the crime? She had everything to gain by its successful completion, she would get rid of a husband with whom, in her own words, life was hell . . . Do you think she is resourceful, cool, business-like?' The sordid life to which she was subjected by her husband was described by Sheila Garvie during the trial in some detail, no doubt in an attempt to counter the automatic disapproval it was anticipated the jury would feel about her affair with a younger man. The Solicitor-General was then able to describe her defence as a double-edged sword, on the grounds that 'it may show you she would have a very strong motive to seek her husband's destruction'. This is a Catch 22 situation which faces many women on trial who try to expose their husband's rotten behaviour.

Where Ann Jones's theory has most potency is in the legal response to women who are depicted as 'women's libbers'. For a while the theory that women's expanded horizons led to more female crime had some currency, but examination of the data showed that women are no more criminal now than they have ever been. The number of reported cases has increased in the last 30 years but this is consistent with more effective policing of the kinds of crime traditionally committed by women, largely offences of dishonesty.

As well as witches, we have amazons: the women who have most seriously confronted the male authority of the court are those whose offences emanate from their political beliefs. In the 1970s and 1980s we saw many waves of political women coming before the courts, involved in anti-nuclear campaigns like the women's peace camp at Greenham Common, or feminist demonstrations such as Reclaiming the Night and Women's Right to Choose on abortion. These public campaigns echoed the suffragette campaigns of the beginning of the century. The response of the court had changed remarkably little, and women voiced very similar criticisms of the patronising and paternalistic nature of the system.

The operation of the criminal justice system in public order cases always produces feelings of anger. The mass-processing involved in dealing with so many cases arising out of the exercise of political freedom inevitably creates a sense of injustice. In most circumstances the response of the court is no different whether you are male or female, but some other component does come into operation when the demonstration is actively organised by women for women.

In the early days at Newbury Magistrates' Court, where the Greenham campaign cases were tried, the celebratory atmosphere of women coming together demanding peace penetrated the courtroom. The magistrates were perplexed and unsettled by the motley collection of women who appeared before them: women of all classes, ages and marital status, gay women, nuns, mothers. I was instructed to appear for a group of peace women. After making the legal argument in relation to the right of way and not succeeding, we had agreed that I would withdraw and no longer act so that the women could make their own political statements. I stayed to watch, and it was quite extraordinary to see how the traditional regimented courtroom procedure was changed. One after another, the women gave forceful explanations of why they were involved. Their large numbers together in the dock meant that they were not intimidated and were able to express themselves freely in what is normally an inhibiting male theatre. They gave each other encouragement and support.

Apart from the male magistrates and a few police officers, the only other man in the court was the court interpreter, who was there to translate the incantation of the Japanese Buddhist nuns. He had learned his Japanese in a prisoner-of-war camp and he entered into the spirit of the event as few interpreters do. Instead of sounding like the speaking clock, he charged his translation with some emotion and enthusiasm, and spoke with deep feeling about the horror of war. The women were all found guilty, but my last memory of the courtroom was of a great festival of kissing and hugging, with the little interpreter getting his fair share of the affection.

However, this female insurrection had to be contained, and a decision was made to separate the women so that only one or two were tried at any one time in the courtroom. The variety of the women involved was soon homogenised by the popular press into the 1970s stereotype of the political woman in dungarees, spiked hair, non-matching earrings and no trace of lipstick. The legend was created that this or that woman was a man-hater, an iconoclast with no respect for the institutions, a woman who abandoned her responsibilities of home, hearth and children to haunt the perimeters of legitimate male activity in defending the realm. The antagonism towards the Greenham women was soon tangible in the courtrooms; in the most minimal of obstruction cases, questions would be asked about whether women had children and who had been caring for them at the time of their arrest. No miner on a picket line would ever be asked to account for himself in this way.

Women who enter the political arena are either mythologised or marginalised. Greenham moved from being portrayed in the press as legitimate peace campaigning to a sideshow, and eventually a freak show. This process of marginalisation was completed in the courts. However, contemporary politics threw up a different kind of she-devil.

The trial of the Price sisters in 1974 for bombing the Old Bailey court was the first of a number of cases, alleging acts of terrorism, against women involved in Irish republicanism. The surprise and sense of horror that women were playing a prominent role ran right through the trial and the publicity which surrounded it. The headlines on 11 September 1973 blazoned the significance of their leading roles: DOLOURS BOSSED THE IRA BOMB SQUAD (*The Times*); THE TERROR GANG WAS LED BY A GIRL CLAIMS QC (*Daily Mirror*) – and she was 'a pretty 23-year-old redhead' to boot, according to the *Sun*.

The terrorist woman is a new category of female offender, in that she challenges the pathos of so much female crime. Her attack upon the state is dual, assaulting the institutions both directly, in bombing attacks, and indirectly, by confronting the traditional role of woman as a cornerstone of established society. Some women criminologists perceive a 'unisexing' of terrorists, with women activists being denied their gender. I have always found the opposite, that in fact women involved in terrorist trials stimulate enormous prurient interest. Their womanliness is described in detail, with accounts in the press of the clothing they wear and their appearance in the dock.

There seems to be a sexiness about the combination of women, so long as they are young, and power: possibly the idea of a bossy, pretty woman like Dolours Price summons up repressed sexual feelings about dominant women. The words 'cold', 'calculating' and 'ruthless' are often juxtaposed with 'attractive', 'vivacious' and 'pretty'. The men involved in these cases – police, lawyers, judges and reporters – are titillated by images of the Armalite rifle in feminine hands, but they are also fearful of its implications. Running through most of the cases of IRA activity involving women is a sense of horror that women should use the very attributes which make them so appealing to men to undermine their guard.

In the Price sisters' trial in 1974, evidence was given that Dolours was asked by police about a photograph in which she was seen smiling in the company of a British soldier. It was maintained that she flirted with the army to get information, ruthlessly exploiting her charms. According to press reports she had 'fluttered her long natural eyelashes' at army officers.

Being duped by men is one thing, but to be taken in by a woman particularly rankles with men. Judges frequently become exercised that women provide cover for activities which are traditionally seen as within the province of men, presenting as half of a married couple, as Martina Anderson did in the Brighton bombing conspiracy, or as half of a courting couple for the planting of a bomb, as was alleged against Carole Richardson in the Guildford bombing trial. It was alleged by the prosecution that when Marion Price was being interrogated after being arrested for the Old Bailey explosion and was asked about other possible bombs, she looked at her watch at 2.50 p.m. and smiled. At 2.44 p.m. a bomb had exploded in Great Scotland Yard. Her image as an ice-hearted maiden was reinforced by the claim that she was known as the Armalite Widow because of her reputation as a crack shot against the British army. Whether this was because she made widows out of military wives, or was a woman no longer dependent on a man, or was as deadly as the Black Widow spider was never made clear, but one was left in no doubt that this young woman was lethal.

Women like Ulrike Meinhof and Gudrun Ensslin, who led the German Baader Meinhof group of urban guerrillas, Bernardine Dohrn and Kathy Boudin of the American Weather Underground, the Angry Brigade women, Anna Mendlesson and Hilary Creek, or Patty Hearst, have all provoked more interest and speculation than their male comrades. All were educated, middle-class women who became involved at the extreme end of the radical politics which grew out of the anti-Vietnam war movement. However, it was their sexual liberation, rather than their class analysis, that seemed to interest the male voyeur.

This response may have been influenced by some of the cultural images which were prevalent at that time, in the late 1960s and the early 1970s, images of leather-clad Diana Rigg in *The Avengers* or 'Pussy Galore' in *Goldfinger*, physically able to floor men without losing any of their sexual charm. These women also functioned alongside men, introducing exciting possibilities about what they got up to sexually, in contrast to women-only politics like Greenham Common, which are at best boring and at worst involve sexual activity that few want to hear about.

The domination imagery is interesting because it has to stay on the right side of the narrow line between attractive sado-masochistic fantasies and the fearful domineering form of control. Evidence was adduced against Dolours Price that she had ordered Paul Holmes, a co-conspirator, to take the considerable risk of going back to prime the Scotland Yard bomb when he had forgotten to do so. The impression given was of a woman who expected manliness of her men, a challenge that few can resist. But the dividing line is very narrow. The seductiveness of powerful women is mesmerising but also frightening because of the unspoken notions that such power is won at the expense of men, and that powerful women consume and destroy. The need to show who is master (the same dynamics which underlie domestic violence) is played out publicly in the courtroom, as women are reminded of their proper place.

The theatrical convention, from Jean Genet to Monty Python, in which the judge indulges his fetish for sado-masochism with some beautiful, scantily clad dominatrix spanking him in the wings of the court, has its roots in the complicated relationship between sex and guilt, punishment and power. These elements charge the atmosphere at the trials of political, independent women, and as a result subtle and insidious inferences undermine the proceedings. There is no difference in the way women are sentenced – the courts cannot be criticised for inequality on that score – but the sense of alarm that they should be involved in such warlike activity infects the rhetoric of the courtroom. In summing up to the jury, or in sentencing, judges almost unconsciously single women out for comment. When Martina Anderson and Ella O'Dwyer were sentenced after the Brighton bombing trial in 1986, the judge made a special comment about their cold-heartedness. On the evidence, they were no less feeling than their male co-accused, but of course 'caring' is not the province of men.

However, although the IRA women invoked complicated responses, their commitment was understood. The calculated nature of their offences means they acquired the 'bad' rather than 'mad' label, but their motive was appreciable. The support they received from their own community helped them maintain dignity and self-esteem, and they were acknowledged as a special category of prisoner within the penal population itself. They may have been perceived as a monstrous regiment, but they do not fill the nightmares of the public in the way that Myra Hindley, Rose West and female child abusers do.

11

The Myth of Post-feminism

The fashionable claim is that feminism has had its day. Women have pulled down all the barriers to their aspirations, have renegotiated their relationships with men and are now scaling the heights that were formerly beyond their reach. The 'f' word cannot be mentioned without a boo from the sidelines. Girls are doing better than boys in education; they are filling the universities; they are becoming priests. Childcare is being shared, new men are staying at home while their women bring home the bacon. If we are to believe certain newspapers, our preoccupations are to ensure our pay is high and our weight is low. A few more legislative changes and all will be well with the world.

Yet the gains for women have been very uneven and the genderquake, ending the world as we all knew it, has been much less seismic than was predicted. We may be more aware of violence against women and the extent of abuse, we may exclaim about the problems surrounding rape prosecutions and we may recognise the need to reform institutions but for many women the changes that have taken place have not reached into the dark places where primordial power-play still simmers.

Some young women eschew feminism because they think it means man-hating rather than ending the ways in which relationships between the sexes have been blighted by inequality. We should not be surprised, given the way feminism is portrayed as unsexy, no fun and the road to a lonely middle age. In fact, men and women both are beneficiaries in an environment where there is no automatic hierarchy or prescribed roles and no dominion claimed because of gender. Human rights is all about the recognition of another's essential humanity. Like Mary Wollstonecraft, I want women to have power not over men, but over themselves. However, while today's young women may be unenthusiastic about organising under women's banners they are just as keen to confront unfairness when they see it. Political activism has diminished in an era of broader general prosperity, which has made it easier for people to insulate themselves from the social problems of the disadvantaged; yet those problems do require a political response. Increasingly, the arena of political change has moved to the courts, where individual cases become a way of raising wider political issues. As Rahila Gupta of Southall Black Sisters says, 'it is as though individual pain is the only point of entry into an understanding of a systemic disorder'. Law has become a political space for women that is capable of being used as an engine of change. Some of the most high profile and important cases heard in the courts in recent years, aside from criminal cases, have involved women asserting their rights and testing the boundaries of the law: Dianne Pretty's case over the right to die, Diane Blood over the right to conceive using the sperm of her dead husband, the women in the military who were dismissed once they became pregnant.

In many respects the battle for formal equality has been won. For the most part, old-fashioned rank prejudice has gone, since the laws which underpin formal equality were introduced in 1976. Examples of crude, in your face prejudice are much more rare. The case which now has to be made is for substantive equality – treatment as equals, taking account of the real experiences of women and the context of their lives. There has to be greater understanding of the differential effects of policies, which on the surface are neutral. It is also important to acknowledge that women are not just one homogeneous group. Discrimination now is much more subtle and nuanced and often operates most fiercely at that junction where different forms of prejudice intersect. When race and class overlap with the social vector of gender, we see in sharp focus the disadvantages still suffered by so many women.

The backlash against feminism takes many forms. Men are the ones we are now to be concerned about. They are being battered; they are having false claims made against them of child abuse because of false memory syndrome; they are being refused access to their children; they are falling prey to shameless hussies who try to get money out of tabloids for their stories. All of it does happen. Men can be used and abused too. Their pain at false accusation is no less. Their loss of their children is just as raw a wound. But the smoke and mirrors used to enlarge these claims are the products of fear that the old arrangements between the sexes might be reconfigured in ways that may be less to the satisfaction of some men. After September 11, American evangelical preachers claimed that the events were a punishment for the behaviour of feminists and other deviants.

I do not want to minimise the many gains that have been made over the last decade. There are causes for optimism. The creation of pilot programmes, where special domestic violence courts will operate a speedy, multi-agency response to abuse, is a major development. The many projects within the police, prosecution and penal service to address women's concerns are to be welcomed. There is a desperate need for special units to deal with rape cases and the Crown Prosecution Service is putting them in place. A lot has improved within the courts and legal system. There is no doubt that government has taken on many women's issues and taken women's experience of victimisation to the heart of criminal law policy. However, women's concerns have been rolled into a generalised rhetoric about victims. All victims are bundled up together, when the government should be brave enough to say that cases involving abuse of intimacy and the historic discrimination against women deserve special treatment. But ministers live in fear of being ridiculed as being in the thrall of 'feminists'; they recoil from the reality that the most ill-treated victims within our system are women and children, and that this is still a reflection of some very disconcerting facts about male violence. What is the gender of most children abused over a long period and eventually killed by parents, from Jasmine Beckford to Victoria Climbié? Go through the files of the NSPCC and you will find that they are almost invariably girls. Of course, boy children are also killed in outbursts of rage or to wreak revenge but the slow torture of children is most often directed at girls. What is the gender of the partner most often beaten in a relationship? What is the gender of those most often sexually violated? When we hear a body has been found, someone killed in a park by a stranger, what sex is the victim? When we hear of honour killings who is found dead? The gendered nature of certain crimes and their victims and the gendered nature of so much law, because it is largely created and administered by men, is still insufficiently recognised or discussed.

Instead of debating all these questions boldly, ministers hide behind the much more acceptable cloak of the generalised heading, 'Victims'. The most troubling and pressing question is never asked. What is it about men that they are so much more disposed to criminality? Is masculine violence perhaps a necessary feature of a patriarchal culture and why is so much of it directed at women? Discussions about violence never get to the heart of these issues because they are so disconcerting for us. Criminal law has proscribed anti-social violence in a highly selective manner. If we consider just how our law has criminalised aggression – how certain types of anti-social behaviour have been targeted, while others have been either formally or practically left unregulated – then it seems that such law is about male patterns of behaviour and about male standards of acceptable conduct. The law is gendered, especially in relation to violence, and the gender-neutral language of legislation does not fully disguise this fact. It is why male violence in the home was until so recently beyond the province of the criminal law. It is why rape law has remained so mysteriously ineffectual.

Despite the fact that we really know that men and women behave differently and seem to act for different reasons we still watch governments provide universal theories of crime and formulate general criminal laws that are meant to work in a gender-neutral manner. We are just not prepared to face the facts of crime. Sex is the most salient variable when it comes to offending.

Until women and children get justice in the system certain special processes are justified, including anonymity for complainants in sexual offence cases and anonymity for children at all times. However, at regular intervals we have to rehearse the arguments about why accused men should not be given the cover of anonymity in some spurious call for equality. Open justice means anonymity should be used sparingly. The coverage of a rape case at times leads to the discovery that the male accused is a multiple offender, because other women are given the confidence to come forward.

Redressing the profound historic failures in relation to women means having to take special steps and the government should say so clearly. 'Gender bias' does include bias against men, and there are cases, particularly those involving child custody, where this certainly applies. The difference is that the majority of men in court are stereotypically viewed as powerful, credible and independent. The men who do invoke negative stereotypical assumptions – homosexual, black, Irish, Arab, vagrant, gypsy, unemployed – can suffer just as women do.

When judges were first challenged about gender bias they refused to recognise there was a problem. Indeed, many women did too. They could not see that change had overtaken our political and social institutions – that male behaviour which was once considered acceptable is no longer so, or that what was deemed chivalrous or courtly is now patronising. Conversely, we hear male judges, in relation to women lawyers and defendants alike, asking why they are so aggressive. 'Why can't they act like women? Why must they act like men?' In fact, they are acting like lawyers or independent human beings.

We have reached an extraordinary impasse, for example, in sentencing policy: the prison system is in crisis because of over-crowding yet the judges continue to sentence as though oblivious to the fact, or its serious implications. The compartmentalising of the criminal justice system – police, prisons and the courts – means that devising a coherent law enforcement or penal policy can be undermined by lack of co-operation between the parts. There is small point in introducing a progressive police policy on domestic violence if the courts do not reinforce it, nor is there any sense in the penal system working to maintain family relationships, if those same relationships play little part in the considerations of the court.

Reviews of the prison system often neglect women, because they make up such a small part of the whole and because there are rarely disturbances in the female jails. However, given their limited size and the varied nature of the population in women's prisons, it should be possible to try out new initiatives amongst women first, such as small satellite units instead of the few large prison institutions which currently exist. In hostel-type units women could have their children with them on a more prolonged basis and gain work experience where appropriate. The increased number of small prison units would mean less dispersal to remote parts of the country, something that has a fatal impact on many relationships.

Before any woman with a child is sent to prison the burden should be upon the court to obtain full information on the impact of separation upon the child and reasons should be given for rejecting an alternative to incarceration. Once that process had begun the same arguments could then extend to men coming before the courts, but a start should be made with this small proportion of defendants and the effects monitored. Crucially, women should be sent to prison only in exceptional circumstances where they have committed serious crime. Repeated low level crime and drugs offending should not lead to incarceration.

However, while the fact that there has been some change shows that movement is possible, this shift will be marginal, destined to solidify like lava, if the institutions are left to their own accord. The legal system has an astonishing power to revert to type. The underlying culture ensures that. Many judges remain blinkered and are at times arrogant. Just as can happen to children in care, hospital inmates, long-term prisoners and mental patients, they become institutionalised, dependent on known forms and reluctant to contemplate change. The power of the system to turn any free spirit into a conforming replica of those who went before is considerable, and it is often not long before the great new hope on the Bench begins to look very like the old vintage.

In *The Bar on Trial* Robert Hazell highlighted a problem which starts at an even earlier stage:

There is one other way in which the conventions and traditions of the Bar affect the development of the law and its institutions, and that is by ensuring that barristers who challenge the conventions do not reach positions of importance in which they can influence matters. Outwardly the Bar has a reputation for tolerance . . . but this tolerance can only exist within clearly defined limits. Most barristers are conformist by training, if not by temperament, and for those few who are not, the ceremonies, rules and patterns of behaviour in the Inns soon ensure that they pay proper respect to the ethos and traditions of the Bar which are inculcated into them by their elders.

Even the good ones succumb to tunnel vision. They do not see that the very notions which are idealised by the law deserve examination. The ideal of objectivity, for example, is a masculine value which has come to be taken as a universal one. Often when the law fails people it is not because of some lack of objectivity but because judicial objectivity has meant a denial of the female or black or working-class experience. There is a systematic exclusion of other perspectives. Insisting on equality, neutrality and objectivity is not to insist on judgement by the values of men of a particular class. It is, therefore, important that truly universal values are created.

In fairness to judges, the judicial role has become more difficult at a practical level, because courts are so much busier. Management is required to get through the list, and the pressure is considerable. It is one of the reasons why I think women often make good judges because without realising it women with families, who juggle double lives, acquire good management skills and have no difficulty running a court to time.

Judges are also isolated and receive very little feedback. The people they mainly mix with socially are their own peers, who do not see them doing the job. In David Hare's play, *Murmuring Judges*, which was performed at The National Theatre in 1991, an elderly member of the judiciary responds to the suggestion that judges are 'out of touch' with the claim that he and his brethren are very familiar with common folk since they see them in court every day. (A familiar utterance at the Bar.) Coupled with this isolation is the enduring characteristic of judges: they are in charge and wield great power over people's lives. They are not used to being challenged and it is hard for them to accept questioning of their function as creative.

*

The reason why the arguments for more women on the Bench must continue to be made with vigour is that public confidence demands it. Legitimacy comes from many sources but one index is the diverse nature of those who sit in judgment. People should see that adjudicating on the serious stuff of people's lives is not the sole province of white men.

Whenever there are discussions about whether women judge differently there is always a rush to say 'no'. However, everyone brings their own life experience to their work and it is no accident that Lady Hale in a case in the House of Lords on medical negligence was able to speak with such authority about pregnancy and childbirth. The women on the Canadian Supreme Court are perfectly confident about the impact they had on the court because they know that they changed the nature of the discourse. Women educate men for the most part about sexism. Men then educate other men.

One Canadian lawyer was in Britain when the rituals of the opening of the Law Courts took place at the beginning of the legal term. This is an extraordinary occasion when all the Law Lords and the Judges of Appeal and the High Court downwards process publicly in their robes with full-bottomed wigs and knee breeches and silk stockings. He was shocked that this full display was so barren of women, having become used to the near equality of numbers in his own country. The sprinkling of women was so thin that he had almost missed them.

The Department for Constitutional Affairs has accepted that the process of women becoming judges and reaching the top of the legal profession cannot be left to chance or the passage of time. Those on the outside of exclusive networks feel uncertain about attempting to join. Although the door may have been opened, women still stand outside asking to be invited in. There are many senior women solicitors who have never been considered and who would not dream of suggesting themselves. Women often do not have a career plan and have to be encouraged to think of sitting. Solicitors, male and female, provide an enormous pool of potential judges but they have to be urged to think of judicial appointment if they have established busy, lucrative practices. Positive action has to be taken to get women on to the Bench in real numbers, and that will only be achieved by removing blinkers about what constitutes merit and experience and by fast-tracking talented younger women. A critical mass of at least 30% of women is needed on the Bench before tokenism ceases to function and a real difference is felt.

The creation of the Judicial Appointments Commission will continue the process of reforming the judiciary. By introducing outsiders to the decision-making process, the old tendency towards judicial cloning will become less likely. The Commission will include members of the legal profession – solicitors and barristers, judges and legal academics – but there should be a majority of lay representatives who are able to insist that best practice selection processes are put in place. It is important that the Commission has the final say on appointments and not the Secretary of State or Prime Minister, however senior the appointment. For too long the system has been perceived to be one based on patronage, which is unacceptable. There must also be an independent audit function so that there is oversight of the new arrangements by an ombudsman, with the criteria for appointments made public. Until now not many human rights lawyers, otherwise known as public interest lawyers, have appeared on the secret lists which circulated among the judicial fraternity for their comment. This is probably because they are perceived as too liberal. One of the strange things at the Bar has been the belief that only people on the left are political. When I was a pupil barrister I remember being advised sternly by a senior member of the chambers not to mix politics with a career at the Bar. He was a Conservative MP.

I have always supported the extension of rights of audience, enabling solicitors as well as barristers to act for clients in courts at every level. In the interests of consumer choice it is a crucial development, but it means the breaking of the charmed circle which binds judges and barristers, often contrary to the interests of justice.

At the moment, the earliest age at which judging can begin is 35 but it is much more usual that the lawyer is in his or her forties or even fifties. There is no valid reason why judges should not begin this training at 30. Women with young families, for example, may be particularly interested in using this time for acquiring judicial skills, sitting part time in the lower courts. The resistance to reducing the age is based on a view of the world from the far end of the telescope, where the ageing judges who currently run the show look down on someone in their early thirties as a mere child.

The entry of women would be easier if the job were attuned to more realistic living arrangements. Circuit and district judges are locally based, but the grander office is that of High Court judge; these are the people who set the judicial tone. On appointment they receive a knighthood. Rather than basing High Court judges in a particular part of the country, they are all centrally located in London at the Royal Courts of Justice, but those who deal with criminal cases travel to the different circuits for stretches of a month or two at any given time. Sometimes, if they are handling a long trial, they may spend many months away from home. During these periods they live in special judges' lodgings (rather grand houses with a cook and butler and other staff). It is not a life that can easily be combined with the care of a family. For the majority of women, for men whose wives have demanding careers, or who themselves wish to be involved actively with their children, it is an unacceptable lifestyle which urgently needs to be changed if the people who take office are not to remain unrepresentative and remote from the changing world. It is perfectly feasible to appoint local High Court judges and to restructure the court system.

Effective judicial training is a crucial part of judicial reform. The Judicial Studies Board has changed beyond recognition in the last decade with courses on sex and race awareness. An equal-treatment benchbook has been created which, although a source of mirth to the media, has given judges food for thought and stopped some of the off-the-cuff remarks which used to get them into trouble. No more suggestions that a convicted rapist had shown concern by using a condom. It urges judges to be aware of their own assumptions: such as that full-time working mothers are neglectful of their children or that homosexuality is catchable or a pathological condition. It tells them that black people often mind being referred to as coloured.

Not all judges by any means are dyed-in-the-wool reactionaries: they too can suffer from stereotyping. There are real signs of movement. Judges are becoming sensitised to the arguments about accountability and are seeing the need to present a more human face to the public. Sleeves are being rolled up and efforts made to reach the people. All practitioners have their own favourites who epitomise good judgement, intellectual honesty and humanity. Chief amongst the good guys must be Lord Woolf, the Lord Chief Justice. He is one of the few judges who has publicly expressed real concern about the system and is suggesting methods for improving it. Most of the judges currently sitting at the Old Bailey are fair and conscious of how people really live. There is a clutch of fine judges in the higher courts and the current team in the House of Lords is enlightened and impressive.

A new generation of men are now taking their place on the Bench, with different views about the world. They are more used to working alongside women as colleagues and come from more varied backgrounds. The English Bar has been renowned for its integrity and high level of professional competence, but this new generation has a particular dedication to their clients and a special commitment to the meaning and quality of justice. It was this generation which first challenged the orthodoxies of the Bar, setting up new chambers which organised democratically, and challenging the attitudes in conventional sets. They have largely been responsible for a political shift within the Bar Council, and for the shaping of a less entrenched profession. It is claimed that the apotheosis of this group will be the class of '68, with their very different views of social mores and class divisions. They will surely make some difference, it is said, when their time really comes.

The Bar is already engaged in continuing learning for the profession but it still meets some resistance from practitioners who can see no advantage for themselves; a sure way of compelling practitioners to acquire new skills is to preclude them from remuneration if they do not have them. I am firmly of the view that there are special skills when handling child abuse cases and mental health cases which advocates should be required to learn. The way in which vulnerable witnesses are cross-examined is often unacceptable; the assumption that techniques which work with armed robbers should be used in sensitive cases is ludicrous. Legal aid in cases involving children should only be available to those barristers and solicitors who are certificated to handle such trials. To obtain the additional certification the lawyers should be required to take specialised courses.

Young women coming into the profession ask me whether it is possible to have a fulfilling career and a contented family life. I can honestly answer in the affirmative, though it helps enormously if you have a supportive partner and earn enough for good childcare. Women find their own individual way of making it work; some take several years out of practice when children are small, others take just a few months off. There is no right way or wrong way. Either choice induces wrath in some quarters, as even women can be competitive when it comes to what makes for better mothering. Doing what makes you feel good is always the best option if it is open to you, and both chambers and law firms should be challenged to make it possible. Until there is a fairer sharing of work burdens and domestic organisational burdens, women will feel under pressure. New technologies can make it possible to spend much more time working at home, preparing cases. Children are often happy just to know you are in there tapping away at a keyboard, even if you are not on the floor with the Play-Doh. However, the machismo of late hours and the expectation of global law firms that lawyers should be prepared to offer a 24-hour service is ludicrous. Choices should be available and chambers should never require women to pay rent when they are not earning fees.

In the training of young lawyers, greater store is now being set on putting the client at ease and trying to ensure that they appreciate the issues and the procedure. Victim Support, an organisation which supports the victims of crime, has made enormous headway in its efforts to reduce the terror for witnesses, negotiating with courts for better facilities, providing a knowledgeable volunteer as a support, taking the victims into courtrooms to familiarise them with the room and the box in which they will stand, and explaining procedure.

Many defendants as well as victims need support. They would welcome the opportunity of sitting close to their representative so that they can communicate more readily, rather than remaining in isolation in the dock. This step has already been taken when children are on trial in adult courts but it could be extended to other defendants in appropriate circumstances. Defendants frequently do not have a clue who is who and the distinctions between barristers and solicitors escape them. (The public often believe barristers are solicitors with a few more years' training, an illusion which barristers are happy to maintain.)

The medical and teaching professions have already gradually lost much of their mystique through greater public awareness and criticism: it is no bad thing that a new value system is created for professionals. Authority and status should not come from a job title or a fancy costume but should emanate from the way in which the job is performed. People are entitled to knowledge about the processes to which they are exposed: professionals need to have their authority challenged if it is used inappropriately.

Televising the courts would be a different way of significantly reducing the mystery of what goes on in the halls of justice, although I am firmly of the view that the cameras should only be allowed in to the Appeal Court where there are no juries and rarely witnesses. The spectacle of the O.J. Simpson trial in the United States was convincing testimony of the way that selecting the day's highlights gives the impression to the public that they are seeing the whole trial and are surrogate jurors, when they are only seeing the editor's cut. High-profile, salacious cases provide such potent material for the prurient and voyeuristic that the admission of cameras would have to be carefully regulated.

The hype which surrounded the media announcement that barristers' wigs might be abandoned was met with terror in certain ranks of the legal profession. Large numbers of barristers are wooed to the fancy dress because of the very mystique it introduces; the abolition of the wig, gown and wing collar will undoubtedly be resisted in some quarters. (A survey showed that 70% of criminal barristers want the wig retained.) But the arguments for keeping it, which stress dignity and authority, are snares. It is as though the costume is some sort of legal corset or scaffold, required to sustain the edifice. The judges in the House of Lords wear no stuffed shirts or horsehair, yet the show still goes on. In wardship proceedings involving children, robes are never worn and the quality of justice has not been undermined: indeed, it has greatly improved.

Another argument for the retention of wigs is that the judges and the barristers benefit from the anonymity afforded by a uniform. It adds to the illusion of the neutrality of the law. If judges are dressed in an abnormal way they are not ordinary men who might have human frailties and prejudices. It is a pretence which simply adds to the whole fictional quality of the court. Judges need to be seen as real, as professionals doing a particular job. Wigs and regalia and dining may seem irrelevant eccentricities of the system, but it is these obsolete adhesions which hold the structure in place; their removal enables essential cultural change.

Commercial lawyers who have to compete in international markets and function alongside bankers and industrialists have been among the first to recognise that the uniform of old, far from enhancing their image, is more than faintly ridiculous, and unsuited to modern commercial litigation. Now, quite a few senior judges would be happy to see the wig resigned to the dressing-up box. It is practitioners at the Bar who oppose change. The real reason is professional pride and rivalry: some barristers want to keep the wig because, once it goes, so does a major artificial distinction between barristers and solicitors.

The reforms of the legal profession which began in the Thatcher years brought the winds of the marketplace into the profession: professional clients such as accountants could have direct access to a barrister without incurring the cost and involvement of the solicitor as intermediary; barristers could publicise their specialities and solicitors would be given rights of audience in the courts. The new philosophy – that monopolies had to be broken and competition should dictate the terms of engagement – achieved, for rather different reasons, some of the changes I believe were crucial to a modern legal system.

It became clear to the Bar Council, for example, that survival in this new competitive climate meant addressing some of the criticisms. But changes should not be driven by public relations advisers, who see the value of 'cosmetic' changes on race and women whilst remaining over-sensitive to the traditionalists' desire to preserve the status quo.

The Human Rights Act has provided a new language for reform.

There is no hierarchy of human rights and women cannot be relegated to a second division in the protection of their rights; indeed the state has a duty to ensure that women are not treated as second-class citizens or subjected to violence even within the private domain of the home. There is no sovereignty of home or nation when abuse is actually taking place.

The present spirit of reform has opened the doors to ideas which would have caused mass hysteria only a decade ago; the gap between the two branches of the profession, solicitors and barristers, is closing, and the requirements of those who use the law are becoming the priority. My focus has been on women throughout this book. However, the failures I am seeking to describe are about more than sexual bias, racial prejudice or a narrow class perspective. I have sought to show the legal processes which produce injustice and the mindset of lawyers and judges which allows the law to be reproduced in an unfair way.

The law is changing but the process is slow and sometimes cosmetic. Women are not going to settle for a legal system that does not listen to them or take account of their lives, and the system is becoming wise to that fact. Women have gone through the stage where they did the adjusting; now it is time for the institutions to change. The symbol of justice may be a woman, but why should we settle for symbols?

Index

ALSO BY HELENA KENNEDY

MISJUSTICE

'Fascinating and chilling'
Caroline Criado-Perez, author of *Invisible Women*

Two women a week are killed by a spouse or partner.

Every seven minutes a woman is raped.

The police receive one phone call per minute about domestic violence.

Now is the time for change.

Helena Kennedy forensically examines the pressing new evidence that women are being discriminated against when it comes to the law. From the shocking lack of female judges to the scandal of female prisons and the double discrimination experienced by BAME women, Kennedy shows with force and fury that change for women must start at the heart of what makes society just.

'Helena Kennedy has written a chilling exposé of how the law has historically failed women. Taking no prisoners, Kennedy outlines the damage we must undo, and the changes we must make'
Amanda Foreman